How to Write a
Damn Good
Mystery

Also by James N. Frey

Fiction

The Last Patriot
The Armageddon Game
U.S.S.A.
The Elixir
Circle of Death
The Long Way to Die
A Killing in Dreamland
Came a Dead Cat
Winter of the Wolves

Non-Fiction

*How to Write a Damn Good Novel: A Step-by-Step No
    Nonsense Guide to Dramatic Storytelling*
*How to Write a Damn Good Novel, II:
    Advanced Techniques for Dramatic Storytelling*
*The Key: How to Write Damn Good Fiction
    Using the Power of Myth*

How to Write a *Damn* Good Mystery

A Practical Step-by-Step Guide from
Inspiration to Finished Manuscript

JAMES N. FREY

ST. MARTIN'S PRESS ❦ NEW YORK

www.stmartins.com

Designed by Sarah Maya Gubkin

Library of Congress Cataloging-in-Publication Data

Frey, James N.
    How to write a damn good mystery / James N. Frey.—1st ed.
        p.   cm.
    ISBN 0-312-30446-3
    1. Detective and mystery stories—Authorship.   I. Title.
PN3377.5.D4F74 2004
808.3'872—dc22

                                                        2003058633

First Edition: February 2004

10   9   8   7   6   5   4   3   2   1

In Memory of

Raymond Chandler (1888–1959)

Contents

Introduction

Why Every Mystery Writer in the World Should Read This Book

Most books on how to write mysteries are chock-full of great tips on what to do and what not to do, sage advice about clues, red herrings, and where to find out about picking poisonous mushrooms and the fine art of lifting fingerprints. When reading such books, you might get the idea that a mystery is a mix of ingredients that you measure out judiciously and toss into a bowl, beat with a wooden spoon until all the lumps are smoothed out, bake in an oven at 350 degrees for a few months, and violà! A great mystery is born.

Sadly, it doesn't work that way.

How to Write a Damn Good Mystery is *not* a collection of tips on what to do and what not to do. It's a guide to brainstorming, planning, plotting, drafting, rewriting, and polishing a mystery. It's a how-to book that shows you how to write a damn good mystery, step-by-step, beginning with creating fascinating, three-dimensional, dynamic dramatic characters, who, if you let them, will create a complex yet believable damn good plot for you. A damn good plot is one that's full of mystery, menace, suspense, and dramatic conflict.

Next, this book will show you how to write gripping scenes and exciting narration, and will tell you all about rewriting and polishing, and, when you're done, strategies for placing the manuscript with an agent.

Will reading this book and applying its principles guarantee that you will write a damn good mystery? Nope. Sorry. Too much depends on you. But if you apply the techniques in *How to Write a Damn Good Mystery* scrupulously, let your characters work out their own agendas, and write, write, write, write, and rewrite, rewrite, rewrite until your story sizzles, you may well have *big* success. Many mystery writers do—why not you?

Learning to write damn good mystery fiction is something like learning to roller-skate. You try, you fall on your keister, you struggle to your feet and try again. Then you repeat the process over and over. Eventually, you'll give your work to someone and she'll say, "Hey, this reads just like a *real* mystery!"

Writing and plotting a mystery should not be seen as drudgery or even very hard work; creating a mystery is an adventure and should be done in the spirit of adventure. That stuff about writers staring at blank pages until blood comes out of their foreheads is a lot of bunk. Bloody foreheads are for literary writers. For mystery writers, the creative process ought to be, well . . . fun. Making up interesting characters and fictional towns, even whole societies, and contemplating murder and how to get away with it—murdering people who resemble your loutish ex-spouse, your cranky boss, your nasty mother-in-law—what could be more fun than that?

We'll begin our adventure in Chapter 1 with a discussion of why people read mysteries, the place mystery fiction has in modern literature, and how it functions as cultural mythology—all important things to know when you're planning to write a damn good mystery.

How to Write a
Damn Good
Mystery

Why People Read Mysteries and Other Useful Stuff for Mystery Writers to Know

First, the Classic Answer. (And it's still true.)

If your aim is to write a damn good mystery, the first thing to get straight is why people read them.

The usual answer is that people read mysteries as "escape," as a form of entertainment. Reading a mystery is a good way to spend a few quiet hours away from the hubbub of real life—it's diverting. But there are a lot of things that are diverting that aren't as popular as reading mysteries. Mud wrestling, as an example.

Ed McBain (author of the 87th Precinct series) once said in an interview that we read mysteries because they "reconfirm our faith that a society of laws can work." Indeed, they do that.

It's usually assumed that most readers enjoy "solving" a

mystery the way people enjoy "solving" a crossword puzzle. They say a mystery is an elaborate puzzle carefully constructed to baffle the reader, and that the writers of mysteries are playing a sort of game with their readers, hiding clues in plain sight, presenting suspects who couldn't have done the murder, but act as if they did, and so on, so the reader will go down what will very likely be the wrong path. The detective in a mystery almost always beats the reader at the game of who-done-it.

But if the love of a puzzle were the principal reason most people read mysteries, the mystery would have died out with the "locked-room" mysteries of the 1930s and 1940s, which were perfect puzzles, ingeniously devised. The murder would happen, say, in a room locked from the inside, with only a corpse inside—or some other devilishly devised perfect puzzle that at first would seem impossible to figure out. A bullet wound with no bullet. A body disappears from a rooftop. Any reader who could unravel one could be justifiably proud.

A damn good mystery is far more than a clever puzzle.

Marie Rodell, in *Mystery Fiction* (1943), gave the following four classic reasons that people read mysteries and the reasons haven't changed much since. People, she said, read mysteries to get:

1. The vicarious thrill of the manhunt . . . carried on intellectually in the cleverness of detective and reader.
2. The satisfaction of seeing the transgressor punished.
3. A sense of identification with the people [the hero principally] and events in the story which will make the reader feel more heroic.
4. A sense of conviction about the reality of the story.

And, Ms. Rodell goes on to say, "The mystery which fails to satisfy these demands will be an unsuccessful mystery." This is just as true today as then, maybe more so: Because today's readers are more skeptical, more in tune with police procedures and forensic science, the "sense of reality" needs to be greater than in days gone by.

THE MODERN MYSTERY AS HEROIC LITERATURE

Barbara Norville, in her very helpful and informative *Writing the Modern Mystery* (1986), claimed that the modern mystery story had its roots in the medieval morality play, but, she said, "today's literary culprit works in a framework of felonious assault against neighbor . . . rather than, as in the morality play, against the sins of pride, sloth, envy, and so on."

While it is true that the two forms—the medieval morality play and the modern mystery—have elements in common, the modern mystery has its roots, I believe, in far older stories. The modern mystery is a version of the oldest story ever told: the mythic journey of the warrior hero.

When I refer to "myth" or "mythic forms" in reference to mysteries, I mean that mysteries echo mythic forms and that the mystery is a modern retelling of a very old form of literature. The hero of ancient myth slew dragons (monsters who threaten the community) and rescued damsels in distress; the contemporary mystery hero captures murderers (monsters who threaten the community) and rescues damsels in distress. Ancient heroes and modern mystery heroes share many qualities: courage, loyalty, a determination to defeat evil, the drive to sacrifice for an ideal, and so on.

Best-selling mystery writer Robert B. Parker (the Spenser series) has called the mystery novel "one of the last refuges of the hero." Fortunately, for those of us who write mysteries, it's a large refuge indeed. In the publishing world, mystery fiction attracts immense audiences, and accounts for more than a third of all fiction sold in the English-speaking world.

In *The Key: How to Write Damn Good Fiction Using the*

Power of Myth (2000), I showed how a modern writer can tap into the power of myth and use ancient forms and motifs that readers unconsciously respond to in a very deep and powerful way. These forms and motifs are called "functions" by mythologists, and, remarkably, the same functions are seen in every culture on earth, through every age. These functions might be characters, such as the "trickster" or the "mentor," or they might be actions, such as "the hero has a special birth" or "the hero is imprisoned." These functions are repeated over and over again, and form the patterns of myths and legends found in all cultures. As an example, some mythologists claim that there is a recognizable version of "Jack and the Beanstalk" in the Americas, Europe, Asia, Africa, Oceania, even in places where there are no beans and no stalks.

Lord Raglan, a British mythologist, claimed in his book *The Hero* (1956) that the "myth of the hero king" (where the hero becomes the ruler and lawgiver, falls out of favor, and is killed) has appeared in an easily recognizable form in every culture on earth without exception.

Often, myths and legends are in the form of what mythologist Joseph Campbell called the "hero's journey," which he described in detail in his famous *Hero with a Thousand Faces* (1948). Christopher Vogler, in *The Writer's Journey* (1992)—a book aimed at screenwriters but a must-read for any fiction writer—applied Campbell's insights to the art of screenwriting. The hero's journey is the most common of all mythic forms and is the basis of most literature, both ancient and modern, according to Campbell. The modern mystery is an incarnation of the mythic hero's journey.

For mystery writers, the important thing about the hero's journey is that its mythic form and the mythic functions that appear in the modern mystery have a powerful pull on the reader. Carl Jung, the Swiss psychologist, thought of the functions of myth as corresponding to structures in the mind—structures human beings are born with—that he called *archetypes.* In other words, the attraction to the mythic forms is inherited, a part of the human psyche—hence, universal. I find his arguments extremely compelling—and for a mystery writer, very useful. The hero of the ancient myth in pursuit of golden fleece or the elixir of life, the medieval knight pursuing dragons to slay,—today these are the detectives in pursuit of justice.

The usual pattern of the hero's journey is this: The hero has a call to adventure, which is generally some kind of a mission on behalf of his community; the hero goes forth into a strange land where he or she learns new rules, is tested, encounters various archetypal characters (the woman as whore, the woman as goddess, threshold guardians, magical helpers, and so on), has a death and rebirth, encounters the evil one, defeats the evil one, and returns with a boon that will be a benefit to the community.

There are variations within this basic design. Some heroes resist going on the journey, as an example, and may suffer guilt for refusing the call. Some heroes have to be dragged kicking and screaming onto the path of their journey. Some heroes fail to defeat the evil one. Some are killed.

In the modern mystery the hero/detective has a mission to find a murderer and goes forth, not to a strange, magical land as in the ancient myths, but to a place of lies and deception, a place foreign to the hero, where he or she encounters the evil one—a murderer—and, using courage and reason in a clever and resourceful way, defeats the evil one. Then the hero/detective returns to his or her community, bringing the "boon" of justice.

The weapon the mystery hero uses is never luck, chance, or intuition (though these things may play a part); the modern mystery hero/detective's weapon is *reason*. The almost universal premise of a mystery—using the term "premise" as I defined it in *How to Write a Damn Good Novel* (1987)—is *reason conquers evil*. The nature of the evil will, of course, vary from story to story, but that same basic premise is the foundation of all damn good mysteries. The hero/detective, through the use of reason, will bring a murderous evil one to justice.

Why Is the Injustice a Murder?

In modern mysteries the crime to be solved is nearly always a murder. Couldn't you write a clever burglary story where the crown jewels were stolen from a room locked from the inside and it's the hero/detective and the reader's job to figure out how it was done? For most readers, figuring out who committed a burglary wouldn't hold much interest. Why is that? you ask. This is an important question.

In a mystery, death, which to all of us seems so arbitrary and irrational, is made logical and rational. The hero, using reason, triumphs over irrational death in a symbolic way. The mystery touches us in the deepest part of our being because it shows that death is accountable to reason. When we finish a damn good mystery, we feel that the human condition is not entirely at the mercy of irrational forces set on destroying each of us. Readers, I believe, find the dramatic presentation of reason conquering evil profoundly satisfying.

Modern mysteries are not just diverting entertainments and puzzles to solve, but important contributions to our cultural life. Culture is based on myth. Heroes are not just comic-book characters to entertain children. Mythic cultural heroes are as important to our civilization as yeast is to bread. Heroes are role models. As Marie Rodell said over half a century ago, reading a mystery makes the reader "feel more heroic."

There are other cultural values associated with mysteries as well. Take a look at the tough-guy mysteries that appeared in the 1920s in America. It was the heyday of the dime mystery and cheap pulp fiction magazines like *Black Mask*, featuring comic-book-type mythic heroes like "The Shadow" and "The Spider." It was a time when America was going through vast changes. America was the victor in World War I and was trying to come to terms with its new role as a leader in the new world. It was a time when industry was booming and farms in the Midwest were facing hardship. A devastated Europe was not buying American farm products, and the drought that caused what became known as the Dust Bowl had already begun. It was a time when a vast number of people from the farmlands of America were moving into already-overcrowded cities where factories were humming and where the 1919 Volstead Act, which, with the 19th Amendment to the Constitution, had made alcohol illegal, was spawning a speakeasy subculture of fast money and easy virtue.

People caught up in these changes felt lost in these fast-growing, dirty, clogged cities. The individual felt helpless. Later, in the Great Depression of the 1930s, this feeling of helplessness was greatly exacerbated and the tough-guy detective came into a full flowering with the likes of Dashiell Hammett and Raymond Chandler.

The tough-guy detective became the most widely recognized American cultural hero. He was a loner and he was tough, but—damn it—he cared about the little guy. He was tough-talking and if need be he could punch or shoot his way out of trouble with his ole reliable .38 snub nose.

The wonderful thing about the tough-guy detective was that even though on the outside he was hard as pig iron, inside he was soft as goose down.

An outstanding example is Sam Spade in *The Maltese Falcon* (1930). He's a loner and tough and, damn it, he cares for the little guy. He's up against tough cops and tough bad guys, but he falls in love with Brigid O'Shaughnessy, who, it turns out, is the murderer. He has to send her over—it's his duty—but, get this: He'll wait for her, he says, even if it takes twenty years. Now that's an old softy.

Robert B. Parker's Spencer is an example of a modern incarnation of Sam Spade, only Spencer's outer softness conceals an inner toughness, instead of the other way around.

It's not surprising that in the 1970s and 1980s, when women were moving out of the home and into the war zone called Corporate America, the tough-talking, tough-guy model of the cultural hero of the past did not fit. A new cultural hero arose, the tough-guy *female* hero.

Take Kate Scarpetta, Patricia Cornwell's series detective. Kate's a modern female cultural hero. She's a hero who has long ago entered the jungle known as Corporate America and now she's a top forensic pathologist. She's a cultural hero for women who have found their place in Corporate America and are battling pervasive sexism. She's a typical American cultural hero: She's a loner, tough, brilliant, educated, and can punch or shoot her way out of trouble if the need arises. Now there's a hero millions of women—and men—can identify with.

This phenomenon is not limited to America. Lynda La Plante's *Prime Suspect*, a made-for-TV film (1981) which won an Edgar (Edgar Alan Poe Award from the Mystery Writers of America), is about Deputy Chief Inspector Jane Tenneson, a British woman hero/detective, who is in conflict more with her own male chauvinistic department than she is with suspects and culprits, truly a cultural hero for our times.

Cultural heroes embody the values of the culture, which change from time to time, but the core of the heroic character remains the same. DCI Jane Tenneson, Patricia Cornwell's Kate Scarpetta, Sue Grafton's Kinsey Mullhone, and Sara Paretsky's V. I. Warshawski are modern incarnations of Dashiell Hammett's Continental Op and Sam Spade and Raymond Chandler's Philip Marlowe.

Modern mythic detective heroes share the same core traits as other mythic heroes that I described in *The Key*. They are courageous, good at what they do for a living, have a special talent, are wounded, and are almost always an "outlaw" in some way. Modern mystery cultural heroes are not slaying dragons; they're pursuing justice. The mystery is a story in which a cultural hero, in the face of a grave moral wrong, seeks justice, not for himself or herself, but for others. The mystery hero is self-sacrificing; that is the key to the hero/detective's character.

In *The Key*, I referred to Ian Fleming's James Bond as an example of a cultural hero. He was created in the 1950s, when it looked as if communism were going to take over the world. James Bond certainly embodied bourgeois cultural values: He had his silk suit tailor-made in Hong Kong, he drove a Bentley, and he knew which grape was used to make the brandy in his glass by the bouquet alone. And he was licensed to kill (making him, in one sense, an outlaw).

Agatha Christie's Miss Marple is a cultural hero. She was created in the 1930s when England was still trying desperately to return to normal after the ravages of World War I and was facing both a deepening depression and a new threat from the Nazis in Germany. Miss Marple was a member of the gentry and exhibited the virtues the English people have long held dear: She was loyal to king and country; she lived in an idyllic English village; she was shrewd, but kindly; she had a sharp eye, a keen wit, and was 1,000 percent English, right down to her sensible shoes. She indulged in her ritual afternoon tea, and always carried her sturdy umbrella.

Many of the most popular and enduring characters in fiction endure because they are cultural heroes, even though these characters are somewhat cardboard, some would even say "cartoon." James Bond is but one well-known example. Indiana Jones is another. Such characters have very few inner conflicts, doubts, misgivings; rarely do they suffer from guilt. Many popular hero/detectives are of this ilk. Perry Mason and his sidekicks Della Street and Paul Drake are examples, yet they endure. They endure because they embody the universal heroic mythic values, even though as characters they're one-dimensional, and as flat and thin as a credit card.

There is in the writing game—especially among book critics and college professors, literary writers, and other snobs—much prejudice against books with such heroes; they are derisively attacked as "junk" or "popcorn" fiction. Most of these literati, of course, could not construct a decent plot for a damn good mystery if you gave them twenty years in solitary.

One theory, sometimes discussed in whispers among mystery writers, is that thin characters hook the reader in a strange way. Since such characters have little or no inner life themselves, readers project their own personality onto such characters. Comic-book heroes are such characters. The same is said of abstract paintings: Viewers project their own formed image on a formless work. Alfred Hitchcock, the great director, said he preferred a blonde for his female lead, one who seemed to have little or no personality, because, he said, audiences would then project their own personalities onto the character.

As a matter of taste, I usually prefer characters to be more fleshed out, to be three-dimensional and fully rounded. I'd rather read about John le Carré's George Smiley than about Fleming's James Bond, though I have to admit I've read a lot of Ian Fleming's works. They're like driving a sports car around a tight track. Fast is sometimes fun. If this is the kind of fiction you want to write, that's up to you. The critics may scoff, but your creditors may someday be as happy as a kid sucking on a ten-foot fudgesicle.

A good dramatic story is about the transformation of a character through a meaningful, dramatic struggle. Mystery fiction is a special kind of dramatic fiction. While there may be the same kind of dramatic transformation—an atheist finds religion, say, or a drunk sobers up, or a reprobate finds honor, or the like—the transformation of the hero in detective fiction is often simply from bafflement to certainty, from not knowing who in the community is a vile murderer to finding out the murderer's identity and seeing that the S.O.B gets what's coming to him—or her.

TYPES OF MYSTERIES

For the purposes of this book, a damn good mystery is defined as any story that fits this paradigm: A character called the villain, the murderer, commits a murder and is pursued by another character, the hero, who brings the murderer to justice. The word *detective* in this book means the person who solves the murder. I call this character the "hero/detective." He or she is the protagonist of the story whether he or she is a college student, a prisoner, a dentist, a ditch digger, or a bum. The hero/detective may, or may not be, an "official detective," either a police officer or a private eye.

Damn good mysteries are, first of all, damn good fiction. All damn good fiction has a moral purpose because damn good fiction says something about what it means to be a human being and how we ought to live our lives and treat other human beings. Mystery fiction is about murder and the pursuit of justice and is very serious moral fiction indeed.

But mystery writing is also popular fiction and all popular fiction is written to be entertaining. The mystery writer needs to approach this work in the spirit of an entertainer, an entertainer with a serious purpose.

Often in books designed to teach writers how to write mysteries, mysteries are put into categories. These include "police procedural," "private investigator," "amateur sleuth," "cozies," "hard core," "soft core," "puzzles," "comic tongue-in-cheek," "science fiction," "fantasy," "historical," "romantic suspense," and sometimes crime novels, with the murderer as protagonist, such as James M. Cain's brilliant *The Postman Always Rings Twice* (1934). These are useful categories for the publishing industry and it's good for the writer to know which type he or she is writing, but from an aesthetic or creative point of view, there are but three types: *genre, mainstream*, and *literary*.

Genre mysteries (sometimes called "category mysteries") focus on the mystery: the clues, the witnesses, the cat-and-mouse game the hero/detective is playing with the murderer. They're often highly suspenseful, often have a lot of menace and skulking around, and may have many elements usually found in thrillers: bombs that might go off, assassinations, and so on. The characters in the best ones are *theatrical*, but avoid being total cartoons. They're theatrical in the sense that they are colorful and somewhat exaggerated and have quirks of character and behavioral eccentricities. Genre mysteries are usually sold in rack-sized paperbacks and are marketed to airports, bus terminals, newsstands, drugstores, and supermarkets, as well as to bookstores. Sue Grafton and Tony Hillerman write damn good genre mysteries.

Mainstream mysteries are published first in hardcover and only later in rack-sized paperback. The mainstream mystery has many of the same elements as the genre mystery—clues, suspects, suspense, menace, and so on. However, the characters in mainstream mysteries are generally more "textured"; hence, they demonstrate more facets of character than characters in genre novels. Like other mainstream novels, characters in mainstream mysteries are more like "real" people with "real" problems. Mainstream mystery novels will often have a subplot involving, say, an ex-wife or a problem child, that has nothing to do with the murder. Mainstream mysteries are stories about characters involved in the solving of a murder. Scott Turow, as an example, writes damn good mainstream mysteries.

Literary mysteries also have many elements of a genre mystery—dead bodies, clues, suspense, menace, and so on—but they're often written with a somber, brooding tone. They are darkly poetic and are usually thought of as taking a walk on the dark side. Often, the heroes are tough, brutal, and lawless, living on the edges of society. Literary mysteries are usually sold in trade paperbacks (paperbacks the size of hardcover books) to bookstores. Raymond Chandler was the consummate master at writing them.

Whichever type you're going to write, you're going to start with a damn good idea, which is the subject of Chapter 2.

Ideas to Get You Started—The Good, the Bad, and the Ugly

THE GOOD

What's a good idea for a mystery? Better yet, what's a damn good idea?

You'd probably like me to tell you all the damn good ideas I know that, with absolute certainty, will make New York editors flip over backwards in ecstasy. An editor-flipping-in-ecstasy idea is, after all, what most writers think of as a damn good idea for a story.

Sorry.

I've been in the writing racket for a few decades now and, the horrible truth is, I've never been able to figure out what editors will find mildly interesting story-wise, let alone what will make them flip.

I've heard other writers, agents, and even editors say that they know this trend is hot, this other trend is not; that small-town mysteries, say, are in, hard-boiled are out; that cross-genre books or some such are the next trend, the wave of the future. It's all a bunch of pap. The truth about New York editors, as far as I can tell, is that they are hired by publishers because editors are supposedly expert at finding out which way the fickle finger of public taste is pointing. What drives editors nuts, I think, is that they can never quite be sure of the public taste's fickle finger, even though some of them will tell you with absolute confidence—as if they heard it directly from God—that they can.

The truth is, every book is a roll of the dice unless it says on the cover that some superstar like Robert B. Parker, Sue Grafton, Dick Francis, or Patricia Cornwell wrote it.

So where do you look for a damn good idea to start your novel if I'm not going to give it to you? It's really quite simple: A really damn good idea is one that takes hold of you and won't let you go. Sara Paretsky in *Writing Mysteries* (1992), an anthology of articles on craft put out by the Mystery Writers of America, says, "Writing to a hypothetical, unknowable marketplace instead of from your interests is the best way to produce flat, uninteresting work."

I've seen it a hundred times with my students. More than a hundred.

A damn good idea is the one that comes to you and hits you like a lightning bolt: "Wow, I could build a damn good mystery out of this!" George C. Chesbro in *Writing Mysteries* wrote: "The mystery novelist begins her or his quest by coming up with a single notion that can be squeezed, patted, poked, and fondled by the mind (a process I call noodling) to see if it might possibly yield up the spectral entity we call a plot."

This, I've found, is exactly the process.

Okay, you might read in the newspaper, say, that the ancient Mayans used a certain kind of poison that kills instantly upon touching the skin and suddenly you know how your victim died. You might have a neighbor who has a dog who barks too much and you ask yourself, Could this be a motive for murder? Maybe your Aunt Zelda is paranoid about the weird neighbors who moved in downstairs and you think, What if these weirdos really were plotting to murder my aunt?

Mystery writers are always thinking like this. Why, why, why, why oh why would someone want to commit murder? And how, oh how, do they plan to get away with it? Brainstorming a lot of ideas will help you find an idea that you'll want to develop.

Maybe you go on vacation to the Adirondacks and see a limestone cavern and you think, Wow, you could hide a body down here and nobody'd ever find it. A friend buys a house and finds an old trunk in the attic. You think, What if there's a body in it? You see a big bowl of mayonnaise at the PTA potluck and you think, Somebody could drown in that. Great mysteries are born in the flash of such inspiration.

A mystery writer, alas, thinks of murdering somebody most of the time.

In *How to Write a Damn Good Novel* I called the idea that gets you started writing your novel the *germinal idea*. It's the idea that will germinate and take root deep in your psyche and grow and blossom into a damn good novel.

A damn good germinal idea can come from anywhere.

Religion doesn't often play a role in murder, so there might be some fertile ground there. How about a priest giving last rites to a man he's just murdered? I had this idea once, might still use it. It's traces of the oils he uses for the last rites that provide the hero/detective with the clue that traps him. Who this hero/detective might be, I have yet to figure out. But the last rites given by the murderer sounds like a damn good idea to me.

How about a story in which a wicked stepmother gets her due? Wicked stepmothers are always good as murderers. Nobody likes their stepmother. Well, almost nobody.

How about a woman who seems perfectly sane to all but those she marries?

How about a story about an idealistic young man searching for his long-lost grandfather, who turns out to be a killer?

How about a story about a body that's found in one place, say New York, and the poor fellow's head in another, say San Francisco? I like ideas like this. The murderer has done something symbolic, but only the murderer knows the meaning of the symbol, and the detective has to figure it out. Must be the poet in me that goes for these metaphorical murderers.

Okay, then, a damn good germinal idea is any idea whatsoever that excites you. It may be an unusual motive for murder, a murder weapon, a nice locale, an interesting character, a little-known murder investigation technique, a legal maneuver—anything. What's important is that it's the spark that ignites your creative fire.

Okay, pay attention: If you are going to write mysteries, you should write them because you feel passionate about writing them. You should love reading them, you should love creating them, and you should think mysteries are "real" novels, serious literary works written by "real" novelists. And because you're going to love writing your damn good mystery, the damn good germinal idea you start with should grab hold of you like crazy glue. You don't really have to go out and choose a damn good idea—it will choose you.

If you have no ideas that you think might develop into a damn good mystery, not one idea that you feel passionately about, you should take up macramé. You have no business being a mystery writer.

Since the idea that gets you started might be nearly anything, and since, as we'll soon see, the idea might be profoundly transformed once it undergoes development, like one of those kids' toys that starts out as a truck and "morphs" into a spaceman, it really only matters that you have strong feelings about the idea that will fan the creative fire and fuel your enthusiasm for the project. Once the creative fire is blazing, all kinds of good things can happen; the story may go off into great places you never dreamed it would go when you started.

You might, as an example, have an idea for a unique hero. One of my former students at a University of California Extension workshop I conducted, Michael Mesrobian (who writes under the pen name of Grant Michaels), created as a hero/detective a gay hairdresser named Stan Kraychik, who is the hero of *A Body to Dye For* (1990), *Love You to Death* (1992), *Dead on Your Feet* (1994), *Mask for a Diva* (1996), *Time to Check Out* (1997), and *Dead as a Doornail* (1998). A hairdresser has a unique insight into people: The hair tells all. They're light, comic mysteries, very entertaining.

You might get turned on by an unusual locale. An underwater laboratory, say, or a Zen monastery, or the Rose Garden at the White House. Michael Mesrobian's hairdresser hero/detective goes into the gay scene in Boston, Yosemite Park, the Florida Keys, places where many of his readers have never been.

Betty Winkleman, who writes under the name of Loren Haney, was in my UC Berkeley Extension workshop. She sets her series of novels in ancient Egypt, in the days when the Pharaoh was a god; her hero is an army officer named Lt. Bak. So far, he's the hero of *The Right Hand of Amon* (1997), *A Face Turned Backward* (1999), *A Vile Justice* (1999), and *A Curse of Silence* (2000). There are more on the way. An avid, amateur Egyptologist, Betty has a vast knowledge of her subject and a great passion to learn more.

Cara Black, another participant in my UC Extension workshop, does a series about Aimée Leduc, a half-American, half-French private eye working in Paris in *Murder in the Marais* (1999), *Murder in Belleville* (2000), and *Murder in the Sentier* (2002), with *Murder in the Bastille* on the way. How'd she get the idea for this series? She simply loves Paris, she told me, and once on a visit there she thought, Gee, what if . . .

Now that she's sold four novels in that series, she tells me she just has to go to Paris twice a year for "research." Poor thing.

Another writer I worked with, Dr. Margaret Cuthbert, wrote *Silent Cradle* (1998), which is about skullduggery at a hospital. In the story, tiny newborns are the victims. She was very passionate about writing this book. Though it is very entertaining, with some of the most exciting operating room scenes you're likely to ever read, the book is a critique of the dollar-driven politics that goes on in a big city medical center. This is what fired her enthusiasm for the project.

You might have an idea for a fresh motive. Let's say a murder is committed to save the family honor or to prevent a child given up for adoption from finding his birth parents. The possibilities with family troubles causing a murder—especially in these days of surrogate mothers and sperm-donor fathers—are endless.

You might figure out a clever way to commit a murder. You might come across a chemical that will make the victim kill himself, say, or you've found a poison that can be squirted from a squirt gun. In Patricia Cornwell's *Cause of Death* (1997), the murder is committed by putting cyanide gas into the breathing tube of an underwater diver. Perhaps this was Ms. Cornwell's germinal idea. It's a damn good one. Very fresh.

Your germinal idea might be a great opening. Shelly Singer, in one of her Jake Samson novels, opened with her PI being called to the scene of a crime where the victim, a senatorial candidate, is hanging naked from a tree limb by his ankles. Hard to top that one.

Your germinal idea might be for a book with a great climax. In *Curtain* (1975), Agatha Christie has her series hero,

Hercule Poirot, commit a justifiable murder just before he
dies a natural death. How's that for a smashing climax and
an end to a series?

Cara Black had the idea for the climax for *Murder in
Belleville* (2000) before she had any idea what the story
might be. She'd read in the newspaper about some terrorists
holding a nursery school class hostage and having dynamite
planted all around. In her book, she knew her hero/detec-
tive, Aimée, would save the children in the climax. Who the
terrorists were and what they wanted, well, that came later.
She had an idea for a gripping ending and built the story
from the climax backwards.

Writers are usually advised to "write what they know."
Cara Black knows Paris; Michael Mesrobian knows Boston
and Key West and Yosemite; Betty Winkleman knows
ancient Egypt; Dr. Margaret Cuthbert knows her way
around an operating room; Patricia Cornwell knows her way
around an autopsy room.

I can only write what I know now. However, I could be
in trouble, because I don't know all that much. Happily, the
library is full of books. What I don't know, I can find out. I
read once that if you nest in a great library and work like a
madman, you can become an expert on virtually any subject
whatsoever in sixty days. That's right, in sixty days of
intense study you will know more than 99.99 percent of the
people in this country on any subject whatsoever, including
nuclear physics, existential philosophy, abstract expression-
ism, whatever. My experience has been that it doesn't take
half that long because I'm very good at using a library.

Write what you know about is good advice, but you can
always learn what you don't know. And after you study it,
you will be writing about what you know.

In the plot that you will be reading as a demonstration of
how to construct a plot in this book, the hero/detective is
involved in things that I've never experienced or even read
much about. One of the best things about being a writer is

that writing will take you places you perhaps never expected to go. The writing life is an endless adventure.

Okay, so a damn good germinal idea is one you feel passionate about, one that stirs your creative fire.

Now then, what's a bad one?

THE BAD

Say you get this brilliant idea that the hero should be psychic so that he or she does not bring the murderer to justice by reason, but by psychic means. Such an idea would produce a mystery that is messing with the form. Not a good idea.

Or say you have this great idea, you think, that the killer did not commit a moral wrong. Say he murdered to save his baby? This, too, is messing with the form and it's a damn *bad* idea.

You're writing in a tradition, and the readers who will buy your book have certain expectations that you, in good faith, should fulfill.

Then there are the folks who might not have a bad idea, but they have a bad motive for wanting to write a mystery.

In my mystery-writing workshops I've sometimes had participants who want to write a mystery because they've tried other forms, usually literary, and have not found success writing what they consider to be "real" novels, so they deign to write a mystery in hopes of getting published. I have the security guards remove these people from my immediate presence for their own safety because of the murderous impulses they arouse in me.

But before I have them tossed, I tell them how stupid they are. In literary novels you don't have to worry about a plot, motives can be foggy or even nonexistent, you don't have to worry about the story moving forward, you don't have to worry about the protagonist acting heroically—in fact if the protagonist doesn't act heroically or doesn't even act at all, so much the better. I tell these dumbos that even though creating a mystery may be fun, it is far more challenging to write a mystery than to write a "literary" novel.

Most alleged literary novels aren't even novels at all, because they don't tell a story. What they do is depress the reader for, oh, about three hundred pages, then the writer mercifully kills off the main character at the end. This proves what? Life sucks, then you die. How very dreary.

True, these story-less literary novels are almost always beautifully written and are often brimming over with wonderful insights about life and human character, but since they have no drama—no tests of character and no moral dimension—they are not in any sense dramatic, and it is my belief that any work of fiction that aspires to be damn good, better yet, be deemed "literary," will be intensely dramatic.

Certainly any work that aspires to be timeless will be dramatic. Dramatic storytellers such as Dickens, Tolstoy, Hardy, Austin, Conrad, Poe, and dozens more who wrote the works we now regard as classics, were dismissed in their day by snobbish literary critics as hacks pandering to the popular taste.

Mystery writer Elizabeth George, whom I had the honor to meet at a writers' conference in southern California a few years ago, told me that people often ask her when she's going to write "real" novels. She said she just gives them an icy look (and she has an icy look that would sink the *Titanic*) and says, "But I do write 'real' novels, with 'real' characters in 'real' dramatic situations in 'real' settings: 'real' novels that 'real' people—not intellectual snobs—like to read."

My sentiments exactly.

When asked why he wrote detective fiction instead of serious fiction, Robert B. Parker said, "Detective fiction *is* serious fiction."

Of course it is.

Teaching beginning mystery writers for over twenty years has taught me that mystery writers need to know that even though creating mysteries should be done in the spirit of adventure—perhaps even fun—mysteries are a serious art form and should not be approached with condescension.

Ed McBain once said the modern mystery is "a running commentary on our times, an attempt to illuminate those times, to filter it through the writer's imagination and illuminate it for someone else." A wonderful way to describe it. As a running commentary on our times, mystery writing is just as serious as any other kind of fiction. Sue Grafton wrote in the preface to *Writing Mysteries* that a mystery "is a way of examining the dark side of human nature, a means by which we can explore, vicariously, the perplexing questions of crime, guilt and innocence, violence and justice."

THE UGLY

One ugly idea is to create a hero/detective like the wimpy housewife/wimpy accountant type characters (often found in literary novels) I ridiculed in *How to Write a Damn Good Novel II: Advanced Techniques* (1994).

The impulse to create such a character is this: that the germinal idea has to do with creating an amateur detective, part of a fine old tradition in the mystery-writing game, and so, if the hero/detective is going to be an amateur, he or she needs to be a regular person—hence, inept and a wimp. No so. This is a deadly mistake.

The amateur detective needs to be just as clever and resourceful as a pro. The difference is, the amateur doesn't know anything about detective work except for what he or she has seen on TV and in the movies; therefore, the amateur has more of a challenge when it comes to finding the murderer. But the hero/detective of the amateur mystery needs to be just as heroic in every other way, a larger-than-life character whom the reader or viewer can identify with. Identification with the heroic qualities of the hero/detective is one of the chief reasons the reader is reading the book.

Another ugly germinal idea is one that has been used before and has become trite and stale. Your readers will tell you when you've done that. The tip-off is when they say, "I saw something like this on *Matlock*."

The ugliest idea is to start without an idea at all. Hard to believe, but I've known some fools who've tried this. I tried it myself, once or twice, and ended up with a large pile of manuscript pages to be recycled. Some athletic shoe company has as their slogan, *Just do it*. If that's your idea, it would be far better if you *just don't do it*.

Once you have your germinal idea, you'll need to sit down and start plotting. No matter what the idea is, you'll first have to work out the plot behind the plot, which, happily, is the subject of the next chapter.

3

The Plot Behind the Plot

There are two possible approaches you can use when writing a mystery novel.

1. Have a plan.
2. Don't have a plan.

I've heard writers coming through town on promotional tours at mall bookstores who say, No, they never plan—it hurts their creativity. To them, they say, writing is a wonderful process of discovery, blah, blah, as if their books wrote themselves. Following their bliss, I guess, kissed by the muses, gets the job done for them. I think they make these claims because if they admitted to writing from a plan—

which I'm sure 99 percent of them do—people wouldn't think they were the creative geniuses they pretend to be.

Following one's bliss has been, for any writer I ever knew personally, a colossal disaster. Creative suicide.

When you don't make a plan, of course, the first draft, no matter how chaotic, becomes the basis for the rewrite plan for the subsequent drafts. You might call the no-plan approach the let's-make-several-drafts method.

Writers I've known who use the let's-make-several-drafts method write reams of pages that eventually go into the recycle bin. To end up with an 80,000-word novel, they often write 200,000 to 300,000 words or more, and take from two to five years, or longer, to finish a novel, slogging through draft after draft.

This method is sort of like setting out to build a house without a blueprint: You just start sawing and nailing willy-nilly, tearing down and putting up until the house starts to take shape, then doing more tearing down and building up until you hope you have it right. I don't know anyone who would build a house that way, yet there are writers who try to build a story that way.

The process recommended in this book is to start with an idea, then create biographies for the major characters, including, of course, the murderer. The murderer has a plan for murder, "the plot behind the plot."

Once you have the plot behind the plot and know what the murderer is up to, the next step is to make a stepsheet for the plot, which is a detailed, comprehensive plan for a damn good mystery. After the stepsheet is finished, the next step is doing a rough draft, then a working draft, then perhaps a second working draft, then a final draft, and then a polish or two to make the prose gleam. By going about it in such an organized way, it should take, for an 80,000-word novel, about three to five months, full time; six to eight months, part time.

George C. Chesbro in *Writing Mysteries* put it this way: "The first step for me [is] a plot *outline*, a step-by-step description of how my story will unfold. I try to make this outline as detailed as possible, for I have learned that, for me at least, the more I put into these preparatory phases, the fewer problems I will have in actually writing the book."

I absolutely, totally, 1,000 percent agree.

Just doing it may feel creative, but it's really a huge time waster; the finished manuscript will not be as well executed no matter how many drafts it goes through. If you plan your story carefully, not only will the process be faster, but the finished work will be far superior.

What? you say. How can that be? How can faster be superior?

Okay, for the past ten years or so I've been doing what I call "intensives" here where I live in Berkeley at the University of California Extension, at the Oregon Writers Colony, and at other places in the United States and in Europe. In these intensives, I conduct group brainstorming sessions where the workshop participants and I make up a couple of characters, then we create a plot, then we draft some scenes—pretty much as we'll be doing later in this book.

Now all the participants in these workshops had sent in manuscripts to be evaluated before coming to the intensives. Most of the participants have been pretty good, if not damn good, writers. But almost without exception, the participants in these workshops produce far better writing in these exercises than they did in the manuscripts they'd written before coming to the workshop. The improvement is often astounding.

The reason for this? For one thing, because we talked about the back story for the characters and their ruling passions, they knew the characters extremely well. And we wrote "journals" in the voices of the characters to become more intimately acquainted. Then, when the participants wrote their scenes, they knew the purpose of the scene, what the characters wanted, what conflicts were to be exploited, and how the scene advanced the story. They were in control of their writing; they were not on a fishing expedition to "discover" what it was they were going to write and groping to understand the characters. Their writing became "sure-footed," confident, vigorous, alive. And they wrote these scenes very quickly.

If you have not tried writing from a plan, you might amaze yourself at how powerful a tool it is. Being in control is what really separates the professional fiction writer from the amateur hack.

Okay, I will now get down from the pulpit and stop all this damn sermonizing.

We're ready to begin creating a (hopefully) damn good mystery step by step, as a demonstration of how the process works. So let's begin.

First Things

To start a mystery, before you create the author of the plot behind the plot, there are two things you need to know: when and where the story will take place.

I'm planning to write my mystery in the present, but you may want to write your mystery in the past or in the future. It's a subjective choice. Write what you like to read—that's the best advice I can give.

Okay, my time is the present. How about place?

While doing a workshop in Montana a few years ago, I thought it would be a great place to set a novel. The scenery is strikingly beautiful, and the people are open and friendly and independent-minded. Self-sufficiency is a virtue. You don't find a lot of phoniness in people there. For somebody who lives in the hubbub, glitter, and crush of the San Francisco Bay Area, visiting Montana was like going back in time to the frontier days. I found a lot of colorful characters there, right out of Zane Grey.

Okay, pardner, I'm going to set my damn good mystery in Montana. In fact, this is my idea to get me started, to get my creative fire lit. I want to write about Montana.

Hey, you might say, that's not much of an idea. Well, it's enough to get my creative fires lit, so that's enough for me.

When you create your mystery, you should create not just a place, but *a place where dramatic events are happening besides the mystery*. It will give the story a greater sense of reality and there will be conflicts happening besides the ones involved in the investigation. Creating such conflicts in the background will give your story depth. Some of these actions will impact the murder mystery, but most won't.

Here's one of the greatest examples of dramatic events happening in the background: Hans Hellmut Kirst's *Night of the Generals* (1963), which was made into a gripping film starring Peter O'Toole and Omar Sharif. The hero/detective is after a psychotic murderer of prostitutes, while in the background an assassination plot against Hitler is being planned and carried out by high-ranking officers in the German army. Officers who are suspects in the murder investigation. How's that for a damn good idea?

The Maltese Falcon is a murder mystery being conducted against the background of the search for a fabulous jewel-encrusted statue of a falcon.

In Cara Black's *Murder in Belleville* (2002), the murderer is being sought against the dramatic background of a siege situation involving terrorists who have taken over a school and are holding the children hostage.

In Scott Turow's *Presumed Innocent* (1987), there's a dramatic political campaign going on in the background.

There are, of course, good, damn good, and even great mysteries where there are no dramatic events unfolding in the background. But having them is a way of giving your story more drama and complications, which will make it more exciting. Anyway, it is one of the options you might consider when creating the setting for your damn good mystery.

Okay, so for my fictional purposes, I'll make up a place in Montana. A small town. Let's call it "North of Nowhere, Montana." Let's say there once was a town called "Nowhere" and this is just north of there, so they called it "North of Nowhere." Nowhere was, let us say, mostly destroyed by fire in 1894; now the only thing that's left is a brothel. We'll have the story take place during elk-hunting season. A friend of mine is vehemently opposed to blood sports and I think this, too, is good stuff for the background: an elk-hunting protest.

So far, then, I know when the story is going to happen (the present), where this story is going to happen (Montana), and I know the drama in the background, a protest of elk hunting. For a title, let's call it *A Murder in Montana*.

Next, who will be our murderer?

How to Create a Damn Good Murderer

Okay, as I wrote above, the murderer, not you, my friend, is the author of the plot behind the plot. The plot behind the plot is the murderer's story: why he or she murders, whom he or she murders, and how he or she intends to get away with it. The murderer's motive is the driving force, the engine of any damn good mystery. Our murderer will need to be passionate, consumed with greed or ambition, perhaps, or lust, or hate, or an all-consuming desire for revenge.

The murderer is the pivotal character in a damn good mystery. A pivotal character is one who *pushes the action*, one who makes things happen that other characters, including the hero/detective, must react to.

Of course, the murderer will need to be a good dramatic character, as any other character would be.

In *How to Write a Damn Good Novel, How to Write a Damn Good Novel II: Advanced Techniques*, and *The Key: How to Write Damn Good Fiction Using the Power of Myth*, I stressed the need to write complete biographies of characters in order to fully understand them. These biographies should include the characters' *physiology* (physical appearance, IQ, scars, mode of speech and dress, way of holding themselves, and so on), their background or *sociology* (social status, early training, and experiences: the events that shaped and formed each one's character), and their *psychology* (the product of the physiology and the sociology).

A character might grow up, say, tall and lanky and awkward (his physiology) in a family that smothers him with mother love (his sociology) and because of his awkwardness and smothering, he becomes, say, a self-centered introvert (his psychology). Another character might be a natural athlete (physiology) and grow up in a family that prizes athletic prowess (sociology), so he becomes an egotist and a braggart who always has to be the center of attention (psychology).

A character's physiology, sociology, and psychology are the three "dimensions" of character described by Lajos Egri in his classic *The Art of Dramatic Writing* (1946). This is a very effective way of creating characters.

Egri also recommended that writers create characters with a "ruling passion." You might think of the ruling passion as being a dramatic force that is driving a character's personality. A murderer with a strong ruling passion might want to be president, say, or a great artist, or maybe he or she just wants to dominate everyone. A character might have a ruling passion to be well liked, or to get himself killed—it can be anything, as long as it is a dynamic force that energizes a character to take action.

Beyond being a good dramatic character, fully rounded, with a ruling passion, our murderer has other aspects of character that need to be taken into account.

Our murderer will be evil. We know a murderer is a mythic "evil one" and an evil one always *acts out of his or her own self-interest*. An evil one is the golden star at the center of his or her own universe. Our murderer will be selfish. Sure, we've all read books in which the murderer does the deed for a good cause, heroically, but this motif almost always results in a weak climax. As Marie Rodell said in *Mystery Fiction*, readers want "the satisfaction of seeing the transgressor punished." If the murderer is not acting out of his or her own self-interest and instead is self-sacrificing and acting heroically, the reader is robbed of this satisfaction, which is, after all, one of the principal reasons the reader bought the book in the first place.

Our murderer will not appear to be evil. There are two reasons for this. One, of course, is obvious. If the murderer looks evil, the hero will have no trouble picking him or her out of the crowd of suspects. There is also a psychological reason to have the evil nature of the murderer hidden. We have a greater fear of evil people who are pretending to be good. The impact of the revelation in the end will be greater if the author has cleverly concealed the evil one's murderous nature from the reader.

Our murderer will be clever and resourceful. Remember Marie Rodell's first reason that people read mysteries: the thrill of the chase. It is only a thrill if your murderer is clever and resourceful.

Our murderer will be wounded. In his or her background, the evil one should have a deep, psychological wound. Our murderer, say, was at one time wrongly condemned or badly treated. This wound is often the driving force behind the murderer's actions. This wound, in the murderer's mind, often justifies the murder.

Our murderer will be afraid. Fear can be added to almost any other motive and make the other motive—say, jealousy, ambition, greed, revenge—even stronger.

Now that we know in theory how to create our murderer, the author of our plot behind the plot, the next step is to do just that.

Creating a Murderer

THE MURDERER AS A "BELL CURVE" CHARACTER

Who will he or she be? As yet, I have no idea. Not the
slightest. It gives me a little tingle to think that I'm going to
make up this character out of the mud of my imagination
and he or she will come to life. Making art is really an amazing process.

I know this character will need to be, as I explained in
How to Write a Damn Good Novel, an "extreme of type." I
have discovered in my classes that there is another way to
think of characters as being an extreme of type; that is that
they're "out on the ends of the bell curve." They are what I
call "bell curve" characters.

Okay, what exactly is a "bell curve" character?

If you take any trait, such as "honesty," and you put people on a scale that goes from one extreme to the other, you

will find very few people at the outer ends. St. Simon the Pious—who was so honest that if he found a $5 bill in the street he'd ask everyone he met who owned it—would be at one end and, at the other end, you would find people who were so dishonest that they would tell lies even if the truth served them better. I have a cousin like that who sells roofing and siding and he'd steal the gold fillings out of your teeth if you slept near him with your mouth open.

Most of us, of course, fall in the middle of the bell curve of honesty. We might cheat a little on the ole income tax and we might lie to our spouses about what time we got home from Dinty's Bar, but if you averaged it all out, most of us are pretty much in the middle and would make pretty dull fictional characters.

Ah, but the truly interesting characters are found at the ends of the bell curve. They are extremes.

We'll start, then, with our murderer's background. I'll need to find out how he or she ever got to North of Nowhere in the wilds of Montana. Our murderer must want to go there for his or her own motives, not because I say so.

We're going to create a real human being (species *homo fictus*) who is a pivotal character, one who takes actions to push the plot forward and is motivated by selfish interests that he or she is passionate about. This character will be three-dimensional, will have a ruling passion, will be clever and resourceful and deeply psychologically wounded, and will not appear to be evil. And he or she will probably be living in morbid fear of something.

Okay, let's start with a name for our murderer. Let's call him *Forest*. He'll have to take a lot of kidding about Forest Gump, but that's his name. Okay, let's give him a last name. How about *Volner*?

I've never known anyone named *Forest* or *Volner*, and have no idea how those names sprang from the mud of my imagination. But somehow the name appeals to me, so I'll go with it.

Okay, we have a name for our murderer, Forest Volner of North of Nowhere, Montana. Since he is our murderer and he is going to be the author of our plot behind the plot.

THE BIRTH OF A MURDERER

Now, as you create a murderer, you should remember that the whole process is flexible and fluid—that's part of the fun. We might make changes in a character, large or small, at almost any stage of the game, right up until the final draft. Sometimes, later in the creation of our plot, we may want to go back and insert certain items into a character's back story, even change the character's personality somewhat—that's fine. When we create a character, we're a god; he or she is ours to do with as we please.

We'll start, then, with Forest Volner's physiology—his physical body.

As an adult, let's say, Forest Volner is a big man, well over six feet and weighing three hundred pounds. He has a trick knee that goes out on him once in a while. He has a thick beard and small, dark eyes, and the easy, friendly smile of a con artist. He claims to have a little gypsy in him, but it's not true.

Let's say the story takes place when he's forty-three.

By then he drags one foot slightly when he walks. An old football injury. Volner has large tombstone teeth, and thinning, reddish hair streaked with a little gray. His shoulders are rounded and he has a lumbering gait. He has a few scars on his face, debris left over from a few barroom brawls and his high school days playing football.

So far, then, we have a brief sketch of his *physiology*.

Let's take a look at his *sociological dimension*, his background.

Let's say he grew up in a suburb of Cleveland, Ohio. His father was a welder and his mother, a bookkeeper. He had no siblings. His mother and father did not get along. His father drank and his mother had a series of boyfriends she met in her church group or in the choir where she sang second soprano. A seductive woman, she got a kick out of seducing churchgoers. She finally seduced the pastor and ran off with him when Forest was thirteen. This is his wound: He had a no-good mother and suffered the shame of it in a highly conventional suburb where the gossips showed him no mercy.

Forest hated his mother for sleeping around—everyone knew it and pitied him for it—and he hated his father for being weak. He swore he would not be weak when he grew up.

Although he was friendly and joked around a lot, he had a savage temper that would erupt from time to time in terrible violence. Once, over a dispute about a yo-yo, he broke another boy's shoulder and six ribs.

His father tried to bond with Forest by playing sports with him, throwing the football around, and taking him to his practices. Because of Forest's size (tall then, but not heavy) and agility, Forest excelled at football. He played hard and became something of a local legend, the best high school tight end in the state. His teammates called him "Swifty." Later, when his weight shot up, he'd have a good laugh about that.

He had a love/hate relationship with football. He liked being a star—the girls wanted to date him and he even managed to have sex with a few of them, though having sex only made him feel inept and clumsy. But he liked it that they wanted to be with him; it made him feel important. He didn't understand girls, didn't know what they wanted. He hated his mother—of course he would have problems with girls.

Okay, we now have some insight into his *sociological* dimension. Now for his *psychological* dimension—beyond this hatred of his mother and loathing of his father.

Forest became a dreamer.

As far as his schoolwork went, he was bright, but an

indifferent student. He dreamed of being a treasure hunter; this becomes his *ruling passion*. It seemed to him that he was destined to find treasure. He often had dreams of finding treasure in the depths of the sea or in caves. Then he'd return to Ohio and he'd "show them" that he'd done it.

The idea of college scared him, even though Ohio State recruited him to play football. He worried that things would be expected of him at Ohio State that he wouldn't be able to do. He was tall and quick, but the guys on the teams that Ohio State played—Notre Dame, Alabama, Michigan, Michigan State—were big and could hit you like an army tank. He didn't know what these things he would be expected to do were exactly, but the idea that he wouldn't be able to do them scared him.

Other things scared him, too. Fraternities, things like that. He made friends easily, but the college kids, they seemed somehow above him; he didn't quite fit in. And there was something scary about college girls that he couldn't quite identify. They seemed so . . . so sophisticated.

Then, in the last game of his senior year in high school, he suffered a knee injury. He had surgery and the doctors thought he could still play, but he claimed to have a lot of pain. He used this as an excuse for not going to Ohio State. He dragged his leg as a sympathy ploy.

Forest was always pulling off clever scams. In his early teens he figured out ways of paying little kids to do his paper route so all he had to do was collect the money. He figured out ways to make firecrackers and cherry bombs that he sold at a handsome profit to other kids, and even set it up for another kid to take the fall when the cops closed in. He paid a girl to write his English papers.

One night Forest was at a party and overheard a guy talk about how his uncle had gone to Montana and gotten rich and was now living in a house in Miami so huge that he had an Olympic-sized swimming pool inside. As soon as he graduated from high school, Forest borrowed some money from some friends and off he went.

Okay, so far Forest is beginning to feel like a three-dimensional, fully realized character. You might not want your sister to marry him, but he's a human being, not a cartoon.

THE ADVENTURES OF AN ADULT MURDERER

I know it sounds like a lot of work is going into this and very little of it will find its way into the story, but it is extremely important that this preliminary work be done. Your murderer is the author of your plot behind the plot, and what he does and thinks, what he feels, how he changes and develops both before the story opens and afterwards (on or off stage) is critically important for you to know. Knowing your murderer thoroughly is key to plotting your damn good mystery.

Okay, after Volner went off to Montana, what happened to him?

Let's say he worked at menial jobs, washing dishes in Kallispell, clearing brush for a farmer, cooking at a lumber camp, sweeping up saloons after hours. On his days off he'd pan for gold in mountain streams and was absolutely thrilled when he found even a tiny speck of it. In the winter he'd pore over maps, charting where gold strikes had been made in the past, looking for a pattern, studying geology books, eager to learn all he could about the gold rush days.

One spring, he got caught in an ice storm, took refuge in a snow cave, got frost-bitten, and lost two toes.

It was in the clinic where he was treated that he met Sam Hegg, who'd lost a hand in a dynamite accident. Sam Hegg, it seemed, had a gold mine, hidden away, on a federal game preserve. And now, because of his injury, Sam Hegg needed somebody to help him. Volner, strong and full of romantic notions about treasure hunting, dazzled by the glitter of the precious metal, was just the ticket.

So Volner went to work for Sam Hegg in his mine deep in the wilderness.

The mine was not a rich producer. It took days of back-breaking work to get a few nuggets of gold. Sam Hegg was a vile man: He drank, he was mean and foul-mouthed, and when he went to town, which was seventy miles away over dirt roads, he left Volner to keep working at the mine. Volner felt he was left behind because Sam Hegg didn't trust him not to run off and tell somebody about the mine.

Volner stayed and worked for Sam Hegg for three years. Both of them were forever hoping that just a few feet more and they'd hit a pocket or a thick vein of pure gold. If they did, Volner was promised a third of the profits—enough to make him fabulously rich.

The vein they were following was widening, a sign that they were about to make a big strike. Volner started to fear that Sam Hegg wouldn't keep his word and pay him what he'd promised. When he'd see Sam Hegg wander off into the woods for a break, he'd think he was hiding gold. Sam Hegg was going to cheat him, maybe even kill him.

And that's why Volner started thinking of murder. He was in *fear*.

When Volner, spying on Sam Hegg, saw him sharpening a knife, he felt panic. Sam Hegg was going to kill him for sure, he thought. Why else would Sam Hegg not take him to town? No one even knew he was there. Volner's imagination ran wild. Why, Sam Hegg could kill him and bury him and no one would be any the wiser. And Sam Hegg could do it, too. Didn't he say he had a brother in prison? Violence runs in families, they say.

Volner's fears were born of greed and insecurity, and they were intense.

One night Volner was coming back from chopping some firewood. Sam Hegg was sitting on a stump smoking his pipe, watching a beautiful sunset, having a taste of whisky. Volner came up behind him and whacked him in the head with his ax and killed him instantly.

Volner buried the body, took the gold he found in Sam Hegg's stash, and concealed the mine with brush. He drove almost all the way back to town and pushed Sam Hegg's Jeep into a ravine and, after camping out for a few weeks, made his way into town on foot.

He was smart enough not to be too flashy with his gold. He got a job as a swamper in a saloon and kept a low profile. He boarded with a woman named Ruth, who had a daughter, Penny Sue. Penny Sue was homely and shy, and after a while Volner started taking long walks and canoe trips with her. One summer day they went skinny-dipping and found themselves making love in a pine grove.

Soon after, they married. And not long after that Volner moved up to bartender, and, when business got bad, he bought a piece of the Eagle Tavern from the alcoholic owner. He eventually ended up owning the place.

The years rolled by. Volner and his wife had two daughters, and Volner got elected to the town council, became a volunteer deputy sheriff, and gradually bought an interest in a hotel, bought the liquor store, and became a 50 percent silent partner in the brothel in Nowhere.

Okay, this is Forest Volner as we find him at forty-three. He's changed a lot over the years. He's no longer the wild-eyed dreamer. He loves his daughters, but he rules them and his wife with an iron hand. Penny Sue is afraid of him because she has seen murder in his eyes. He's never hit her, never even threatened to hit her, but she's been afraid of him for a long time. She knows he goes into the mountains and comes back with nuggets from time to time. He's secretive and sly, and she senses the potential for violence in him.

Occasionally, over the years, he's been in fights, but he's tried to control that part of him. Twice, he's beaten prisoners in his custody, and both times the review board found in his favor. Hey, he's one of the boys who run everything in the county.

There we have Volner's back story at the time our story starts.

Whoa, you say. What about Sam Hegg's murder? Well, they found Sam Hegg's Jeep, but thought he'd had an accident and some wild animal dragged away the body. So Volner got away with one. At least for the time being.

Everything up to now has been back story for our character, who is about to become a murderer a second time. The next step is to get into Forest Volner's mind, to try it on for size and see if we really like him as the author of our plot behind the plot.

What I've done here is somewhat abbreviated. I suggest you create your character biographies in much greater detail. Really get into your characters; know them well. The work you do creating them will pay big dividends later when they actually appear in your novel. They will seem more real to you—and to your reader.

Now that we've created him, let's hear Volner speak so we can become more intimate with him.

5

How to Become Intimate with a Murderer

A MEETING OF MINDS

As I advised in *The Key*, writers should write journals from the character's point of view, in the character's voice. Participants in my creative-writing workshops, and I, have found this to be a wonderful technique for getting into their characters' heads.

I encourage the people in my workshops to write these journals as if they were being written by the murderer to the author. In the journal, the character should be absolutely truthful, honest, and open—after all, this is just an exercise.

Here's what Forest might write:

Forest Volner's Journal:

Okay, so you're the mystery writer that's made me up and so I got to tell you the truth. No problem. I ain't ashamed of nothing I've done.

I'll start with when I was a kid. I never liked my old man and old lady, neither one of them. Lots of people feel that way, but they never admit it. I had a feeling like I was born in the wrong family. They were dull people—not dumb, dull. And my old lady was nothing but a slut. I think it was Ohio did her in, living there in a square little town like Jenkins Corners, a dumb suburb—it can do things to you. Takes your edges off. It's like living with a blanket over your head.

Okay, so my ma did try to get me money sometimes after she ran off with that dick-head reverend, but that don't matter. She was still just a slut. I was hoping when I left that I'd never see her again and so far I haven't. Yeah, my own old lady, she loved to be in love. Love— what bullshit! I never believed in that crap. A mother's love, what crap! She could have done better by me, that's all I know.

You, Frey, wrote that biography of me—you made me seem like I was scared of girls when I was in high school. I wasn't scared of them, they was scared of me on account of me being so, well, strong, and a big football star, and yeah, I didn't know what they was after, but I know now. They was after my friggin' money. Women only think about two things—their kids and money. They want you to help them make babies and to pay the bills, period. You want a little lovin', what do they say? They got a headache, they're on the rag, or they've got some damn women's monthly thing that gets them bent out of shape. Screw them! You know what, the only honest woman is a whore. You can trust a whore 100 percent. They sell themselves for a buck, it's a straight-up, honest deal. They don't pretend they love you. Oh, yeah, they say it but you never believe them 'cause they say it to every guy they shack up with. That's okay, it's like a game.

You think it's wrong, me being on the town council and me being a silent partner with Lady Ames in the whorehouse? I mean it ain't that big a deal. Four washed-up old whores that couldn't get laid for free in Missoula don't exactly make me Al Capone. I feel we're offering a service to guys who don't have women. Guys who work hard, mining, hunting outfitters, being guides, ranching, just trying to keep alive. The whores give them a little lovin' and a little comfort and there ain't nothin wrong with it.

That business with Sam Hegg and the mine. Okay, I killed a guy. You made it sound in my biography like I did it because I was chicken or something. But it wasn't quite like that. I did what anybody with a brain in their head would have done. It was the smart thing. I swear, he was getting ready to kill me and so it was nothing more than an act of self-defense. I'd swear to it on a stack of Bibles.

Okay, Frey, you want me to say something about my wife, Penny Sue. She's okay, we get along. There ain't no real spark of love there but, hey, I never did believe in that stuff. And my two girls, I love them to death, but that's different. They love me because I'm their father and that means everything to me. You mess with Annie and Frances and I'll break your head.

But who would mess with them? That's one good thing about living in North of Nowhere and owning a good business—everybody looks up to you. Nobody messes with you.

You want me to say something about how I feel about my life. All right, I'll tell you. I feel it's turned out okay.

So I didn't find the treasure. The gold I got out of Sam Hegg's mine ain't been more than about a hun-

dred and fifty grand, total, and that ain't no lie. But I've been real careful not to do anything stupid like spend a lot in one place. I sell the nuggets off as I go—telling people I bought them at the bar off guys who bring it in.

I'm content, a happy man. I blow my cool and have to beat the crap out of somebody once in a while when I'm acting as a deputy, or in the bar with some drunk, but most of the time I keep a lid on my temper. I take my family to church every Sunday. I help the town with a little donation once in a while, a few grand, so everybody will think I'm a pillar of the community—which, by God, if you think about it, I am. Nobody better come along and try to screw it up. To protect what I got I'd do what I did to Sam Hegg ten times over. I mean it. I don't give a damn who you are.

Character Check

Okay? He seems like he could do for our purposes. Let's see if he passes muster:

- Is Forest Volner driven? That is, is he motivated to take action? You bet. Just as soon as somebody comes along who's going to threaten to upset his nice, comfortable life, he'll be off committing another murder.
- Is Forest Volner well rounded? That is, is he, in Lajos Egri's sense, a three-dimensional character? He seems that way to me.
- Is Forest Volner clever and resourceful? Very. He's been clever and resourceful enough to get away with one murder and to hide the fact that he has a gold mine.
- Is Forest Volner wounded? He's got a mother who walked out on him and he had his chance for college gridiron glory wrecked by a knee injury. He's deeply wounded.

- Will Forest Volner act out of fear? He's afraid of losing what he has; he'll kill to protect it.
- Is Forest Volner's true evil character hidden? Pretty well, I think. He seems to be a model citizen for a rough town like North of Nowhere. He has a bit of a temper, is not well educated, but he's a well-liked bar owner and a good volunteer deputy sheriff. Most people in that town would see him as a good citizen, making a positive contribution to the community, despite the rumors that he's got an interest in a whorehouse in another town. He obviously loves his daughters and is a good provider, a churchgoer, and gives to charity.

Okay, I think we've got ourselves a murderer for a damn good mystery. Now, let's let Forest create the plot behind the plot.

THE PLOT BEHIND THE PLOT

You've noticed, no doubt, that here we are talking about plotting when we have not even mentioned the most important character in any mystery, the hero/detective. Of course we will need to have a hero/detective who will solve the crime and bring the murderer to justice. The hero/detective is the most important character when it comes to actually writing the story, but when plotting the plot behind the plot, the murderer is the one who counts. We'll be deciding who we're going to have for a hero and for suspects and all the other assorted characters after we know the plot behind the plot.

Much of the plot behind the plot may happen before the "point of attack," the moment the story begins from the reader's point of view. We don't know yet what the point of attack will be, or who our hero/detective is going to be, but it really doesn't matter. What's important is to find out who and why Forest Volner is going to murder in the plot behind the plot.

Remember now, no decision has yet been made on what

incidents and developments of the story we will show the reader and what incidents and developments of the story we won't show the reader. Here, then, is how Volner commits the murder in the story we're going to tell.

Okay, Volner thinks his life is bountiful and counts himself a lucky man.

Then into his Garden of Eden comes a snake by the name of Caleb Hegg, forty-eight, recently out of prison in Indiana. He's nasty, surly, mean, and he's looking for his brother, Sam. Volner is shaken, but there's no connection between him and Sam Hegg, so he plays it cool. He'd never even told Sam Hegg his real name; he was called "Swifty" then. Caleb Hegg is looking for a fellow named Swift or Swifty but no one knows the three-hundred-pound Forest Volner is Swifty.

The police tell Caleb Hegg they found his brother's Jeep all smashed up in a ditch, and he was presumed dead and dragged off by an animal.

Caleb Hegg doesn't buy this story. He goes out into the wilderness for days at a time looking for something, but no one knows what. Volner guesses he's looking for the mine.

At Volner's bar one night, Caleb Hegg tells Volner that he got a letter from his brother saying that he had found gold and was looking for someone to help him dig it out; he didn't trust the young punk working for him, and was hoping Caleb would be out of prison soon. But that was not to be—Caleb got into too many fights to win an early release. That letter was the last time Caleb ever heard from his brother. He figures that someone might have killed him for the gold.

Volner is stunned. Everything he's worked for over the years, building his comfortable life, could be lost if he were connected to Sam Hegg. Volner is not just living in fear; he's terrified.

The next day Caleb Hegg goes back into the wilderness—he has some clues where the mine might be from his brother's letters and he's systematically tracking them down. Volner follows him, not certain what he might do. He knows already in his heart that he's going to have to kill him—it's just a matter of how and when. Caleb Hegg is looking in the wrong area for the mine, so Volner feels safe for the moment.

A few nights later, Caleb Hegg is back in Volner's bar. He's drunk. A stranger, about thirty, comes in and asks if anyone owns the old pickup outside with Montana plates; he's scraped the fender and wants to make it right. He's a photographer for an outdoor magazine that runs frequent articles against blood sports, and this community lives on the annual elk hunt, so the patrons in the bar—all elk hunters themselves—give him a hard time. The photographer has scraped Caleb's truck. He offers $50 for the small scrape, but Caleb, taking advantage of the situation, demands $200. The photographer says he'll turn it over to his insurance carrier.

The surly Caleb Hegg takes a swing at the photographer and a brawl starts. The photographer, using judo, does well in the fight. Volner, as a volunteer deputy sheriff, arrests the photographer and hauls him off to the jail. The elk hunters in the bar are delighted. Volner has, he figures, the perfect patsy. He'll kill Caleb Hegg and the young photographer will take the blame.

That night there's a freak, early-season snowstorm. Volner searches the young man's car and finds a handgun cleverly concealed in the trunk. Perfect. His training as a volunteer deputy has paid off.

Closing time at the bar. Volner locks up, but tells Caleb Hegg to hang around a minute—he wants to talk to him. Volner would rather not kill him if he doesn't have to, so he tells him that he was the one who was working with his brother out at the mine that turned out to be worthless. He says he was a great friend of his brother and would be happy to let him have a couple of thousand dollars to help him get a new start. Caleb Hegg says he knew what his brother thought of the guy who had worked for him—besides, Sam was a miserable bastard and never had a friend in his life—so he figures Volner must have killed him. He wants half of everything Volner owns. Volner shoots Caleb Hegg in the chest and then drags his body outside and dumps it by his truck in the empty parking lot.

Volner puts the gun back in the young man's car, hidden in the trunk.

It's 3 A.M. Volner lets the young man out of jail, saying he only arrested him to keep the drunks from beating him up because he's a damn animal rights activist.

Volner figures all he has to do now is let nature take its course.

Okay, we now know how the murder happens and why. We're not through with this, though; there are still more details to be worked out. Perhaps we can do something to make it more bizarre, more mysterious. Everything we do in these preliminary stages can be changed or deleted, as you will see. Creating a mystery is an evolutionary process.

So far, I've had a pretty good time with Forest Volner. I even like the idea of the patsy being associated with the blood sport protesters. Because of the conflicting values and contrasting worldviews, there are a lot of possibilities here for conflict.

Every chance you get when developing your plot, look for opportunities for more conflict.

Okay, we have our murderer and our plot behind the plot. Now we finally have gotten to it. Our hero/detective. Ah, the subject of the very next chapter.

The Hero/Detective

One of Marie Rodell's four classic reasons a reader reads a mystery is that it makes the reader feel "more heroic." This is because of the phenomenon of identification, which is one of the primary reasons that readers read fiction. Readers feel what the hero feels, and it feels pretty good to be a hero, especially in a mystery, when the hero/detective will be bringing justice to a situation of grave injustice, a murder.

The hero/detective, though not the author of the plot behind the plot, is of course the most important character in your book because this is the character your reader will identify with most. This is the character your reader will have the most intimacy with.

Many authors of damn good mysteries have given a lot of

thought to what it takes to create a damn good mystery hero. Gregory McDonald (the Fletch series and the Flynn series) has been quoted as saying that, for him, "character comes first, and from the characters come movement, the electricity." Robert B. Parker once said, "The crime is the occasion of the story, but the subject of the story is not the detection, but the detective." The importance to your story of the character of the hero/detective cannot be overstressed: He or she will need to be a dramatic, fully rounded, and interesting character who is living a life that the reader will want to read about.

"Plots," Sue Grafton tells us, are "limited," but "characters are limitless."

Therefore, take care with the creation of your hero. If your book is a hit and becomes a series, you may have to live with him or her day and night, in sickness and in health, until death do you part.

How to Create a Hero Worth Reading About

The hero is a dramatic character who should be created as a fully rounded, three-dimensional character. We will need to create a biography for the hero/detective, and fully detail the hero/detective's background and his or her physiology and sociology, which will give us a deep understanding of the hero/detective's psychology. The hero/detective will need, of course, to have a ruling passion.

We will then need to write a journal entry in our hero/detective's voice so that we can get in sync with the hero/detective's personality and the rhythm of the character's voice, much as an actor must figure out the voice and mannerisms of a character to be played.

In *The Key: How to Write Damn Good Fiction Using the Power of Myth*, I wrote about what, for untold centuries in Western culture, have been the qualities of a mythic hero. As I discussed in chapter 1, the hero of a mystery—the hero/detective—is an important cultural mythic hero. Mysteries are powerful mythic stories. To qualify for inclusion into the mythic hero fraternity, our modern hero/detective in addition to being a well-rounded, dramatic character with a ruling passion, should:

- have courage;
- be good at what he or she does for a living;
- have a special talent;
- be clever and resourceful;
- be wounded;
- be an outlaw; and
- be self-sacrificing.

I'll explain what I mean by each of these qualities. Please note that the hero/detective is the hero of a mystery and is not necessarily a paid detective (public or private). The hero/detective is the character who is the protagonist of a damn good mystery, the one the reader identifies with as the hero/detective who is tracking down the murderer.

The hero/detective must have courage. If the hero/detective does not have courage, he or she will not be able to do the investigation needed to find the murderer. The hero/detective must act in the face of mortal threat and that takes courage. Without it, the hero will not act, and if the hero of any story fails to act, then the story does not move forward.

There's another problem with the lack of courage, and it has to do with reader identification. The reader finds a lack of courage—cowardice—to be repellent and can't identify with such a character. If the reader fails to identify with the hero, he or she will lose interest in the story.

I know, there are always exceptions; that's one of the reasons fiction writing is such a great art form. There are comic detective novels, some quite successful, with a cowardly hero. Often, though, the hero may claim to be a coward, but is not. On *M*A*S*H*, the TV show, Hawkeye Pierce was always claiming to be a coward, but the audience perceived him as courageous because he always did the brave thing when the chips were down.

Literary fiction sometimes features heroes who are cowards (called *antiheroes*), who will not act when the situation clearly demands it, but most sensible people find reading about such characters as pleasurable as listening to a symphony of fingernails on a blackboard.

The hero/detective must be good at what he or she does for a living. This is also a matter of reader identification. Readers do not respect heroes who are not good at what they do for a living. If your sister is dating a janitor, say, who comes in late for work, is messy, and doesn't care, you will find that you're not too attracted to the guy. But say instead the guy is never late, does a good job cheerfully, is careful not to spill the trash, mops the corners expertly. This man has your respect.

In comic mysteries, of course, the hero does not have to be good at what he or she does for a living; often the hero is a bumbler, such as Inspector Clouseau in the Pink Panther series. And even in a serious mystery you might get away with having the hero/detective not good at what he or she does for a living if it is clear to the reader that the hero/detective is not in the right job, or is being forced by circumstances to be working at the wrong job. Say, a conscript in the army. Or the hero/detective is being forced into a totally unsuitable occupation by a tyrannical father, as an example. But, in general, if the hero/detective is a standard hero, the reader will identify far more strongly with one who is good at what he or she does for a living.

The hero/detective should have a special talent. The hero/detective's special talent may be *any* special talent. It may be related to the job of tracking down the murderer, or it may not be. Joseph Campbell claimed in *The Hero with a Thousand Faces* (1948) that a special talent alone will put the reader on the hero's side. This special talent can be virtually anything. In the film *Lawrence of Arabia,* as an example, when we first meet Lawrence he demonstrates that he can hold his finger in a flame. Not much of a special talent, is it? But it is enough to show the viewer that Lawrence is indeed a special person and that is enough to make the viewer identify with him.

Let's say you open a book and find that the hero is a regular guy: He works in the produce department of a grocery store. He has courage, but we don't see it because he has little opportunity to display it. He's good at what he does for a living—he knows his peas and carrots from his eggplant and rutabagas. The reader might like the guy okay, but there's no real attraction. Now let's say he has a photographic memory and has memorized the entire *Encyclopaedia Britannica.* Suddenly, he's a lot more interesting.

Let's say our hero/detective is a nurse. Mary C. Dobbs. Mary works for a doctor. She's efficient and kind and the doctor and his patients all like her—and the reader will, too. Again, there's no real attraction to this character; there's nothing to make her special. But let's say she has an oddball talent. Let's say she can hit a tennis ball blindfolded. You blindfold her and serve her tennis balls and she hits them back every time. Not a useful talent, but it does make her special, and like magic the reader will be attracted to her and identify with her because of it.

The hero/detective is clever and resourceful. As with the murderer, this quality is extremely important for the hero/detective. Remember, Marie Rodell's four reasons people read mysteries. The first one is "the vicarious thrill of the manhunt . . . carried on intellectually in the cleverness of detective and reader."

If either the murderer or the hero/detective is not clever and resourceful, there is little vicarious thrill. Your mystery will be dull, and no damn good mystery is dull.

The hero is wounded. Heroes have been wounded since way before Achilles ever took an arrow in the heel. The hero's wound creates an emotional link between the hero and the reader's heart and is therefore an important aspect of the hero/detective. Also, a wound often creates suspense. The reader wonders if the wound will be further irritated, cause more pain, or bleed, or if it will be healed in the course of the story, fully or partially.

The wound may be physical or psychological. The hero/detective may be recovering from, say, being shot, or being run over in the line of duty. Or the hero may have lost a loved one or have been fired or prosecuted unjustly, or may have made a big mistake or committed a great sin and is in deep remorse. The wound may have happened in the past, or it may happen as a result of the events in the story. However it happens, or whenever it happens, the wound will trigger the reader's sympathy.

One interesting thing in myth-based stories is that a hero's wound is often fully or partially healed because of his or her self-sacrificing actions, while the evil one's wound that often is his or her rationale for being selfish and doing evil, is never healed.

The hero/detective should be an outlaw. The hero/detective needs to be an "outlaw" in the sense that he or she is somehow operating on the outskirts of normality. This is especially true for a detective. Columbo, as an example, is an outlaw in the car he drives and his lack of adherence to the L.A.P.D.'s dress code.

Did you ever notice that TV detectives are often named after guns? "Cannon," "Remington Steel," "Magnum." Have you ever in your life heard of anyone named Magnum? One of the first PI shows on TV back in the fifties was *Peter Gunn*. TV detectives are never married, you may have noticed, and they don't have children. They never live in the suburbs; some live on boats, or motor homes, or in their office. They never drive an ordinary car. Magnum drove some sort of fancy sports car or flew in his pal's helicopter; Jessica Fletcher rides a bike or takes a cab; Columbo drives an old Peugeot. This is all the stuff of myth: The heroes of yore all rode special horses, some with wings.

The outlaw status is also reflected in the hero/detective's regard for the law. The hero/detective in a mystery novel is pursuing justice, and is not necessarily after legal prosecution of the murderer in the courts. In my own *Came a Dead Cat* (1991), it was clear to my hero/detective, Odyssey Gallagher, that the confessed murderer was going to escape justice, so she put the murderer in her car and pushed it over a cliff and into the Pacific Ocean. Readers cheered (though some myopic critics did not).

The hero/detective as outlaw is often an outlaw in the sense that he or she is an outsider, someone who comes into a society that is different from the hero's. Columbo, as an example, is a blue-collar kind of guy; he likes bowling and picnics, and he has a dog. He's always being called on to solve a crime that happens at a place like the Playboy Mansion or a TV production studio, places where he is what's called in Hollywood "the fish out of water." The mythic hero is often a fish out of water. That's the very point of the hero's journey: The hero is going to learn the new rules and be tested and forced to undergo a transformation in a mythological woods that is not like his or her everyday world. In the mythological woods, the hero will encounter people and challenges he or she would never find in the world of the everyday.

The hero/detective needs to be self-sacrificing. The hero/detective is pursuing justice and is not out for himself or herself. Sometimes the hero/detective gets involved for a greedy motive—to earn a reward, say—but at least at some point in the story the hero/detective will be self-sacrificing. Sometimes the self-sacrificing nature of the hero is revealed in the hero/detective's professionalism or even professional curiosity. The hero/detective does not have to be on a crusade or throw himself or herself in the line of fire for altruistic reasons—it might be enough that he or she wants justice done.

OTHER COMMON BUT NOT NECESSARY TRAITS OF THE HERO/DETECTIVE

The hero/detective is usually a loner. Since the hero is an outlaw, or at least an outsider, it's not surprising that the hero would also be a loner. The hero may also be a loner because society has cast the hero out, and that might be part of the hero's wound.

The hero/detective is often not financially secure; sometimes a hero/detective may even be flat broke. Being on the fringe is often not financially remunerative. The hero plays by his or her own rules, and since he or she does not play by everyone else's rules, it's often tough to make a living.

The hero/detective is loyal to old friends and forgotten, even lost, causes. If the hero/detective is your friend, you can count on him or her to be true blue.

The hero/detective is usually sexually appealing and sexually potent. This is not always the case, of course, but it usually is. Miss Marple, even though she was an old prune, was always being proposed to.

You will notice that "amiable" or "likable" or "admirable" was not included in the list. You often find in how-to-write-a-mystery books a section on the amiability, likability, or admirability of the detective. That is a bunch of hooey. The hero does not have to be "likable" in the least. If your hero has a special talent, is clever and resourceful, is wounded, and so on, it does not matter one whit if the reader thinks he's likable. Your hero could be a mean, rotten, low-down, dirty dog and the reader will identify and sympathize with him or her as long as he or she has the heroic traits outlined above and is pursuing justice. If you don't believe me, watch a Dirty Harry movie, or see *The Laughing Policeman.* Or *The Maltese Falcon.* Many detectives are alcoholic, degenerate misanthropes—so many, in fact, they've become a cliché.

CREATING A HERO FOR A GENRE MYSTERY

Okay, here's what we all want: the genre hero who's not just damn good, but unforgettable. Most of us in the murder-for-hire racket dream of creating a hero/detective readers will be dying to become attached to so that they are breathlessly awaiting the next book. A hero/detective who stands out in the field: a Hercule Poirot, a Sherlock Holmes, a Kinsey Millhone, a Kay Scarpetta, a Perry Mason, a Philip Marlowe, a Spenser, a Columbo. How do you create such a character, and what traits would such a character have beyond those the run-of-the-mill damn good hero/detective would have? Sometimes the hero/detectives of the genre mysteries are very theatrical, such as Sherlock Holmes with his fiddle playing and shooting up with drugs; Hercule Poirot sleeping with the net over his mustache and his gourmet cooking; and Columbo with his rumpled raincoat and stinking cigars.

If you're creating a genre mystery, you should think of your characters, particularly your hero/detective, as being theatrical and give them a few exaggerated, theatrical traits. It's one of the things that make them memorable. But they should have no serious problems in life. No sick kids, alcoholic spouses, or mental illness in the family. Genre novels are entertainments: People buy them and read them to *escape* from such problems as sick kids, alcoholic spouses, and relatives with mental problems. Most hero/detectives of genre novels seem to have no close relatives and only one or two close friends, but they seem to know almost everyone on planet earth, and have thousands of casual friends and acquaintances. As a mythic cultural hero, the hero/detective is, after all, a man or woman of the people and is firmly rooted in a community.

Genre hero/detectives need to be *extremely* clever and resourceful. In fact, the chief reason people read genre mysteries is to be dazzled by just how clever the heroes are at digging up the clues and interpreting them so the murderer can be discovered. There is almost always in the genre mystery the "ah-ha" moment, when the detective finally figures it out.

If you want to succeed with a hero/detective series, find some oddball quirks that label the detective as not just an outlaw, but maybe even a little on the weird side. I've been pondering the weirdness of the detective for some time and it seems to me that this weirdness not only makes the detective an outlaw, it also in a strange way isolates the reader from the horror of what they're reading. A mystery is about a murder, and if a murder happened in real life to someone we knew, it would be horrible.

The reader of a genre mystery is fascinated by the horror, yet repelled by it, the way rubberneckers on the freeway are attracted to a wreck, yet if they see blood they might retch.

The reader's desire to be isolated from the horror might be a reason that readers of detective fiction are more accepting of thin, superficial characters than readers of other kinds of fiction. These thin, theatrical, even cartoon characters have an *unreal* quality about them that distances the reader and may make the horror of the murders they're reading about less horrific. Perry Mason was an icon of detective fiction in print and on radio and TV for over fifty years, and was perhaps the largest-selling series character of all time— over a hundred novels—yet the character of Perry Mason was as thin as tissue paper. He had very little reality. He was a machine that cleverly and resourcefully solved murder mysteries.

When concocting the weirdness and quirkiness of your genre hero/detective, let your imagination run wild.

Say your hero/detective, Martha Mavin, is a lady librarian—quiet, shy, bookish—yet she owns a Harley, say, and is the mascot for a motorcycle gang on weekends.

Say your hero/detective, Ernestine Cline, is a forensic pathologist, very scientific and rational. How about on the weekends she does stand-up comedy?

Say your detective, Louie Krep, is an over-the-hill private eye of the old school: tough, drinks whisky straight, and sleeps in his car. How about on the weekend he goes out into the outdoor splendor of the national parks and collects butterflies?

Often, of course, when authors do this, they just pull a quirk out of thin air. Consider TV's *NYPD Blue* that has tough-guy Andy Sipowitz tending to his tropical fish, which, as the blown-away alcoholic that he was at the start of the series, doesn't ring true.

The weirdness or quirkiness of the character needs to grow naturally out of the character's physiology and sociology; it must be included in the character's biography. In the case of Sipowitz, he'd no more have an interest in tropical fish than he'd have in medieval French poetry. The fish were tossed in to give him a quirk. Dennis Franz, the actor who plays the part, does his best to make the audience believe it, but even a very good actor like Dennis Franz can't quite pull it off.

Okay, so how did the bookish librarian, Martha Mavin, ever get involved with a motorcycle gang? Let's say it started with her brother, who used to take her riding, and when he went off to Vietnam, he left his bike behind. When he never came back, she started riding to bring back the memory of her brother. She rides with his old gang, who are hard guys, outlaws, but not criminals, who think of her as a kindred spirit despite her bookishness.

How about Ernestine Cline, the scientist: How the hell did she ever get into stand-up comedy? Let's say her grandfather was a borscht-belt comic in the Catskills and when she was a little girl, he used her in his act and she got hooked. It's her release valve from the pressures of her work.

Ah, and the grizzled old detective, Louie Krep—how did he ever get into collecting butterflies? I haven't been able to figure that one out yet, but I'm working on it. Stay tuned.

Quirks, eccentricities, and contradictions of character, then, help to create unforgettable characters. That the extremely cerebral Sherlock is a dope addict is an example. That Columbo can trap the cleverest of criminals and yet can't seem to get his pants pressed or his car washed is another. Find such quirks if you want to make your characters unforgettable.

THE MAINSTREAM HERO/DETECTIVE

The mainstream mystery novel is entertaining, of course, but it is not an entertainment in the sense that a genre mystery is an entertainment. The mainstream mystery novel is a mainstream novel. Mainstream fictional characters do have sick kids and relationship problems. The mainstream hero/detective often has moral dilemmas, as Robert B. Parker's Spenser does concerning the use of violence (*ad nauseam* to some of his readers, including me). In *The First Deadly Sin* (1973) Lawrence Sanders's hero/detective Francis X. Deleny has a wife dying of cancer, as an example.

Rather than being focused on a murder and the clever and resourceful machinations of the murderer and the hero/detective, the mainstream novel is about a hero/detective and his life, which includes the solving of a murder mystery and other problems that mainstream novel heroes often have—problem marriages, psychological hang-ups, difficulties with kids.

Mainstream fiction teaches us something about life, about who we are as human beings and how we're supposed to act in a moral universe. Mainstream mystery hero/detectives are not only clever and resourceful in bringing justice to the community, they suffer along the way. They have real moral quandaries and death is very real. Unlike the genre mystery, the mainstream mystery does not have the unreal quality that comes from populating it with theatrical characters. The mainstream mystery is painfully real.

THE LITERARY HERO/DETECTIVE

The hero/detective of literary mysteries slogs around in the sewers. Life in the literary mystery is, at best, bleak. These are most often novels of existential angst and moral ambiguity.

The literary hero/detective is generally a dark figure, occasionally extremely violent. He does not fear death; he or she may even long for death. Often the literary hero/detective is far, far out on the bell curve, sometimes half-mad, often manic-depressive or dope-addicted, sometimes a criminal.

The hero/detective of the literary mystery is living in a world in which there is very little joy or even hope; the characters he or she encounters are living in a moral void amid civilization's decay. People read these mysteries, I suppose, to feel better about their lives—because even if the world we live in has its problems, it's not as gloomy as the literary mystery.

Be warned: If you're going to write a literary mystery (and I hope you won't), your prose better be better than just damn good. It better sing.

Now then, having sketched out what we want in a hero/ detective, the next step is to create one.

Creating a Damn Good Hero

When creating a mystery hero/detective, you may be creating a character that will be for this book only or, if this character becomes part of a series, you may be working with this character for the rest of your life. You'd better give the creation of this character a lot of thought.

What are our choices here? Let's do a little brainstorming. Brainstorming is one of the most important skills a fiction writer needs to cultivate. In *The Elements of Mystery Fiction* (1995), William G. Tapply (creator of the Brady Coyne series of mysteries) describes this process as "disciplined free association" and says, "If anyone watched me do it, they'd accuse me of daydreaming."

What you do when you daydream or brainstorm is let your mind churn up ideas, images, and feelings, and you do it without being critical, without editing what you come up with in any way. It's like throwing mud on the wall; some of it will stick, some won't. Just write down anything you come up with so you can edit and judge it later.

After doing a bit of brainstorming for *A Murder in Montana*, where I considered a lot of possibilities—the local lawyer, the local sheriff, a state cop, a local PI, and so on—I hit on one that I liked.

Here's how I found her:

Let's say the photographer, Bentley Boxleiter, who is going to be falsely accused of the crime, has a sister, Kathy, who lives in Berkeley (where, coincidentally, I happen to live). Let's say she is on a spiritual path and a follower of an Indian yogi, Punjan Singh. She's extremely religious, way out there on the bell curve. I think such a character would be wonderfully orchestrated and contrasted with the rough Western town and our murderer. Seems to me, a woman on a spiritual path with a trained, focused, meditative mind would make a damn good detective, too. A focused mind— that might be her special talent.

I phoned a friend who knows about Eastern spirituality and she suggested I name my hero *Shakti*. People who devote themselves to Eastern spirituality, I'm told, often change their name as a way of announcing to themselves and the world that they are a new person. Okay, that sounds good to me. She changed her name from *Kathy* to *Shakti,* which, in Sanskrit, I'm told, means "feminine life force." Sounds good to me.

She's going to make a wonderful hero/detective.

THE BIRTH OF A HERO

Creating characters always begins with their *physiology* and *sociology*. That's where we'll start creating Kathy/Shakti Boxleiter, the same way we did with Forest Volner. From her physiology and sociology will emerge her psychology and her ruling passion, and of course she'll be way out there on the bell curve. When you create one, say, extremely honest character on one end of the bell curve, it's often very good to create another character at the other end, which means they will be well orchestrated. Say one important character is book smart; let's pair him or her with a character who is illiterate but street smart. One character is outgoing and gregarious; the opposite character is self-absorbed and taciturn.

As we create our hero and other characters, we'll need to keep the bell curve and good orchestration in mind.

When I was first starting out as a fiction writer, I'd have simply said, "Oh, I want a character to be into Eastern spirituality, I'll just dress her up in Indian garb and have her go around saying mystical stuff and be as calm in her demeanor as a potato. A female Gandhi." But I know now that's the way you create flat, clichéd characters who will have no depth or reality to them.

I'll have to reverse-engineer this character; that is, I know I want her to be the sister of Bentley Boxleiter and I know I want her to be on a spiritual path. I won't show you all the brainstorming and all the details that I'll make up about her; I'll just tell you what I've settled on. You'll find a detailed discussion of the process in *How to Write a Damn Good Novel* and *How to Write a Damn Good Novel II: Advanced Techniques.*

So, here's what I've come up with after going through the brainstorming selection/rejection process.

ALL ABOUT OUR HERO

Our story takes place in 2002 and she's twenty-seven, so Shakti, who was christened Kathleen Loren Boxleiter, was born in 1975.

As an adult, Shakti is 5-foot-6, thin, tanned from working in the garden, and very straight, with a calm, peaceful expression. She moves gracefully, effortlessly, and has large, brown, warm, intelligent eyes and an easy smile. She has an IQ of 129, in the "gifted" range.

Kathy and Bentley's father, Bristol Boxleiter, was stinking rich with old, old money (which he gradually lost through bad investments and a profligate lifestyle). Bristol was what was called in the fifties and sixties a "lady's man" and is now called a "sex addict." He was suave and loved fine wines, fine women, and Arabian horses. He did not love his wife, Jennifer, who was from an old money family Bristol's father had ruined in a stock swindle. Bristol and Jennifer Boxleiter hated each other deeply and were rarely together, except on family holidays, which made such affairs torturous for Kathy and Bentley.

Jennifer Boxleiter—Kathy and Bentley's mother—frequently went off to clinics to be treated for an imaginary weight problem. Once past thirty, she was obsessed with staying young. She did not enjoy being with her children—they reminded her that she was getting closer to the grave by the minute. Kathy and Bentley were sent off to separate boarding schools and rarely saw each other, except to spend miserable holidays with their family. They did, however, spend some of their summer vacation at the home of a woman they called "Aunt Hatti," a down-to-earth, hardworking African American woman, once the Boxleiters's maid, who had married a successful professional baseball coach and moved to a large farm in central California. Kathy's time there with her brother was the only happiness she ever knew as a child.

Kathy grew up a rebel. She felt she was born into an emotional refrigerator. Her family had everything in a material sense, but no human warmth. At school she was always leading small rebellions: She was caught smoking and drinking in junior high; she shoplifted, raised hell, disobeyed her teachers. She lost her virginity to a senior when she was a freshman in high school. She seduced a sixty-one-year-old teacher when she was fifteen. She had to change schools four times before she got into college—which she soon quit to go hitchhiking in Europe. She had "born to wreak havoc" tattooed on her left breast, with the picture of a fist holding a hammer.

In France she met economic globalization protester Norman Hacket, an American, who was ready to commit any kind of mayhem to bring down the system of what he called international corporate greed. She believed in Hacket. She loved striking blows against the international corporations and the World Bank, symbols to her of her absent, neglectful father. Once, she served four months in a Swiss jail for resisting arrest at a protest demonstration.

When they were not protesting, she and Hacket were doing recreational drugs, mainly amphetamines and crack cocaine, and drinking heavily. Life's a party.

When Hacket and Kathy returned to the United States after being kicked out of Europe, Hacket needed money and, he said, the big companies had plenty of it. He planned to kidnap a corporate executive and hold him for ransom. He was always making grandiose plans and Kathy never really thought he would go through with this one—it was mere braggadocio, she thought. Protest was one thing; kidnapping was another. When she finally did wake up to the fact that he was really going to do it, she bailed out and he went ahead without her. When he was caught, he said his woman, Kathleen Loren Boxleiter, was in on it. He had carefully set her up. After all, she was from an old money family and the media coverage was extensive. Hacket testified against her at the trial, where she screamed invectives at him and the judge and kicked her attorney before being gagged and shackled. She was sentenced to ten to twenty-five years in prison for conspiracy to commit kidnapping for ransom. Norman Hacket got five to ten and was out in three on good behavior.

At age twenty-one, Kathy started serving her sentence at the federal prison for women in Pleasanton, California.

She was an angry, bitter woman when she went to prison, swearing blood oaths of vengeance, lashing out at the guards every chance she got. She had never planned to kidnap anybody, but no one, not even her parents, believed her. Her brother didn't believe her either, but he stood by her nevertheless.

It turned out that prison was the best thing that ever happened to Kathy Boxleiter, she'd say later. In prison, she met a follower of Punjan Singh, Jane Payton, and Jane Payton taught her to meditate, to chant, to find inner peace and happiness. Kathy served four years, four months of her sentence and was released when her conviction was overturned on appeal. Hacket's phoney evidence did not hold up.

Both of her parents, at the time of the present story, are now dead. The family fortune is gone.

Shakti's Journal

I have been asked by my author to tell you about myself. It is difficult, because at one point in my life I became another person. I was a person of darkness and hatred, who thought only of myself and what would make me feel good. In the cold loneliness of a prison cell I was given a great gift. A truly astounding thing happened—it was as if my soul had been purified by a flash of lightning and darkness was turned to light.

I was twenty-one at the time, serving my sentence for a crime I had not committed, and for that I was angry and filled with hatred for Hacket, the man I thought I loved and who had betrayed me. I had hatred for all of society, and my family—everyone except my brother, Bentley. The guards sometimes would salt my food and hose down my cell because I swore at them all the time and called them terrible names. I hated the other inmates, too. And cursed them and spit on them.

There was one inmate, Jane Payton, who was kind to me even though I spit on her repeatedly. She seemed so at peace, and for that I hated her even more. She said I was angry because I did not know my true self and that if I could find out who I really was by meditating and praying, I could be free. She said I could liberate my mind. I said she was a fool—she was in for life without parole for killing her boyfriend. I told her that her only chance for liberation was a bust-out, but she shook her head. She said I could not break out of my prison because the prison was of my own making—only God could break me out.

She loved jokes and she wrote humorous verses and recited them at meals and while she worked scrubbing floors. I began to envy her: She loved life. She was free despite the bars and the guards.

She had this sort of glow about her that I found completely mystifying. If I wanted to be free, she said, free of my own greed and lust and hate, then she could show me the path.

I resisted for a long time, but she persisted. She gave me things to read about finding the spiritual path and because I was bored, perhaps, or perhaps God was already whispering in my ear, I don't really know, I read them. For some crazy reason—perhaps to ridicule her—I started to chant with Jane and then, one night, I started meditating on my own, counting my breaths, and later, I meditated with a simple mantra—God is Love—repeating it over and over.

At first nothing happened. Maria, my cellmate, a Mexican woman who with her son had robbed dozens of banks, was laughing at me, I remember, and I struck her in the face and made her lip bleed. I got thirty days in segregation for that—kept in a four-by-eight cell twenty-three hours a day, with one hour to shower and walk in a small exercise yard. It was in that cell, on the twenty-eighth day of my confinement in segregation, that it happened—my mind was unchained.

I was doing as my friend Jane Payton had taught me, not really believing that any good was going to come of it, half-thinking I was an idiot, when the finger of God reached into my heart and turned on a light in the darkness of my soul and made a new person of me. Kathleen became Shakti in the twinkling of an eye, and the world became a different place, a place of endless goodness and beauty, and I could see for the first time the glory of God.

I remember I burst out laughing, it seemed so absurd at the time. When the correctional officer came to let me out of the cell the next morning for exercise. I kissed her hand.

Once out of segregation, I began to study with Jane and she opened my mind like a flower opening in spring. At first it was difficult, but then I began to see the reality behind the superficial reality of time and space, of place, and temporal being. It was like I had been walking around with a bag over my head all my life, and suddenly the bag was jerked off and I could see and smell and hear and feel!

Then a terrible thing happened. Jane Payton was killed that year. An inmate, Veronica Sales, attacked a guard in the recreation room with a homemade knife and Jane stood in front of the guard and took the knife thrust herself. She died, they said, with a smile on her face because the guard and the attacker were not hurt. They sent Veronica to another prison. I have been writing to Veronica, telling her that there is liberation from her torment if she will but seek it. She writes back calling me a simpleton. Yes, I tell her, I am a simpleton. I know only one thing worth having and that is to see the light of God.

I met Punjan Singh after I got out of Pleasanton; he is an extraordinary teacher. I began attending his meditation class, and after a year he asked me to live at the meditation center, where I now make a modest living teaching meditation and leading yoga sessions. At the center I read and meditate and study the sutras—the ancient holy books. I was put in charge of the center's lovely garden. I knew nothing about gardening when I started, but in the three years I've been there I have learned to cultivate and weed and nourish the vegetables and flowers and now people in the neighborhood seek my advice on how to grow things without using chemicals and pesticides.

I'm often asked what is the biggest change since my "conversion." I do not call it that, but I know what they mean. It is easy to tell them about the biggest change. What I thought was important—getting even for real or imagined wrongs, hating people, being angry about abuses I suffered as a child—I now see as a waste of time. I can see clearly that evil people create only bad karma for themselves, and it's sort of well, humorous. Yes, it's funny. People who think they're gaining great things for their own selfish ends are actually throwing gasoline on the fire of their own private hell. Anyone can see it if they merely open their eyes. You are in the Garden of Eden right now on earth if you will make it so, or, if you prefer, you can make it hell. I go out into the street and I can see all kinds of people who are in hell—their unhappiness is like a plaster cast on their hard, tortured faces.

Since my brother did not believe in my innocence when I was arrested, you may wonder why I will go to help him when he is to be arrested. The answer is simple enough. I was Kathy, then, a person not to be trusted. I was a liar and hated everyone, even myself—it is only logical that he would not believe me. When one is

*spreading bad karma, as I was, it spills out onto others
and infects them like a bad case of the flu.*

*My author asked me to tell how it was when I was
growing up. I hated my mother, but not my father. Since
he was never home, he was a stranger, so I felt nothing for
him. My mother, I think, hated me and my brother, and
when I was growing up I never knew why. I know now
that she was sick with self-loathing because of the empti-
ness of her life. She wanted youth and beauty all her life,
and watching both her youth and her beauty drain away
was, for her, terrible. She had no goals in life—she could
see no future for herself. She died of an overdose of pills
and booze while I was away at college and now I feel
profoundly sorry for her. At the time, in my bitterness, I
called her "the bitch" when she was alive and "the dead
bitch" when she was gone. I am sorry now I called her
those things. I should have pitied her, not hated her.*

*My summers growing up were the only time of joy.
Bentley and I, as you know, went to Aunt Hatti's. We
had known her all our lives. She was the one really
warm, human being we knew.*

*It's strange, but on the farm we weren't allowed just
to play. We had to feed the chickens and shovel cow
manure and tend the garden; we had to help with the
supper and clean up afterwards. The work was hard and
it was often incredibly hot, but even though we were
quite exhausted at the end of the day, we loved being
there. Aunt Hatti's husband, Jefferson, was a nice man,
retired from coaching baseball. He read to us in the
warmth of the evening on the back porch and told us
fanciful tales of knights and ladies in castles and magic.
He had a very deep voice, and though he had very black
skin, he had the bluest eyes I think I ever saw. Aunt
Hatti and Uncle Jefferson had no children of their own,
but their nieces and nephews would come sometimes and
stay awhile and sometimes we'd go up into the moun-*

tains to Yosemite Park. People thought it was funny us being white and Aunt Hatti and Uncle Jefferson being black, but let them stare, Aunt Hatti would say.

But even at Aunt Hatti's I'd sometimes lose my temper and do something bad, like break things. And she'd paddle me and I was glad, because when she'd do it, I knew it hurt her to do it and she was doing it for love. I told her I didn't mind.

She never did paddle Bentley, even though I'd get him to do a little mischief once in a while. I never knew why. Most of the time when he wasn't doing chores he was drawing or petting the barn cat he called Tickles. He wasn't very good at drawing—that's why, I think, he took up photography. He was a good photographer and maybe, someday, he'll look inside and find the new sight that will make him into a great one.

My author wanted me to tell you about my attitude about sex now that I am on a spiritual path. I don't want you to think I'm weird, but my tradition does not allow sexual relations—sex distracts us from our spiritual progress. Falling in love would be a disaster. Yes, I have longings sometimes, but I struggle against them. Often I long just to be held, but I know such longings will diminish over time as I am able to resist the pull of nature on my soul.

My author also wanted me to tell you about my spiritual progress. My problem is focusing my mind. There are yogis in India who, it is said, can focus their minds and melt iron. Not me. I have what is called "monkey mind." My thoughts jump all over the place and it is very difficult for me to get to a point where the world goes away and I can find myself, the truth of my being. But I keep working on it. I am advancing slowly. My teacher tells me that sometimes it takes several lifetimes.

Mr. Joseph Cleemann, the editor of this book at

*St. Martin's Press, has asked my author to ask me how
I now feel about Norman Hacket, and would seeing
him turn me from my path? I have worked hard and
long at forgiving Norman Hacket, and feel that I truly
have, but deep in my soul there might yet remain a
sliver of hatred. I worry about what might happen if I
ever did see him again. Such a meeting would, I know,
be a severe test of my spiritual progress, one I would try
my best to avoid, if at all possible.*

A REVIEW OF SHAKTI

After you create a character, take a few moments to sit back
and reflect on the portrait you've created. Does your character have a sociology? In other words, does he or she have a
solid background? Did he or she grow up in a particular
place with particular parents that he or she had feelings
about? Does your character have a physiology? Do you
know your character's build and appearance, the way he or
she carries himself or herself, and so on?

Shakti grew up in a wealthy, materialistic, dysfunctional
family where her father was mostly absent and her neurotic
mother was obsessed with her looks. Shakti spent her summers with a loving friend of the family on a farm. She has a
slender build, a pretty face with big, brown eyes, and a tattoo
on her breast to remind her of her wild days when she was
"Kathy." She has a quiet demeanor, glides when she walks,
and has a high IQ.

What is the psychology that has come out of your character's sociology and physiology? Shakti became a rebel, wild
and crazy; then, through a betrayal, she became an inmate in
a correctional facility and had a spiritual conversion.

Her ruling passion is to find God through meditation.

Is she an extreme of type? Yes, she is indeed. She's an
extremely devout religious person. She's at the extreme end
of the bell curve, which is just where we want her.

Is she well orchestrated with our murderer, Forest Volner? He's fat; she's slight. He's rough; she's gentle. He's given to rages; she's at peace. He's small-town, corrupt; she's from a big city, but pure-hearted. She's seeking God; he's seeking wealth and pleasure. I'd say they were pretty nicely orchestrated.

Does she have the heroic qualities necessary for a hero? Let's see. Is she good at what she does for a living? Yes, she's a wonderful meditation teacher and organic gardener. Does she have a special talent? Yes, she has visions, as we will soon see. Is she wounded? She was betrayed by the man she loved, but she's been working to heal that wound. She's going to be damn clever and resourceful. And, of course, she's going to be self-sacrificing for others.

In *How to Write a Damn Good Novel II: Advanced Techniques*, I suggested that characters be created not only to be dramatic, but also to be *interesting*. "If you met them at a cocktail party," I wrote, "you'd later want to tell others all about them. . . . A good dramatic character, then, is interesting in the normal sense of what makes people interesting." I think Shakti is such a character.

But some of my readers pointed out that there is one problem with Shakti. Shakti is too perfect. She's a "goody-two-shoes" one of them said. "A real pill," said another. Now of course she's on a spiritual path after all—sweet, kind, loving—but my readers were right: A character that is too perfect starts to lose credibility.

So I thought about it, thought about her having sexual fantasies about monks or avatars, things like that. Or maybe she hallucinates, thinks she sees a black dog following her— a lot of stuff that didn't seem to fit either her character or the tone of the story. I finally hit on it: I'll have her addicted to something. Not dope. Not cigarettes. She's addicted to chocolate ice cream!

Such an addiction would not be an issue with many, but to Shakti, it's a terrible problem. Every time she's tempted and succumbs, she feels that she's fallen off her path, that she's backsliding into the secular world of sensual pleasures.

Okay, when we see her next she will have this terrible addiction that she developed in childhood and it is now a burden to her.

From Shakti's Journal (the section about Aunt Hatti):

Aunt Hatti made her own chocolate ice cream. She had some special ingredients she never told anyone about. It was smooth with tiny bits of chocolate in it. It wasn't overly sweet, and sometimes she put in chopped walnuts. She gave everyone huge bowls of it and we'd sit out on the porch after dinner in the cool of the evening and eat chocolate ice cream and we all felt that nothing in life could ever be better than sitting there and eating that chocolate ice cream a tiny quarter-spoonful at a time to make it last as long as we could.

It's clear, then, where her addiction comes from. How she handles it will have to be added to her biography and more entries will need to be written in her diary about how it disturbs her spiritual practice, but I won't reconstruct it here. I'm sure you get the idea. You'll see her trying to deal with her addiction in the pages that follow.

Now, then, we have the two most important characters for our damn good mystery—the murderer and the hero/detective. Next we'll need to round out the cast.

The Other Characters: Some Mythic, Some Not
and
Mythic Motifs of Interest to Mystery Writers

The hero/detective of a murder mystery is a hero on a hero's journey, so many of the same powerful mythic characters and common mythic motifs that have an irresistible appeal to the reader of ancient stories and myths—as well as most modern commercial and literary literature—might be used to your advantage in your damn good mystery. They are certainly worth keeping in mind. When you're plotting a story, it might be a good idea to check over this list from time to time and see if you can effectively exploit some of these mythic characters and motifs. The list is not exhaustive—there are hundreds more—but I'm giving you the common ones found in mysteries in addition to the hero/detective and the murderer, which I've already discussed.

Common mythic characters found in damn good mysteries:

- *The hero's sidekick*. This character is usually heroic, but sometimes may be an antagonist or even a trickster (see below). As a rule, the sidekick is not quite as skilled as the hero; his or her special talent is not quite as special as the hero's.
- *The hero's lover*. The hero's lover is sometimes also the hero's sidekick and may even be a co-hero. The hero's lover may be as heroic as the hero, a true hero in every way. The hero's lover must be "large" enough to be worthy of the hero. This character is usually very well orchestrated with the hero so there will be a nice contrast.
- *The wise one*. Also called the "mentor." A man, woman, robot, whatever, who is old and wise. The hero's teacher.
- *The trickster*. A fascinating character who loves to play clever tricks. The trickster often changes loyalties.
- *The threshold guardian*. This character warns the hero not to go on the journey. Sometimes the wise one or another character will function as a threshold guardian.
- *The armorer*. The armorer gives weapons to the hero. "Q" in the James Bond series is an armorer.
- *Magical helper*. This character gives the hero magic or magical powers. In ancient stories, the magic was an amulet or a potion. In modern stories, computers or technical people are often magical helpers and their magic comes in the form of some marvelous technological gadget.

- *Woman as goddess.* A saintly woman, usually beautiful, kind, forgiving.
- *Woman as whore.* She's sexually promiscuous. Often a prostitute. Often a temptress. Usually good natured, but not always.
- *Woman as earth mother.* She is motherly, earthy. A plain woman, usually. Solid, dependable.
- *Woman as bitch.* She has a nasty disposition.
- *Woman as nymph.* A young seductress.
- *The loved one.* Not the hero's lover, this is a minor character the hero has a tearful good-bye scene with when going on the journey, and a tearful reunion with when coming home. Usually a relative.
- *The fool.* Only the hero suspects he's wise, and then usually late in the game.
- *The shape-shifter.* This character seems to be one way, then another. A psychotically cruel person who can be sweet at times, say, or a goof-off who is a great surgeon, as in the case of Hawkeye Pierce on *M*A*S*H*.
- *Femme fatale.* A seductress who offers love, but delivers evil.
- *The god with clay feet.* A powerful figure the hero looks up to, admires, even worships, but who proves to be unworthy.

At times, two or even more of these characters may be fused in the same character. As an example, the wise one may warn the hero not to go on the journey, and therefore be acting as a threshold guardian. The hero's sidekick may also be the magical helper.

COMMON MYTHOLOGICAL MOTIFS

Just as mythological characters resonate strongly in readers, so do these common motifs—common scenes or situations—

no matter how many times the reader sees them. Some of them might work well in your story; some may not. Okay, if they don't fit, don't try to shoehorn them in.

- The hero/detective receives a call to adventure. The call to adventure is when the hero is asked to find the murderer. The hero either accepts or declines.
- The hero/detective at first declines the call to adventure and then must be pressured both by inner forces such as guilt and by other people before answering the call.
- The hero/detective seeks advice from the wise one.
- A threshold guardian may tell the hero not to go. A friend, a colleague, a relative—anyone may be a threshold guardian.
- The hero/detective may capture a prize in addition to unmasking the murderer, as in *The Maltese Falcon*.
- The hero/detective may have a showdown with the murderer. This happens in almost every damn good mystery.
- There may be a preparation scene for the showdown with the murderer where the hero may be armed or given magic (technical assistance).
- Someone close to the hero may die: often the sidekick, sometimes the hero's lover.
- The hero/detective often has a "death and rebirth" scene. This is usually where the hero is almost killed and recovers or suffers a symbolic death, such as being disgraced and kicked out of some place and told not to come back. The "ah-ha" moment—when the hero/detective figures out who the murderer is—is a psychological death and rebirth.
- The hero/detective may change costume, which signifies some psychological change; often this happens just after the death and rebirth scene, or just before.

Sometimes it might be the hero/detective giving up or accepting a badge or some other symbol of official authority.

- A common motif is the rescue of the hero by the sidekick.
- Another common motif is the hero rescuing the sidekick—or someone else. The hero's lover is a good candidate for rescuing.
- The hero/detective may invade the lair of the murderer (home, office, corporate headquarters).
- The hero/detective may have to learn some new rules. This is especially true of "amateur" detective stories.
- The hero/detective may have encounters with women— as earth mother, as goddess, as nymph, as femme fatale, as bitch.
- The hero/detective may fall in love.
- The hero/detective may suffer a terrible betrayal.
- The hero/detective may figure out a riddle or other conundrum.
- The hero/detective may come to see that the fool is no fool.

Not all characters have the psychological drawing power of mythic characters, but are nevertheless familiar—the sadistic sheriff, the jocular drunk, the mousy housewife, the anal-retentive accountant. With types, as well as with mythic characters, it's best to try to figure out ways to make them more complex and give them traits that go against type.

When creating semi-major characters (characters we see in the story more than once) it's a good idea to take the time to write a short biography and a journal entry in their voice so that you can get into their heads and give them more complexity and create them with more reality. This is not necessary with minor characters we see only briefly as witnesses or whatever, but I'd still recommend that you think about who they are, give them a few traits counter to type, and think about what they might want—their motivation to act—in the scene(s) they appear in. In other words, give them an *agenda*.

A MURDER IN MONTANA CAST

When creating a cast, some of the characters will be suspects and some will not be suspects.

While the murderer is the author of the plot behind the plot, the murderer is not *necessarily* the most important character after the hero. I know: Most how-to-write mystery books tell you that, but it just ain't so. The hero/detective's chief antagonist may well be another character, say the hero/detective's boss, a suspect, or the official detective on the case—as happened in *The Maltese Falcon*. Take, as an example, Lynda La Plante's *Prime Suspect*. In *Prime Suspect*, hero/detective Jane Tenneson knows the murderer is a thrill killer, and he certainly looks like one to the reader, but she can't prove it and she gets very little cooperation from her colleagues. Her chief antagonists are the sexist idiots who run her department.

You might have a murderer, as an example, who is a sixteen-year-old kid. But the one who's working hardest, the most clever and resourceful antagonist—and the character who is the most active character behind the scenes—is the murderer's mother, say, or the murderer's girlfriend.

You might have a murderer who is, say, a cop, and the whole damn police force is trying to cover it up.

And then, of course, there are all those suspects who might be trying to get out from under suspicion. Hey, for the hero/detective of a damn good mystery, the woods are full of wolves.

You probably know from reading a million murder mysteries that detectives and prosecutors are always looking at *motive, means,* and *opportunity* to determine who their suspects might be. This is a very useful way of thinking about your suspects when you plot your story. *Motive*, naturally, means that the suspect had a reason to kill the victim. *Means* means that the suspect had access to the murder weapon. *Opportunity* means the suspect was in the vicinity and could physically have done the deed.

When a suspect denies having had the opportunity and claims to have been someplace else at the time of the murder, that's called an *alibi*. Now sometimes the alibi given by the murderer or a suspect turns out to be false. In real life and in fiction, a lot of police work goes into checking out alibis.

In a way, your suspects are like your murderer; the only difference between them is that the suspects didn't do it. But, alas, they *could* have done it.

As we shall see when we get to the actual plotting of our damn good mystery, the suspects and other characters should not be just sitting still behind the scenes when they come under suspicion, but should be acting to throw suspicion off themselves or onto others. It's not just the murderer who is actively thwarting the hero/detective in the cat-and-mouse game—other characters can play, too.

Okay, here's our cast:

> *Bentley Boxleiter*, the hero's brother, the photographer, who will be accused of the crime. He has a fiery, combative nature. The sheriff thinks he's guilty; Shakti, our hero/detective, does not.
>
> Bentley was born on July 4, 1973. He escaped from the cold reality of his home life (described above in Shakti's bio and journal entry) and dull boarding schools into art and photography. He was always a wild, impulsive, hot-tempered kid. He was tall and wiry and loud. He loved combat. He joined the judo team and eventually became, at age twenty-five, a fourth-degree black belt. Judo gave him confidence.
>
> The only two human beings on earth he ever loved

were his Aunt Hatti (the black maid who moved to a farm, remember) and his sister. As an adult he became obsessed with becoming a great animal photographer. Always wanting to embrace a cause, he found a home in the animal rights movement. What appealed to him most was the shear audacity of it—demanding equal rights for animals. He hooked up with Cameras-Not-Guns, and became deeply committed to ending blood sports, which he found revolting. He felt loved and appreciated in this group and had a sense of belonging for the first time in his life. When he got the assignment to go to North of Nowhere to photograph the elk hunt, he felt deeply honored.

Bentley's Journal:
Okay, so here I am about to be arrested for murder in a town full of redneck, elk-murdering assholes. I have never killed anyone. I've never even thought of killing anyone. I'm a fourth-degree black belt in judo and I know how to do choke holds, which are deadly if you hold them for about two minutes, and if I was going to kill somebody, that's how I'd do it. But I wouldn't. I'm a photographer—I love taking pictures. I consider myself an artist. I won the Hagadorn Award for the best outdoor photo of the year 2000 by Nature/Art Digest. *It was this incredible shot of bighorn sheep on the side of a mountain in Alaska in a lightning storm. None of it was touched up—I don't believe in airbrushing or using computers—everything I shoot I see through the lens.*

Marshal Dillon, so named by his parents, who loved *Gunsmoke* on TV. Everyone calls him "Matt." He's a country lawyer who loves horses and would prefer to live in the nineteenth century. He's going to be the hero's lover, I decided, even though Shakti won't recognize it until she's known him a while. And, of course, she'll resist having any romantic feelings for him because it would deter her from her spiritual path.

He's tall, lanky, and strong, and, at the time of the story, thirty-four. He has shaggy, long, blond hair and hazel eyes. There is a scar from a bullet wound on the biceps of his left arm.

He was born in North of Nowhere. He loves to ride horses, do amateur rodeo, and is the fastest draw and the best shot in Montana—proved in the last three statewide quick-draw contests. His father was a hard-working, hard-drinking, two-fisted telephone line-man. He died in an industrial accident when Matt was ten. Matt worshipped his dad, but he was killed while drinking on the job so Matt never drinks.

Matt's mother raised him. He had no brothers or sisters, but had a dozen cousins living in the area. His mother was a strong, good-natured, ranch woman who kept the ranch going and food on the table. She made Matt do his homework. He was never a great scholar—he couldn't sit still—but he's smart, so he managed to score high on tests. He played the guitar well and secretly wrote poetry. He still writes poetry, and attends the annual cowboy poetry gathering in Elko, Nevada.

After high school, Matt joined the Marines and served as an M.P. He married while in the Marines. His wife left him three years later. He loved her deeply, and her desertion made him bitter. He withdrew into himself for years. He has a daughter, Destiny (he calls her "Dusty"), who lives with him. When he came home, he became a deputy sheriff while he was going to the junior college. But the petty corruption in the local sheriff's office sickened him, so he went to the University of Montana, finished his B.A., and then went to the School of Law, where he did six years' classroom work in four. He's in demand as the best criminal lawyer in western Montana, but he turns down a lot of work so he can spend more time with Dusty and his Appaloosa horses.

He's still pretty much a loner and, although he does go out with women, he's afraid to love anyone again.

Matt's Journal:
Yeah, I love horses. I'm a criminal lawyer and I love my work. I love Montana, it's big country and it's beautiful. People come here, see the Rockies, it dazzles them.

I had a wife, once, who was great-looking, and she ran off with a tourist with a burgundy Mercedes and a penthouse in New York City. She left me with my daughter, Dusty, who's now nine and can ride as good as anybody. I'd give my life for her; she's nothing like her mother. I've got neighbors a few miles down the road from my place, Maria and Jesus Sanchez, who look after Dusty and my animals when I'm away on business. They're real good people, have four kids of their own. One of them, Diego, is only twelve years old and he's the best calf-roper in the county. I taught him myself.

Meeting Shakti, well, I can't tell you what that was like. She's just a skinny thing with big, brown eyes. She's really something else, coming up here to help her brother, who looks to me as guilty as the day is long, but there's something about her saying he didn't do it that makes you want to believe it.

Sharon Sundance, a resident of North of Nowhere. She's the local "party girl." She had an Indian father and a white mother; she lives in a manufactured home at the edge of town. Hardly getting by on welfare and food stamps, she makes a few dollars selling fake Indian jewelry to tourists in the summer. Now in her thirties, she used to run with the Hell's Angels in Los Angeles and did time for selling crack cocaine in Washington state. She and the victim, Caleb Hegg, hung around together, drank together, but they often fought. He smacked her around a little, but so did some of her other boyfriends.

Sharon's Journal:
"Life without booze is death." That's my motto. I get up in the morning and I feel shitty. I hate this town and everybody in it. I hate the whole damn state and the whole damn Wild West. Fuck 'em all. I hate the whole human race and that includes me. Especially me.

The Indians and the whites both think I'm not good enough. Not pure blood. As if your goddamn blood tells who you are.

Sure, I've been to prison. Sure, I'll go to bed with just about any man who'll buy me a drink. Sure, I'm a whore and a drunk and I don't give a shit.

Some say I might have killed Hegg. Look, you can tell I didn't do it—I'm not smart enough to set it up so that Mr. Twinkle-toes from California gets the heat. I kill somebody, you'd be able to tell right off; his head's gonna be on my mantel.

Lyle Blodgett, sixty-seven, the lazy, boozing, somewhat-corrupt sheriff.

He is personally offended that someone would think they could get away with murder in his town. He's from the area, a former highway patrolman in California and briefly a U.S. border-patrol guard. He keeps getting reelected because he enforces the law the way the citizens of the town want it enforced. He's been married three times and has six kids. He only gets along with one of them, his youngest daughter, Ellen, who works for him.

Lyle's Journal:

North of Nowhere is my town. It's been my town for eighteen sweet years. Some son-of-a-bitch comes to my town looking for trouble, he's gonna get his head broke. One time the state boys came here investigating a complaint of police brutality and nobody, but nobody, would back up the complainant. Everybody in this town knows what I do for North of Nowhere. I keep the peace—keep it the way folks around here want it kept.

I've been known to accept a gratuity. True. Everybody in town knows you can't live on $18,000 a year, which is what it pays to be sheriff. But if something serious needs doing, like a guy ain't paying support for his kids, he can't buy me off—I ain't for sale when it means something. But the petty fines and crap, sure, I'll look the other way. And the folks in town, they appreciate it.

Another thing: This part of the country there's a lot of bad feeling between the whites and the Indians. I figure it is my job to see that no blood gets split on that account. Any Indian in North of Nowhere can go about his business without nobody givin' him so much as a bad look, and I see to it. Any Indian causes trouble, though, he gets the same as a white, a crack in the head and a long, hard stretch in the slammer. We got a judge here, Judge Sims, he sees things my way, and I see to it he has a mighty nice Christmas every year. That's the way it is around here—everybody knows everybody and we watch out for each other. One big happy family.

This Hegg murder. I find this mighty upsetting to the tranquillity of my happy family. The state sends this young Blackfoot with her highfalutin education—gonna show me how to do my job, stickin' her nose in my business. I don't need no help doing my job. I'm gonna catch the guy who shot Hegg and he better not give me no trouble. I've had guys shot trying to escape from my lockup once or twice before, back in the old days.

Molly Runningwolf, a young forensic pathologist with a Ph.D. from the University of Montana. Her job is to assist local officials in making a strong case for the prosecutor. She grew up back East. She's smart as a whip and has a chip on her shoulder.

Molly's Journal:

I grew up in a Catholic orphanage in Vermont, two thousand miles away from my tribe. The sisters were hard as walnuts. They were amazed to find out how quickly I was able to learn. I could do high school algebra by the time I was eight and I learned Latin and French. They used me to prove to the white world how good they were, how really smart I was and how well-behaved. They taught me that we all have a soul and that no human being on earth is any better than anyone else. They taught me to pray to a God I doubted even as a child. I wanted to love Jesus Christ, but it was never in my heart to truly love Him.

They stripped me naked, these nuns. They peeled my Indian skin off me. When I was eighteen and already halfway through college, my cousin from the tribe wrote and invited me to come and meet her and her family in Idaho. I traveled by Greyhound and found once I got to Idaho that I was in another world. My relatives were backward, superstitious, ignorant drunkards living in beaten-up, old, government housing. What they wanted from me, I never did understand, but I fled back to school and buried myself deep in my studies.

A professor, an old Jew, steered me into the study of forensic pathology because, he said, it was an up-and-coming field and I needed a career that would bring me out of the laboratory but not out of science. I thought he was very wise and when I began my studies I found that it was right for me.

Ironically, I got a great offer for a fellowship to work on my doctorate at the University of Montana. It turned out to be one of those chance things that offered me a challenge I could not turn down.

Mike Martin, a local rancher, real-estate mogul, and head of the merchants' association.

His family has been in the Nowhere area for six generations. His family owns half the county. He had a strict Lutheran upbringing: His father demanded that he work hard and obey the rules of God, country, and family. Now, at fifty, Mike Martin is a stiff-necked, overbearing jerk. His alcoholic mother committed suicide when he was ten and his father blamed him for it.

Bad weather, a sickness in the herd, and Mike's father went broke. Mike has been struggling all his life to get back what his father lost—and he's almost made it.

He has a wife who's never home, always on trips back East, Europe—she married him for his money—and a daughter who's away at school and pretty much hates him for being too strict.

Mike's Journal:
I don't care who hates me or who doesn't hate me. Long ago, I accepted the fact that people cannot be trusted under any circumstances. The only thing you can really trust is money.

The people in this town know me. They know that

my word is my bond. They also know that if they cross me, they'll be paid back. I never forget.

I am not a lonely man. People think I am. I am a solitary man—that's entirely different.

Penny Sue Volner, thirty-four, Forest Volner's wife. She grew up in North of Nowhere. Her mother was deserted by her father. Her mother let out rooms and took in laundry, made pies to get by, and spent every evening sitting by the window waiting for her man to come home. Penny Sue was a poor student who could never keep her mind on anything but dolls. She dreamed of a handsome, kind boy, who would some-day sweep her up in his arms. When Volner arrived and started dating her, even though he was almost ten years older, she felt wanted for the first time in her life. Her mother helped convince her that he was the right man to take care of her.

Penny Sue's Journal:

The best things in my life are Annie and Frances, my daughters. They are the only two people I've ever really, really, truly loved.

My life is very pleasant, really. I don't have to work outside the home—in fact, Forest don't want me to. I make pot holders and even won a prize for them at the county fair. Forest sleeps days on account of he works all night sometimes and don't come home till almost sunup. I know he's not at the bar and it's killing me that I don't know where he goes when the bar closes. I know it's another woman, and I really, really want to know who it is so at least I won't have to be nice to her when I meet her at the store.

Forest is good to us, really. We don't want for noth-ing. We got satellite TV, we got a new Ford truck and a

*new big SUV, real nice furniture, the girls wear the
prettiest dresses in the school. He's good to me, too.
Only . . . only every once in a while I get out of line
and he gets terrible mad and sometimes he screams at
me. I got to admit I'm afraid of him sometimes. But
most of the time he's the same at home as he is in
town—he's friendly as a bear. It's almost like he's two
people.*

Clyde Apple, sixty-one, an African-American taxidermist. He's from Mississippi. Raised by an abusive
father and a cruel stepmother on a cotton farm. They
were dirt-poor sharecroppers, He's 6 foot, thin, with
deep worry lines. He's obsessed with owning gold.

Clyde's Journal:

*I learnt my trade from Tom Silverhawk, lived here
in North of Nowhere, who was about the best taxidermist there ever was, and fast, too, lightning fast. Once
he did a 310-pound bear in five hours, dressing out the
meat, too. He taught me three things. One: Keep your
knives sharp as you can. Two: Charge the going price,
no more, no less. Three: Be sure to get paid in advance.*

*I killed a man in a bar fight in 1959, a white man
name of Tate, down in Tupelo, and figured if I didn't
get the hell out of there I was gonna be hung. I was
gonna go west to Los Angeles where I had a cousin. I
was riding the rails, but some rednecks took my money
and tossed me out in Montana. Tom Silverhawk died in
'84, and he left me his business.*

*Sure, I don't have many black friends. Hell, there
ain't but a dozen black families in the whole damn
county. But I do have white friends. Forest Volner—
him and me is friends. He sells me nuggets cheap. Well,
not too cheap, but a little cheap. In the off-season,
when there ain't much work for me, I do some fixing*

up for a widow up on the old creek road who still ain't bad looking and she thinks I'm a stud. I call her Mrs. Hector, even in bed, and she calls me Mr. Apple, formal-like. I think in a weird way we really got something good going.

Then there's the nuggets. I pan for gold in the spring and summer and early fall. I'm a collector, I guess you'd say. There's something about that damn shiny metal that's got a grip on my soul. Keeps me poor—I use every damn penny I can scrape together to buy more. I know it's nuts, but I just can't get enough. I dream of one day finding a mountain of it, enough to buy me a big ole house in New Orleans. I was there once, a great town.

I'm used to the town now, and most of the folks are used to me and we get along. One or two, like Sheriff Blodgett, I'd say, is friends of mine. He's a crook, but he's our crook, if you know what I mean. Most people who bring me jobs like my work. I got respect, I eat well, I live comfortable in a good, warm, double-wide mobile home, and my stash of nuggets keeps growing. What more can a man want?

About Caleb Hegg. Okay, I did meet the bastard when I was out prospecting—claimed I was following him—and he messed up my camp. He was a racist, redneck jerk. I could have killed him easy if I'd have wanted to. He was always going off into the hills. I'd have just followed him and he'd never come back and nobody would ever know what happened to him. But he weren't worth the trouble. If every time a black man got hassled by some stupid redneck and a redneck got killed, rednecks would be an endangered species, let me tell you. I would not kill a man and put the blame on that wrong-headed white boy who calls huntin' a "blood sport." He's just a sorry-ass, mixed-up kid who never learned if you don't thin the herd, the elk will starve. Killing animals, you got to do it so they don't suffer.

Caleb Hegg. He's going to be our victim in the current story, and what a nice victim he's going to be. He's surly, violent, brutal. An ex-con, tough, nasty, a drunk.

Caleb (forty-five at the time of our story) and his brother Sam (who was two years older) grew up in a trailer park in Oak Park, Illinois. Their father was a brutal, petty crook and dope addict, and their mother was a prostitute. Caleb and Sam grew up on the streets, boosting cars, then moved up to armed robbery, specializing in grocery stores.

The Hegg brothers were in and out of prison. Then Sam, in 1992, ripped off a drug dealer and lit out. Out West he met a man who showed him gold ore and eventually sold him an illegal mine for most of the money he'd gotten from the drug dealer, $23,000. Once he'd seen the gold in the rock, he was hooked.

Sam found out later that the mine wasn't worth hardly anything—it was on government land and, except for small pockets that yielded a lump of gold, the ore was useless because there was no way to process it, but he had this idea he was going to hit a vein of pure gold and he'd be fabulously rich. This idea became an obsession.

He barely made enough to live, but the years wore on and he kept hoping. He wrote to Caleb in prison that he was taking out nuggets the size of apples.

Caleb, meanwhile, in prison, had become even more savage and cruel, constantly getting in fights, making slaves of the weaker prisoners. He was the leader of a racist prison gang. The only person on earth he had any warm feelings for was his brother, Sam. He dreamed his brother's dream. When the letters stopped coming from Sam, Caleb figured he had gotten rich and had taken off. He felt betrayed. As soon as he got out of prison, he headed west to find Sam and break his head. He was shocked to find he was presumed dead. He didn't believe the story of the accident and Sam's body being dragged off. He was sure he'd been killed.

Caleb's Journal:

The one thing I learned from my worthless old man was not to take no shit from nobody. And I never have.

I got a real big hate in me. It's like a fire that sometimes burns in a hot glow like a sizzlin' barbecue, and sometimes it burns hot like an arc welder. When I was doing a dime in Joliet, I spent most of the time in isolation, spittin' on the walls and cursing myself. The only light I could see was my brother's dream, that crazy-ass bastard who thought he'd found gold. Sam is the only human being on this planet I give a rat's ass about, and mainly because he gave me something to live for. A reason not to bash a screw's head in and let the fuckers fill my sorry carcass full of lead.

Then he stopped writing. I figured, hell, he hit it big and figured to cut me out. Nobody cuts me out. We had a deal. I figure when I get out, I'll find the son of a bitch and set things right. I never should have trusted him—that was my mistake.

Him and me was different. He loved our ma, that trailer trash slut who spent all her days fucking to get the money for the perfect fix, and she got it, too. Me and Sam was just kids. He bawled for a week.

I never bawled in my life. Whatever comes, I grit my teeth and stand up to it.

I been accused of being a racist, but it ain't really so. The White Brotherhood, the gang I formed in the joint, well, we weren't really hating anybody, but we had to do something. The La Raza gangs and the Black

*Avengers, well, hell, we had to do something to protect
ourselves. We didn't hate nobody, not really. I want to
get that straight.*

DISCUSSION

We now have our cast of characters. The only one who wor-
ries me is Mike Martin, who seems much too stereotypical.
One good test for a stereotypical character is to ask yourself
if such a character would appear on a TV cop show. Mike
Martin would.

Of course, each of these characters needs to be fully
fleshed out to discover their physiology, sociology, psychology, and their ruling passion.

For the purposes of this book, I've kept the number of
characters small, so that it will be a simple design. For your
damn good mystery, you will probably want to have more.
As we go, of course, we'll be inventing more characters. This
is an open process. Some of these characters may not make it
to the last draft, either.

Now that we have the cast assembled, okay, let's plot!

All About Plotting, Stepsheets, Flowcharts, and That Kind of Stuff

or

How to Get the Hell Out of the Way and Let Your Characters Tell the Story

DESIGNING *A MURDER IN MONTANA*

A plot is, according to William G. Tapply in *The Elements of Mystery Fiction*, "a sequence of imagined events which the writer converts into scenes populated by imaginary people. . . . When the writer puts it all onto paper, it becomes a story."

So our plot is a sequence of imagined events. When showing this series of events to the reader, the mystery writer must decide what voice and viewpoint to use. Making that decision takes careful thought. The narrative voice and view-point you choose will determine what scenes you'll be showing to the reader. The factors that need to be taken into account when making that decision will be discussed in Chapter 18. In the case of *A Murder in Montana*, I've decided on a third-person narration from several characters' viewpoints.

Okay, so far we have created a good cast of well-orchestrated characters and these characters will create the story for us, as promised, almost by magic. Plotting now is simply a matter of asking what each character is up to, what they want, what they do, and what happens to them when they do it.

We will keep track of what they do by creating a stepsheet, which I discussed in detail in *How to Write a Damn Good Novel* and *How to Write a Damn Good Novel II: Advanced Techniques*. For those of you who are not familiar with what a stepsheet is, I offer the following example. This is how such a stepsheet would look for Dashiell Hammett's *The Maltese Falcon*:

1. Our hero/protagonist, Sam Spade, a sleazy, hard-boiled private eye, is in his San Francisco office when his secretary, Effie Perine, comes in and says he's got a client, a Miss Wonderly, who is, we're about to see, wonderfully attractive and seductive. Miss Wonderly tells Sam she's got a little sister who's mixed up with a rake named Floyd Thursby. She wants Sam to get her sister away from Thursby, she says. They're interrupted by Sam's senior partner, Miles Archer, who, when he sees the color of the $200 Miss Wonderly is offering as a retainer, says he'll shadow Thursby himself.

2. Sam's asleep in bed that night when he gets a phone call from the police: Miles Archer has been shot dead.

3. Sam arrives at the scene of the crime and meets Detective Tom Polhaus, an old pal. Archer was shot in an

alley at close range by a Webbly automatic, .38. No witnesses.

4. Sam calls Effie, his secretary, to have her call Iva Archer, Miles's wife, to give her the news about her husband's death.

5. Sam, back in his apartment, is having a drink when Detective Polhaus and Lieutenant Dundy arrive. They want to know who his client is, etc. Sam, of course, won't talk. He tells them he'll take care of Archer's murderer. They now give him the news that Floyd Thursby's been shot and killed. They suspect Sam. He denies ever having seen Thursby, dead or alive. But he has no alibi—he says he was out for a walk at the time of the murder. They don't believe him, but they leave.

These five steps in the paperback edition of the book take 21 pages. That would be, at 225 words per page, about 31 manuscript pages.

This stepsheet reflects only what the reader sees. When writing a mystery, the important part of the story for you to know is what the reader *doesn't* see. Many books on mystery writing point out that a mystery is really two stories: one hidden (what the murderer is up to, what I call the "plot behind the plot"); the other on the surface, the scenes that are shown to the reader. There are actually more than just two. There's the story the reader sees unfolding as the investigation proceeds, and then there are the machinations of the murderer behind the scenes both in the past and in the *now* of the story, and the machinations of other characters behind the scenes in the *now* of the story, each with his or her own agenda.

I call the stuff that happens behind the scenes "offstage" actions. When you're plotting a mystery, these offstage actions are extremely important for you to know. Knowing them is really the secret of plotting a damn good mystery.

Here's an example of a stepsheet for *The Maltese Falcon*, which includes what's happening offstage, out of the view of

the reader, starting with the back story of the murderer,
Brigid O'Shaughnessy:

OFFSTAGE (BEFORE THE START OF THE STORY):

- A few months before the point of attack (the scene the
  reader reads first), Brigid O'Shaughnessy met a fat
  man named Casper Gutman and his henchman, Joel
  Cairo, in New York. She was hired to help them pull
  off a robbery scheme. (Notice that the back story is
  written in past tense.)
- Gutman had been looking for a fabulous, jewel-
  encrusted statue called the "Maltese Falcon" for several years and had somehow gotten a lead on it. It was
  supposedly in the hands of a General Kemindov, an
  expatriate Russian living in Constantinople.
- Brigid and Joel went to Constantinople, where they
  decided that if they found the falcon they'd cut Gutman out of the deal and keep it for themselves. Brigid,
  however, was afraid that Joel might double-cross her
  just as she was double-crossing Gutman, so she hired
  Floyd Thursby, a thug, to help her deal with Joel.
- Brigid and Thursby got hold of the falcon (later we
  find out it's a fake, but they didn't know that) and
  took it to Hong Kong, ditching Joel Cairo back in
  Constantinople.
- Meanwhile, in New York, Casper Gutman got word
  from a colleague that Brigid had double-crossed him.
  He discovered she was heading for Hong Kong and
  then to San Francisco, where she planned to fence the
  falcon. He went immediately to San Francisco to
  intercept her.
- Brigid turned the falcon over to a ship captain by the
  name of Jacobi for safekeeping. He brought it on his
  ship to San Francisco. Brigid and Thursby came to
  San Francisco on a faster ship. She planned to double-

cross Thursby just as she'd double-crossed Gutman
and Joel Cairo. Thursby had been in trouble with the
law, so she figured that if he thought a detective was
on to him, he'd get out of town in a hurry, leaving the
falcon to her.

This brings us to the point of attack, the place in the novel
where the reader is invited into the story. Now, then, we'll
proceed with a fully fleshed-out stepsheet, not only showing
what the reader sees, but also including what's going on
behind the scenes.

OFFSTAGE:
Sam Spade, before the opening of the story, has been having an affair with Iva, his partner's wife.

THE READER SEES:
1. Our hero/protagonist, Sam Spade, a sleazy, hard-
   boiled private eye, is in his San Francisco office when
   his secretary, Effie Perine, comes in and says he's got
   a client, a Miss Wonderly, who is, we're about to see,
   wonderfully attractive and seductive. Miss Wonderly
   tells Sam she's got a little sister who's mixed up with
   a rake named Floyd Thursby. She wants Sam to get
   the sister away from Thursby, she says. They're interrupted by Sam's senior partner, Miles Archer, who,
   when he sees the color of the $200 Miss Wonderly is
   offering as a retainer, says he'll shadow Thursby himself. (Current actions, please note, are written in
   present tense; the offstage actions are not numbered.
   This is the way I do it—you can do it any way you
   like.)

OFFSTAGE:
- Brigid has told Floyd Thursby that he's being followed, but he's not scared enough to run—he wants

his share of the fabulous falcon. Brigid decides she has to get rid of him some other way. She shoots Miles Archer with Floyd Thursby's gun, hoping the cops will arrest Floyd Thursby so he'll be out of the way.

- Meanwhile, Casper Gutman, Joel Cairo, and Casper's hood show up and kill Floyd Thursby because he was, they thought, Brigid's partner and had betrayed them.
- A passerby finds Miles Archer's body and calls the police. The police arrive.
- Another passerby finds Floyd Thursby's body and calls the cops, who, at first, don't connect this murder to Sam Spade and Miles Archer, or to Brigid or Casper.

THE READER SEES:

2. Sam's asleep in bed that night when he gets a phone call from the police: Miles Archer has been shot dead.
3. Sam arrives at the scene of the crime and meets Detective Tom Polhaus, an old pal. Archer was shot in an alley at close range by a Webbly automatic, .38. No witnesses.
4. Sam calls Effie, his secretary, to have her call Iva Archer, Miles's wife, to give her the news about her husband's death.
5. Sam, back in his apartment, is having a drink when Detective Polhaus and Lieutenant Dundy arrive. They want to know who his client is, etc. Sam, of course, won't talk. He tells them he'll take care of Archer's murderer. They now give him the news that Floyd Thursby's been shot and killed. They suspect Sam. He denies ever having seen Thursby, dead or alive. But he has no alibi—he says he was out for a walk at the time of the murder. They don't believe him, but they leave.

Discussion

Now then, you can see how the offstage story is unfolding behind the scenes to create the mystery. What is happening is happening because that's what clever and resourceful and determined characters do. The characters are not stiffs being pushed around by the author creating red herrings, as is sometimes recommended by people who write how-to-write-a-mystery books.

When Brigid O'Shaughnessy comes to Sam Spade for help in the opening of the story, there's no mention of Casper Gutman, Joel Cairo, General Kemindov, her trip to Constantinople, Captain Jacobi, the falcon, nothing. Everything she says in the opening is a lie. Her lies, though, are perfectly consistent with the back story and the plot behind the plot.

This lying is what is meant by the "mysterious deflection" often written about in how-to-write-a-mystery books. The reader's attention is being deflected by the character's lying, in keeping with his or her secret agenda. When you know what's going on behind the scenes, behind the lies, behind the deceptions, the mysterious deflection is happening without any need on your part to think up any red herrings—the characters are doing that job for you. In fact, it's when authors throw in a red herring to juice things up that mystery plots start to stink. Let your characters do the work. Think of what they will do, what they want, what is clever and resourceful for them to do, and if you have created dynamic characters, you will have a dynamic plot.

What Goes into a Stepsheet and What Doesn't

Since the stepsheet is for you and your readers, the amount of detail you wish to include is up to you. I have a few select readers read my stepsheet and look for "holes," meaning coincidences, unmotivated events, places where the characters act out of character, lack of maximum capacity, and so on. Even at this stage of development, my readers will often say things like, "Hey, the murderer is murdering out of jealousy—why not have her cut the victim's nose off?" Good things like that.

Some people write stepsheets "fat" and some people write them "thin." I prefer thin, so my readers won't get bored. But it's up to you.

Here's an example of the first step of a stepsheet that's fat:

1. Cinderella is busy cleaning the fireplace, happily thinking of the monthly bath she's going to have on Sunday. She's wearing a red dress, tattered, stitched up the sides, with smudges down the front. There are fleas on her unshaven legs. Her hair is a rat's nest. In comes her stepmother. Her stepmother is plump, stern, wearing tweeds, hair braided. Her stepmother tells Cinderella to go out back and clean the latrine better or she can't have her bath on Sunday. Cinderella doesn't protest, being virtuous in the extreme, but says, "Yes ma'am," and cheerfully heads for the latrine.

The same step, thin:

1. As a filthy Cinderella is happily cleaning the fireplace, she is interrupted by her wicked stepmother, who tells her to go out and clean the latrine again or she won't be allowed to have her monthly bath. The virtuous Cinderella obediently does as she's told.

Whichever works for you, you should use.

The initial steps, the back story, might include not only the actions of the murderer (his or her plot behind the plot), but may include the significant actions of the victim, the detective, suspects, witnesses, and others. As an example, it is important to the story of *The Maltese Falcon* that Sam was having an affair with his partner's wife, Iva, at the time his partner was murdered. I included it because it's one of the reasons the cops think Sam might have murdered Miles Archer.

By stepping your story out like this, when the story opens you will know who has done what, and you won't have much trouble finding ways for your detective to dig up the info. What you want to avoid is losing control of what is happening behind the scenes, or having to invent what happened behind the scenes at the end of the story when you're wrapping everything up. That is how you end up with a story that sounds contrived. Everything that happens in a story should spring naturally from the characters and their wants, goals, needs—their agendas—and actions.

Some mystery writers keep track of what's happening offstage by using a flowchart.

A flowchart is simply a stepsheet that is done in columns. Say Sam is column one; Brigid is column two; Gutman and his henchman are column three; the police, column four. If the story covers a few days, some writers use an hour-by-hour flowchart showing what each character is doing at any given time. Some of my students do this using database software.

Another useful technique is to put the steps on 3-×-5 cards, using different colors for the onstage action and the offstage action. At times you'll want to rearrange the order of the steps; if you've written the steps on file cards, rearranging is a snap.

Now it is a matter of what actions we plan to show the reader and what actions we won't show the reader.

THE FOUR PILLARS OF MYSTERY FICTION

When plotting a mystery, you should keep in mind the four pillars of mystery writing: mystery, suspense, conflict, and surprise. If you keep these four things in your mind as you're plotting, you can't help but make your mystery damn good.

1. MYSTERY

It seems almost too obvious to state, but a mystery is about a *mysterious* happening. If, say, a man is murdered in a bar in front of witnesses, you have a murder but you do not have a mystery. A mystery is an unexplained event or circumstance; something strange has happened that baffles the reader. If a murder victim is found and the murderer is unknown, yes, that's a mystery, but in a damn good mystery there should be more mystery in it than just who done it. Why was it done in this strange, mysterious way? You want your reader to feel this sense of mystery so that he or she will want to read on and see the mystery solved. The mystery will raise story questions about who did this terrible thing and why. The murder itself should create sympathy, and the detective's desire to find the murderer should cause the reader to identify because the reader will be in concert with the hero's goals.

2. SUSPENSE

Suspense has to do with what is going to happen next. Any strong story question creates suspense in the sense that the reader will want to know the answer to the story question. Say, if your hero is going to propose marriage to his girlfriend, the story questions might be: Will she say yes? Will he have the guts to actually go through with asking her? With any strong story question, suspense is created. The strongest story questions and the strongest suspense happen in a climate of menace. A situation of strong menace can create the strongest kind of suspense—"nail-biting suspense," as it is sometimes called. In a mystery, as a general rule, the more suspense the better. You should try to have menace, danger, the threat of death lurking at every twist and turn of the plot. Creative writing coaches have long stressed the importance of making your reader "worry and wonder." The "wonder" is curiosity about what's going to happen next and is therefore mildly suspenseful; the "worry" part is the nail-biting suspense that will keep the reader flipping pages on into the night.

3. CONFLICT

In *How to Write a Damn Good Novel,* I pointed out that the three greatest rules of dramatic writing were "conflict!" "conflict!" "conflict!" Conflict does not necessarily mean bloodshed or shouting and screaming. Dramatic conflict means that the characters are engaged in a conflict of wills: A character wants or needs something and attempts to get it and the effort is blocked by something—bad weather, a big explosion, a mechanical failure—or, more likely, an antagonist, another character. Inner conflict is conflicting desires *within* the character. Conflict gives your story life, causes your characters to act, to feel, and to change and develop. It is the gasoline that drives the story forward.

4. SURPRISE

Elizabeth George, the popular mystery writer, once said that when plotting a mystery, about halfway through she wrote down everything she thought the reader would be expecting to happen.

In a book I was writing, I might make a list like this of what I think the reader is expecting to happen:

- Bob committed the murder and the detective will expose him.
- Joe will ask Mary to marry him.

- Phil faked his own death and is very much alive.
- Al was the real bank robber.
- Denise is really a lesbian and is trying to seduce Bob to ruin his marriage.
- Billy-Bob is the one who escaped from the mental hospital and had his face changed.
- The dead man is really Grace's father.

Elizabeth George said that after she writes down her list, she makes sure that at least two or three of the things she feels the reader would expect to happen do not happen. This is really a wonderful idea. One of the delights of reading a damn good mystery is that surprising things happen. You should make sure that they do.

Designing the Plot for Fun and Profit

A Damn Good Mystery's Five-Act Design

Almost all damn good mysteries (with some rare exceptions and variations) are constructed with a simple, five-act design:

Act I: Tells How the Hero/Detective Accepts the Mission to Find the Murderer

Act II: Tells How the Hero/Detective Is Tested and Changes, and, in the Pivotal Scene, Dies and Is Reborn

Act III: Tells How the Hero/Detective Is Tested Again and Finally Succeeds

Act IV: Tells How the Hero/Detective Traps the Murderer

Act V: Tells How the Events of the Story Impact the Major
    Characters

That's it. A damn good mystery is the hero/detective's
story, even though the author of the plot behind the plot is
the murderer. A damn good mystery traces the progress of
the hero through the five acts. Of course, because fiction
writing is an art as well as a craft, there are some rare, art-
fully done exceptions to the five-act design, which will also
be discussed.

But we'll begin with Act I of the standard five-act design.

ACT I: TELLS HOW THE HERO/DETECTIVE ACCEPTS THE MISSION TO FIND THE MURDERER

In the standard five-act design, Act I begins at the point of
attack (the very first thing the reader reads when opening
the book) and ends at the point where the hero/detective
accepts the mission to find the murderer—no matter how
long it takes. In the mythic paradigm, this part of the myth
is called "the world of the everyday" or "separation"—
where the hero is "separated" from the common world and
begins his or her heroic initiation.

The purpose of Act I, as in the opening of any dramatic
story, is to get the reader involved in the story world and to
get the chain reaction of the events of the plot rolling.

In designing Act I, you should keep in mind that your
mission is to create an exciting experience for your reader or
viewer. To do so, you will need be sure to:

—create powerful story questions;

—put characters in dramatic conflict (characters exercising
    opposing wills); and

—touch the reader's emotions, particularly sympathy.

There are different strategies for designing Act I, but all of them present strong story questions, put some characters in dramatic conflict, and touch the reader's emotions in some way. Here are some of the usual approaches:

- *Show the murder without revealing the identity of the murderer.* Often in Act I of a damn good mystery, the murder is shown without revealing the identity of the murderer by using an objective viewpoint. This can be an effective technique and is often gripping. It creates strong story questions (Who will get killed? Will the killer get away?); it offers intense, dramatic conflict; and, since someone is shown being murdered, it should certainly arouse the reader's emotions.

  The dark figure got out of his car, removed a long flower box with a red bow, went to the edge of the cliff, opened the box, and extracted a Remington XB-42 sniper's rifle with a Higby scope. He put the rifle under his coat and walked over to the retaining wall that ran along the side of the road. From there he could see the apartment building below, where, less than forty yards away, the lawn party was just winding down. He put the rifle to his shoulder and looked through the scope. A blonde young woman was dancing on the lawn by herself, giggling, weaving drunkenly to the music, as he sighted in on her face. . . .

- *Show the murder and reveal the identity of the murderer.* This design obviously kills the two most important story questions in the mystery (Who did it? and Why did he do it?). But there are other story questions raised: Will the murderer get away with it? Will he be caught? An Act I that reveals the identity of the murderer can be effective if the cleverness and resourcefulness of the murderer and the cleverness and resourcefulness of the detective locked in the cat-and-mouse game of deception and detection are dazzling enough to absorb the reader or viewer. This design is used in the *Columbo* TV series.

Macon had had it with Joyce. It wasn't her drinking; it wasn't her whoring around with every man who gave her a wink: it wasn't even the money that she spent like water. It was the lamp she dragged home the night before. He'd never tell anyone: he'd already decided that even if he were caught and tortured, he would never tell why he did it. It sounded crazy to murder someone over a lamp, but the hideous brass monstrosity was the reason, a goddamn lamp that looked like a Komodo dragon. She brought it home as a symbol of one of her sexual conquests, he was sure of that, and as soon as he saw it, he knew not only that he was going to murder her, he knew how he was going to do it—manual strangulation. A gun would be too remote, too distant; to do it bare-handed, that would be exquisite pleasure.

• *Show the body.* This is usually an effective opening. The story questions surrounding the mysterious nature of the murder can be raised right away. Upon seeing the body, the reader is often shocked and horrified, and immediately sympathizes with the hero/detective.

Marjo Applegate awoke about four in the morning to a weird, chomping sound, sort of like somebody hitting soft wood with a dull ax. The sound came from her roommate's room, and there was this other sound: a man's voice. Men were definitely not allowed in the apartment after 10 P.M. and never in the bedroom area.

There it was again—chomp. And then footsteps and a door slamming.

"Linda? That you?" she called out.

Marjo was going to report this, and she was going to tell her roommate, Linda Lawson, who did not think the rules applied to her. Marjo went down the hall. There were drops of something wet on the rug coming out of Linda Lawson's room. Wine, maybe. Another rule broken: The committee was going to hear about this, Marjo thought.

She knocked on Linda's door.

"I know you're in there, Miss Lawson, and I know you've had company. We have to talk."

No answer. Marjo pushed the door open and peeked inside.

"Don't pretend you're asleep . . ."

The light in the aquarium was on, and inside there was something swirling around. The water looked dirty, and some of it had spilled out onto the table because the tank was filled up to the brim, water spilling over. In the tank was something that looked like a ball . . . a ball with blond hair. And, as she got closer, Marjo could see that it was a human head— Linda Lawson's human head.

Marjo stepped back, shaking her head. This didn't make any sense . . . She thought, the committee is going to really—

And then she heard a scream that sounded hollow and far away, and she realized that it was coming from her own mouth.

Twenty minutes later, after the neighbor called the police and the police arrived, she was still screaming.

- *Show the victim alive.* If the reader has seen the victim alive and well before the murder, the reader will have more sympathy for the victim. This will pump up the reader's desire to see justice done, and get the reader more deeply and emotionally involved in the story. If you choose this option, the opening scenes will have to be written in a way that evokes some other dramatic conflict—say, a domestic dispute or lover's quarrel, some dramatic confrontation such as road rage, or the like—to avoid a dull opening. It is possible to have a gripping opening with low levels of dramatic conflict if the coming murder is heavily foreshadowed. Since the reader does not see the murder, the powerful story question of who did it is operational.

The two detectives sat on the couch. Wendy served them tea. One of the detectives—the man—was talking. They checked it all out: There was no one stalking her. As far as they could tell, whoever slashed her tires also slashed the tires of six other cars in the neighborhood that night, and even though they have not caught the punks who did it, they're pretty sure it was teenage vandals.

The woman cop smirked at her, the condescension of an older woman toward a young, pretty airhead. She said they checked out the man Wendy thought might be harassing her, this Brad Norman, and he had an alibi for the evening she said she had been followed: He had spent the night on his boat with two other people.

Wendy said, "I saw him. I know it was him. And he slashed my tires. And he keeps calling me."

"How do you know it's him if he just breathes into the phone?"

"I just know," Wendy said.

"You could ask the judge for a court order," the male policeman said. Wendy liked him; he seemed really concerned.

"He's going to kill me," Wendy said. It was the first

time she'd said it aloud and she was surprised at how even and calm her voice was.

"Perhaps you should take a vacation," the woman cop said. "We talked to your boss. He said you've been stressed a lot lately."

"You don't believe a word I said, do you?" Wendy said.

"We spoke to Brad Norman at length," the woman detective said. "He is really concerned not only for your safety, but for your . . . emotional state."

The man detective nodded in agreement. "He's not really the type," he said.

Wendy thanked them both and showed them to the door.

"After he kills me, will they have you two on the case?"

"Nobody's going to kill you," the woman detective said. "You need some professional help."

Wendy closed the door and went to the window. She watched them get into their car and drive away.

She turned around and gasped. Brad Norman stood in the doorway to her bedroom and he had a knife in his hand.

"Scream," he said. "I want you to scream."

"I won't scream," she said. She turned her back to him and stood listening to the sound of his heavy breathing, just as he'd sounded on the phone, and watching the detectives' car disappear around the corner.

- *Show the hero/detective's call to adventure.* If your damn good novel is a third-person narrative written from the point of view of the hero/detective, or a first-person narrative with the hero/detective as narrator, then the hero/detective's call to adventure is often what you'll be opening with. Usually the hero/detective will be engaged in some kind of dramatic conflict when the call to adventure (the request to become involved in the investigation of the murder or some kind of business that will soon result in murder) comes. Showing the hero/detective receiving the call to adventure can be an effective opening because the reader, through the magic of identification, is living the life of the hero right from the start. When this motif is used, Act I will often be short, perhaps only a single scene. Since we have not seen the body or the victim before death, evoking the reader's emotions will require some thought. Here's my example—hope you find that it works:

Big Jake hated this kind of work, but, what the hell, the rent was due. The next-to-the-worst part of the deal was tailing the poor slob until he hooked up with his honey. The very worst part was telling wifey her suspicions were correcto. Over the years he'd seen some of them bawl for an hour or so; others faint; still others go psychotic. Funny thing, infidelity.

This client was a mousy little number, looked like she might be part Asian, quiet, serious behind her big bifocals, with a round, smooth face that looked like it never had a smile hanging on it. She was wearing a brown dress, plain as butcher paper.

"You have photos, Mr. Winchester?" she asked.

He nodded, tapping the large white envelope on his desk between them. He slid her his bill.

"It's customary to settle accounts first," he said, handing her his bill—$482.10.

She wrote out a check. He hated taking checks, but this one looked like she probably had something in the account besides goose eggs.

She put the check down, but kept her fingers on it.

"The photos?" she said.

"I'll give you a peek at one," he said. He showed it to her. It was of her husband going into the room with the other woman. The client made a gurgling sound in her throat. She snatched the check back.

"What—what's the matter?" Big Jake asked. "I checked that woman out. She's a hundred-buck-an-hour hooker—Sheila Star she calls herself."

"That may well be, Mr. Winchester, but that man— he is definitely not my husband."

"What the hell are you talking about? I saw him come out the back door of his factory—he drove over to her apartment in his Lincoln—of course it's your husband."

"That man is my husband's barber. He drives a Lincoln, too."

She tore up the check. "Make sure you keep the bill, Mr. Winchester, put it down on paper. You'll need it when you sue me for nonpayment."

She stomped out.

He sat staring at the door for a few minutes, shaking his head. Then he poured himself half a water glass full of cheap Kentucky sippin' whisky, sat back, and had a long belly laugh. First time he ever followed the subject's barber.

He was still chuckling a few minutes later when the phone rang. He picked it up. "Winchester Investigations."

"Jake, I got a problem." It was Ted, his brother. Ted had gone off to the Gulf War a bright tech sergeant half-way to his twenty years and had come back in a straight-jacket, claiming he went for a ride with space aliens.

"Your problem is my problem." Big Jake said.

"Remember Linda Lawson?"

"Your latest flame? Sure."

"Somebody cut her head off last night, dumped it in my fish tank—the one I was letting her use."

"You better stay out of it. Ted. Let the cops handle it."

"That's just the problem, Jake. The cops are handling it. They say they can prove that I did it."

"Did you?"

"That's just it . . . I'm not sure."

"Where are you?"

"Hiding."

"Where?"

"In the trunk of my car, across the street. I'm on my cell phone."

"Hug your spare tire. I'll be right there."

This, then, would be all of Act I; the detective has taken the case.

The purpose of Act I is to get the reader involved with the characters and the story. Once the detective takes the case, we move into Act II, leaving the everyday world of the detective behind.

ACT II: TELLS HOW THE HERO/DETECTIVE IS TESTED AND CHANGES, AND, IN THE PIVOTAL SCENE, DIES AND IS REBORN

In the mythic paradigm, this part of the hero's journey is called the *initiation.* It is similar to a coming-of-age story in which the hero gets initiated into adulthood. The hero leaves the world of the everyday, crosses a threshold, and enters a mysterious "mythological woods" that is far different from the hero's everyday world. Here the hero must be initiated— in other words, "learn the new rules"—and be "tested" by the trials presented by the evil one, the evil one's minions, and others.

In a damn good mystery, the hero/detective, like any hero, fails some tests and passes some tests. The hero's character changes in the process; he or she will learn new skills, find unsuspected talents buried within, and gain some insights into his or her own inner nature, becoming more self-aware. In dramatic terms, the hero is undergoing "character growth." Your English teacher in high school called this "character development."

For the professional detective, such as Hercule Poirot, who already has skills, knows his talents and weaknesses, if any, and has a whole lot of self-awareness and self-confidence, these tests do not produce growth. Often, with series characters who don't change from book to book, the "growth" or "development" in the character has to do with how the hero/detective relates to other characters. Friends become enemies, lovers become ex-lovers, trusted clients are found to be murderers, and so on.

Whether the hero/detective is an amateur or a professional sleuth, the tests and trials and the character growth progress until the pivotal scene, which usually comes around the halfway point in the entire story, but may come later. The pivotal scene in the mythic paradigm is what Joseph Campbell called the "supreme ordeal." Gustav Freytag, the influential nineteenth-century German dramaturg, called this pivotal scene—this supreme ordeal—a "catastrophe" for the hero, the "nadir" of his or her fortunes. From then on, the fortunes of the hero, which had been steadily building until that point, will generally improve.

In a damn good mystery, this pivotal scene is usually highly dramatic, and often comes at the nadir of the hero's fortunes, but doesn't have to. It does not have to be the "supreme ordeal" either. There are many stories, Raymond Chandler's *Farewell, My Lovely* (1940) as an example, that have a least five or six severe ordeals. Which one is supreme? Marlowe is shot at two or three times, kidnapped, drugged, beaten, hounded by the cops—hard to tell which ordeal is supreme. But there's no problem at all picking out the pivotal scene, where he's been drugged and comes to, gets his suit pressed as a change of uniform, and returns to work, eager to go on the offensive.

The pivotal scene will reverberate through the rest of the story and stands as a symbolic death and rebirth of the hero. After the rebirth, the hero will see things differently, and perhaps operate differently. The pivotal scene might be, say, the death of someone close to the hero—a lover or side-kick—that will cause the hero to seek not just justice but revenge. It might be a situation of intense menace that changes a flippant, wisecracking hero into a grimly serious one. It might be the surprising death of a suspect the hero was certain was the murderer, shaking the hero's confidence. It might be a serious and menacing confrontation with the murderer that will make the hero realize that the murderer is far more evil and menacing than he or she thought.

The hero/detective after Act II is a very different charac-ter than the one we first met in the beginning of Act II, both because of what he or she has learned incidentally through being tested and challenged, and from the impact of the intensely dramatic pivotal scene.

Since this is a practical, step-by-step guide, after all, I offer three examples:

Max, the PI. The hero, Max, is a former FBI special agent who was kicked out of the bureau because of his drinking problems and his tendency toward insubordination. Now a PI, he takes the case of a wife who thinks her husband is hav-ing an affair and might be planning to kill her. Max thinks it's hooey, but he accepts the job because he needs the work.

Max goes through the motions, interviewing witnesses, not taking his client seriously (flunking the tests), padding his expense account, spending the afternoon in bars. In the evening he's haphazardly following his client's husband and discovers he's going to a secret meeting and figures, Hey, it looks like the guy really is playing around with another woman. He reports this to the client. The client wants to know who the woman is. After a week of following the husband, Max tails him to another secret meeting and finds out the guy is not seeing another woman—he's going to a poker game. Max tells the client her husband does not have another woman, but she insists he does and that her husband and the other woman are planning to kill her, but she has no evidence. She wants him to stick with it, but he thinks she's loopy, so he refuses. Two weeks later he gets a call from a cop friend of his—his former client is dead.

He sees the body; it's horribly mutilated. This is the pivotal scene. The hero gets drunk, gets in a fight, spends the night in the drunk tank. This is the symbolic death. He sobers up, gets his suit pressed, has his hair cut, redeems his gun at the pawn shop, and goes back on the case. He's been reborn a new man. Because of his guilt, he's going to be on fire to solve the case and Act III begins.

Alice Cicero, Amateur Detective. She's a stand-up comic in her fifties, doing biting political humor and redneck jokes. She's been playing to small audiences in smoky clubs, hoping for a break since she was kicked out of college at twenty for smoking dope. She's cynical, road-weary, bitter, feeling that at life's banquet she got mostly scraps.

Her one real friend is Mavis Dancer, a one-time burlesque queen who does a mind-reading act. Mavis is murdered, bludgeoned to death, in the parking lot and the cops in this backwater Southern town don't seem to care.

Alice starts to investigate. She finds some clues: a possible footprint, a Cadillac seen speeding out of the parking lot. Her primary witness is Georgie, a retarded boy who parks cars in the club parking lot, so the police don't think she's onto anything. Along the way, Alice makes a few mistakes—one suspect sics a dog on her, another steals her purse, another sends her on a wild goose chase as a practical joke. Alice finds out that, at her last performance, Mavis quit in the middle and, coming off stage, gasped that she'd really read somebody's mind and he was thinking of murder.

This can't be a lead, Alice thinks.

Alice doesn't believe in mind reading. She always knew Mavis was faking it, but she thinks if she dresses up in Mavis's robe and turban and pretends that she's getting vibes, she might manage to flush out the murderer.

She tries it. Nothing happens for four nights. The next night she gets banged on the head and while unconscious she moves toward a light, as she heard some psychic on *Oprah* say, and in the light is Mavis, thanking her for being such a good friend and telling her to listen to Georgie.

Okay, this is the pivotal scene of her being attacked, followed by the death and rebirth of the hero. When Alice wakes up, the doctors tell her she had a near-death experience. She is no longer cynical—she realizes that Mavis did read somebody's thoughts as he was planning a murder and now, with the wise fool, Georgie, she goes after the murderer with new energy and a whole new set of beliefs.

Simon Craft, Detective. Simon is an experienced detective, but new to homicide (where he will have to learn the new rules and be tested). His first case turns out to be a serial killer of five-to-seven-year-old girls. A sensitive man, Craft begins to crack under the strain. The team he is on believes they have their man, but they don't have enough evidence to convict. Fearful that the system will let a monster go free, Simon, in the pivotal scene, plants evidence so they can at least hold the suspect for trial.

He is caught on videotape planting the evidence and is

subsequently stripped of his badge and gun and kicked off the force. This is his death scene.

He is reborn as a private citizen, determined to stop this monster. This is his rebirth, and Act III begins.

ACT III: TELLS HOW THE HERO/DETECTIVE IS TESTED AGAIN AND FINALLY SUCCEEDS

Act III begins after the hero has survived the pivotal scene and is "changed." The hero goes after the murderer with a new attitude.

Act III is a continuation of the cat-and-mouse game with the murderer. The hero/detective, having survived the pivotal scene and having experienced a death and rebirth, is now going after the murderer with renewed vigor and determination.

Act III ends with the discovery of the identity of the murderer. This moment in dramatic works has traditionally been called the "obligatory scene." The obligatory scene is the scene in which the central, most powerful story question is answered. In the case of a darn good romance, say, that scene would be the moment when the female hero decides she's going to make a lifelong commitment to her lover. In the case of a damn good mystery, this powerful story question is: Will the hero/detective solve the mystery?

The progress of a damn good mystery is this: As the hero makes his or her progress on the case, his or her bafflement is increased and the mystery, as a rule, gets more mysterious. And the situation gets more menacing.

Then, when it looks like nothing adds up, the hero suddenly has a great flash of insight and reasons it all out. This happens in an instant. We now know that the one among us who is evil and has been hiding is about to be unmasked in the showdown scene, which in the mythic scheme of things is the "final confrontation with the evil one."

ACT IV: TELLS HOW THE HERO/DETECTIVE TRAPS THE MURDERER

Now that the hero/detective knows who the murderer is, the question remains: Can the murderer be brought to justice?

In the mythic paradigm, this part of the story is the *return*, where the hero returns to the world of the everyday, bringing the *prize* that is a boon to the community. In the hero/detective's case, this boon is the removal of a murderer from their midst.

In the return portion of the myth, there is the final confrontation with the evil one and that is precisely what happens in every damn good mystery. The evil one/murderer and the hero/detective meet face to face in what Hollywood calls the "showdown scene."

Here, another one of Marie Rodell's classic reasons for reading a mystery is delivered to the reader: The reader has the satisfaction of seeing the transgressor punished. The capture may or may not mean that the murderer is handed over to the law; some alternate punishment may be imposed. But the murderer *must* be punished in some meaningful way.

In the words of William Goldman, the screenwriter of such classics as *Butch Cassidy and the Sundance Kid*, "endings are a bitch." You'll find when you get there, trying to make it all come out right while still playing fair with the reader—having mystery, menace, conflict, and surprises—is a bit daunting. The stepsheet you will read in chapter 11 gave me a bit of trouble and it took me a couple of days of falling on my keister over and over again before I was satisfied.

ACT V: TELLS HOW THE EVENTS OF THE STORY IMPACT THE MAJOR CHARACTERS

After the capture of the murderer, there follows a brief section that shows what has happened to the characters afterwards. Act V is also the resolution to the romantic subplot.

Here the hero might go off into the sunset with his or her lover, or not.

Here, too, we might find out what really happened behind the scenes to some of the other characters.

Oftentimes, this section reflects back on the beginning. Take the Big Jake Winchester mystery above: Act V might go like this:

> *So, now that Ted was getting the right medications and Neal Smookler was in Q awaiting a needle in the arm, Jake was finally back in his office, his feet up on his desk, savoring Kentucky sippin' whisky. The phone rang:*
> *"Yo, Big Jake Winchester."*
> *A woman's voice chimed: "You've got to help me—my husband's seeing another woman."*
> *"Sorry," Big Jake said, "I don't take cases like that any more."*

THE RARE EXCEPTIONS TO THE FIVE-ACT DESIGN

One rare exception is to skip Act I. That's right; there are damn good mysteries that have no Act I at all. These start with the detective arriving at the scene of the murder ready to investigate, having already received the call to adventure in the back story and answered it. This works best with the professional detective kind of story.

Another exception is to start with a prologue, which is a scene that happens previous to the present story. Authors may choose to do this because they do not feel that Act I has strong enough story questions to grip a reader. A prologue may be gripping, but since it may not get the reader involved with the characters in the story at the time of the story, it is not an effective technique. It is better to try to find ways of strengthening the story questions of Act I and skip the prologue.

Occasionally mystery writers will use what's called a

"sandwich." In this technique, the first thing the reader or viewer sees is a scene near the ending, so that the beginning and the middle are sandwiched in between two pieces of the ending. This, like the use of a prologue, is done because of weak story questions at the natural start of the story. The sandwich is sort of a cheap trick, but it can work if the sections following the sandwich have strong enough story questions and strong enough conflicts to hold the reader.

Okay, we're ready, then, to start plotting.

Plotting Theory

THE OPENING ACTION

The very first few words the reader reads may be critical to the success of your novel. The more exciting the opening, the better your chances of hooking the reader into the story, as well as getting an agent to reach for an agency agreement and an editor to reach for a checkbook.

The opening sets the stage for what is to come. It gives the reader a sense that the writer has a story to tell and knows how to tell it. This is the part that telegraphs the way the book will be written—voice, tense, viewpoint, tone, etc.—creating what I called in *How to Write a Damn Good Novel II: Advanced Techniques for Dramatic Storytelling* the "contract with the reader."

In *A Murder in Montana*, we know that a long series of events began years before when Forest Volner murdered Sam

Hegg out at the secret mine. Now the present murder is
going to be committed because Sam Hegg's brother, Caleb
Hegg, has come to town. We know that Volner has to kill
Hegg because Hegg might put it all together and discover
that he, Volner, killed his brother and stole his gold and his
gold mine. We know Volner is going to blame the murder on
Bentley Boxleiter.

In plotting Act I, we need to pick an event in this chain of
events that will be what the reader reads first. What are our
choices? Let's do a little brainstorming and see what our creative options might be. It's always a good idea to look at the
possibilities rather than seize on the first idea that pops up.

- We might start with Bentley driving into town. It's late
  and he's been through a bad, early-season snowstorm.
  He's tired, but there's no hotel or motel open. He sees
  the Eagle Tavern is open. When he parks his car, he
  bumps into Caleb Hegg's pickup. He goes into the
  bar, offers Caleb some money, but Caleb wants more
  than Bentley's willing to pay, so Bentley says he'll turn
  it over to his insurance company. Hegg wants $200
  now, there's a scuffle, and Bentley dumps Hegg on his
  can with a judo throw. Volner takes Bentley to jail.

- How about starting by jumping right into the action
  at the bar with Bentley coming in: The fight starts
  and he's hauled off to jail. Next scene, he's let out
  about three in the morning, goes to his motel, and is
  getting ready for bed when he finds Hegg's body in
  the shower. Realizing he's being framed for murder,
  he takes the body out and puts it in his car and drives
  out of town and dumps the body. He doesn't know
  it, but he's being watched. He heads south, desperately trying to get out of the area, but he's stopped
  by a Highway Patrol roadblock and arrested for
  murder. This opening has a lot of action and I like it
  that Bentley realizes he's being framed and then does

the wrong thing—he acts like a guilty man. It's always nice when an innocent suspect digs a hole for himself.

- How about after he shoots Hegg, Volner puts one of the phony elk heads on him to make it look like the animal rights people did it? Then we start the novel with a minor character finding the body with this stupid elk head on it. Might be good. It would create some nice story questions.

- What if our hero/detective, Shakti, has a dream while meditating? Her dream is strange and terrifying: It's an elk-man and he's bleeding, shot through the heart. I like it because it establishes Shakti as the hero of the story immediately. The problem with it is that it should not feel like she can have these visions at will. Visions should not help her solve the crime. Remember: It's the hero/detective's power of reason that has to defeat the murderer.

- What if our hero/detective Shakti has a vision while meditating—she never had a vision like it before—of her brother being strapped to an execution gurney! This is strong because it involves Shakti's beloved brother and any time a hero's loved one is involved, the stakes go way up.

Okay, I made up my mind and I made my stepsheet. Before you read it, I have a suggestion to make. On first reading, read only what is marked "THE READER SEES:" It is very important that you get the idea of what the story will look like to the reader, who will not know either the back story or what is happening offstage. After all, the good stuff that happens offstage nobody but the author sees.

So keep in mind that the reader knows nothing except that the title of this book is *A Murder in Montana* and that it's a murder mystery. We know that Act I is supposed to get the reader involved in the story, getting the conflicts going, raising story questions, arousing the reader's emotions. Let's see if does.

Stepsheet: Act I/*A Murder in Montana*

THE READER SEES:

1. Shakti Boxleiter, age twenty-seven, is teaching a meditation class for senior citizens in Berkeley, California. Shakti is rather slender, 5-foot-6, with long, brown hair and big, brown eyes. She's a *Bhakta,* a seeker on a spiritual path, content with her life, calm (at least she tries to be), forgiving, emotionally controlled (at least most of the time), at peace with herself and the world—except for an occasional intense craving for chocolate ice cream. As she starts to meditate, she has a vision of a man with the head of an elk. He's writhing on the ground in pain. She's shaken because she thinks it might be some kind of weird portent of evil, which sometimes happens in meditation, but she recovers and manages to go on with her class.

2. After her class, the still-troubled Shakti goes to her teacher, Punjan Singh, who runs the meditation center. She wants to talk about her disturbing vision. To reassure her, he tells her it probably has no meaning, that the vision was merely "mind clutter" that gets stirred up when one tries to do deep meditation. She has not had very much success with deep meditation; she has what is called "monkey mind," that is, when she tries to do deep meditation her thoughts jump all over the place. She's relieved.

3. In her room that night she fights off urges to buy a half gallon of Chocolate Madness. She begins to meditate and has another vision: a prison death chamber. The prisoner is struggling in his bindings and calling for "Kathy," her birth name. Then she sees that the

man on the gurney is her beloved brother, Bentley! Shakti comes out of her meditation, shaken.

4. She rushes to a phone and calls her brother, but his phone has been disconnected.

5. Shakti rides her bike to her brother's place a few blocks away and finds her brother's druggie girlfriend there, half-stoned. The girlfriend refuses to tell her where her brother is, but Shakti goes to her brother's desk and discovers that he had a contract with a magazine to shoot photographs of the protest against the elk hunt, planned in a few days up in Montana. He had promised Shakti that he wouldn't go to any of these hunting protests because of the danger. The druggie girlfriend says he's a big boy and can do what he pleases. Despite the hour, Shakti calls the editor of the magazine Bentley's working for and finds out that he's gone to a town called North of Nowhere and is probably camping out where he can't be reached.

6. Shakti returns to the meditation center and tells her teacher about the vision and that her brother has gone to Montana. Her teacher now thinks that there may be danger for her, but he says if God is sending her messages, she must not ignore them. He opens his thin wallet and gives her what money he has and the keys to the meditation center's van. He also gives her a large gold medallion of the Divine Mother, a goddess, to wear around her neck and to remind her to pray and think always of God. They have a tearful good-bye.

7. We switch to Bentley's point of view. He's twenty-nine, thin, but muscular and wiry—an artist type, but he's deeply committed to animal rights and has a fiery, combative nature. Fatigued from the long drive, he's arriving in North of Nowhere, Montana. They're having an early, heavy snowstorm and he's not used to driving in snow. He's a little skittish anyway about the possibility of counterprotesters, the elk hunters, get-

ting out of hand. It's well after midnight. He sees
anti–animal rights signs that give him pause, but he's
too tired to camp out. He stops at the hotel: A sign
says that at night customers should go to the Eagle
Tavern. He drives his car across to the street to the
tavern and parks out in back in the parking lot. While
he's parking, Bentley, who's not used to driving on
ice, bumps into an old pickup truck. He sees that it's
got a lot of rust and dents and figures to hell with it.
He goes into the bar to arrange for a hotel room.

8. In the bar, one of the patrons, Red Steckles, sees Bentley's "Animals Are People Too" sweatshirt, and they
trade insults. Then another patron says he saw Bentley
"hit and run" Caleb Hegg's truck. Hegg (he's an ex-
con, scruffy, as you'll recall, about forty-five, a real
nasty number) demands more money than the bump
is worth. He loves to pick on the weak and helpless,
but he makes a mistake when he picks on Bentley.
Bentley has a fourth-degree black belt in judo,
remember. Bentley tosses Hegg on his ass with a judo
throw, then, when Hegg gets up swinging, Bentley
puts a judo choke hold on him and Caleb Hegg passes
out for a few seconds. When Caleb Hegg gets his
breath back, Hegg wants to resume the fight, but the
friendly, peacemaker bartender (also a part-time
deputy sheriff and soon-to-be murderer for the second time in his life) Forest Volner gives Bentley a
hotel room key and escorts him out of the tavern.
(Volner, you'll recall, is a bear of a man, over 6-foot-3
and weighing three hundred pounds.)

OFFSTAGE:

- During the fight, Clyde Apple (the African-American
  taxidermist) has gone out into the parking lot, broken
  into Hegg's camper, and taken the old letters from
  Hegg's brother Sam that Hegg was using to find the

gold mine his brother had been working. (Clyde, you'll recall, has gold fever and just a few days before had an altercation in the wilderness with Hegg, so he will later make a fine suspect.)

- After the fight, Forest Volner announces he's closing early and kicks everyone out. The patrons shuffle out. Volner helps Hegg to his cab-over camper on the back of his pickup truck and gets him settled down in the back, then Volner drives off.

- Red Steckles, who had been heckling Bentley about his "Animals Are People Too" sweatshirt, goes out the back to the parking lot, and has trouble getting his jeep started. He sees Sharon Sundance, who had been arguing with Hegg before Hegg's fight with Bentley, as she comes out and gets in her car but doesn't start it. He thinks she's waiting for Hegg. It's snowing hard; he can hardly make her out. Steckles, after a few moments, finally gets his jeep started and drives off.

- Volner figures it's only a matter of time before Hegg figures it out. He decides he's going to take care of Hegg now that he has the opportunity to pin it on Bentley, and returns to the tavern. He's found an animal rights lapel pin on the floor that Bentley must have dropped during the altercation with Hegg. He goes out into the parking lot and tries to open Bentley's car with a "slim jim," a thin bar inserted between the window and the outer door skin that cops use (he's a deputy, remember), but it doesn't work. Volner goes over to the hotel where he has a passkey, sneaks into Bentley's room, and gets his keys. He goes back to Bentley's car, pops the trunk, and rummages around looking for something to use as a weapon. He fails to notice that one of the theatrical elk's heads that the blood-sport protesters use falls out. He takes the heavy camera base for the tripod: It has nice, sharp edges. He climbs into Hegg's camper—the lock was busted by Clyde Apple earlier—and bashes Caleb Hegg's head in. He sees that Hegg is still breathing, so he jerks his head back and breaks his neck. Then he puts the lapel pin in Hegg's hand, drags him out into the snow, wipes the camera base, and puts it back in Bentley's trunk. He tosses Bentley's keys into the middle of the street. Then he drives home, feeling the old familiar power-high that he felt years ago when he murdered Sam Hegg. At home he finds blood on his clothes and shoes and burns them in a potbellied stove.

- Meanwhile, Penny Sue Volner, Forest's wife, is sitting in her SUV across the street (hoping to discover where her husband goes at night when he doesn't come home). She sees Bentley go into the hotel and sees her husband go in sometime later and then come out; five minutes later she sees him throw something in the street (Bentley's keys). When she gets home, she sneaks in the house and sees her husband burning his shoes, his jeans, and his nice, new parka.

- Sharon Sundance, in her car, has been trying to get her contacts right; without them she's blind as a bat. She finally gets them halfway in, sees Volner help the visibly wobbly Hegg to his camper, and watches Volner leave. Sharon has just pieced it together that Volner is the guy Hegg's been looking for. She knows Volner used to play football because she'd seen his scarred knee when they were in bed years ago, and she knows he was originally from Ohio and was a fast runner called "Swifty." She's trying to figure out how she can make a few bucks from Hegg or Volner trading on what she knows. She drives home and waits for Hegg. She expected him to come to her place after the Eagle closed. She's been trying to get a "loan" from him to make her rent. When he doesn't show, she goes back to the Eagle and finds him dead on the ground next to his camper. Fearing that they might think she did it, she leaves. She finds the elk's head nearby and puts it on the corpse. She has two reasons for this: one, to make him look ridiculous in death because she detested him, and, two, to make the killer think there was a witness, because the killer will know he did not have this elk's head thing on when he was killed. She goes back to her car giggling, thinking of all the riches that are soon to come her way. Volner must have killed Hegg, she figures, and he has lots and lots of money.

- Clyde Apple goes home to look over the letters he took from Hegg's truck, searching for clues as to the location of the mine.

Discussion

Okay, there's a lot happening. A lot of scheming behind the scenes, but, as you'll see, it will all pay off with some nice complications and suspense as the story unfolds. If you just take your characters one at a time and ask yourself what they want and what they're up to, you'll end up with lots of nice things happening behind the scenes for you.

Remember: When you make up a plot and the machinations of the characters unseen by the reader, you'll need to play around with it. At first I had Sharon Sundance witness the murder, but then I thought that Hegg would not be so stupid as to commit a murder with a witness around (he would not be at his maximum capacity if he did). And originally I didn't have Red Steckles in the story at all.

Okay, here's what the reader has seen so far:

—Shakti, while teaching a class, gets her terrifying vision of the man with the elk's head.

—Shakti seeks advice from her teacher and calms down.

—Shakti has a second vision, one of her brother, Bentley, about to be executed.

—Shakti goes to her brother's home and finds that he has gone to North of Nowhere.

—Shakti goes to her mentor again and he tells her she'd better go after her brother.

—Bentley, meanwhile, comes to town and bumps a ratty, old pickup in the parking lot of a bar.

—Bentley goes into the bar and soon gets in a fight with the pickup's owner and is ejected from the bar by friendly Forest Volner.

That's it. So far, for the reader there's been lots of action, conflict, mystery, suspense—everything a damn good mystery needs. Even a few surprises. Let's, then, continue the stepsheet:

THE READER SEES:

9. The next morning, we switch viewpoint to a minor character: A snowplow driver plowing out the Eagle's parking lot scoops up a body. When he looks at it, he finds that it's frozen solid, wearing a weird elk's head, and its neck is broken. The snowplow driver runs for the police.

10. Back to Bentley's point of view. Wham! Sheriff Lyle Blodgett, Deputy Sheriff Forest Volner, and a couple of other deputies roust Bentley out of a sound sleep and push him around, demanding that he confess. Volner, the friendly guy, keeps the sheriff and another deputy from going too far with the rough stuff. Bentley's not stupid—he's seen lots of episodes of *NYPD Blue.* He demands a lawyer. He is carted off to jail, vociferously screaming that he is innocent.

11. Still from Bentley's point of view, later that day: He's getting interrogated by Sheriff Lyle Blodgett, who is beside himself that someone has the audacity and bad

manners to kill somebody in his town. Bentley's attorney arrives—Marshal (Matt) Dillon, the only decent criminal lawyer for three hundred miles. Dillon (who will be Shakti's love interest, remember) is a shrewd and crafty country lawyer. The sheriff's deputies have already found out that the elk-head prop was in Bentley's car—he brought along a whole bunch of them. Who else had keys to his car? Nobody. Bentley's story is that he left the Eagle, walked to his hotel room, went to bed, and next thing he knows a slew of deputies are hauling him off to jail. Would he be so stupid as to kill a man and put one of his own elk's heads on him? The sheriff thinks he did it just for that reason, so it would look like he was being framed. Bentley calls him an idiot. Matt desperately tries to get Bentley to shut up. A deputy interrupts: Bentley's sister, Shakti, has just arrived.

OFFSTAGE:

- Despite the snowstorm, Clyde Apple has excitedly gone off in search of the mine. From the letters he got from Hegg's van, he thinks that he's figured out where it is.
- Sharon Sundance is at home carefully crafting a blackmail letter for Volner, using cut up magazines for the letters. She figures if he takes the bait, he's the murderer for sure. She calls him "Swifty" in the letter on a hunch.
- Penny Sue Volner is sifting through the ashes for remains of her husband's burned shoes and clothing.
- Mike Martin (the town real-estate mogul, head of the merchants association, remember) has heard about the killing—he thinks it's wonderful that an animal rights activist has killed a man. He calls in the news media, gleefully thinking this is going to be great for business.
- The state police notify Sheriff Blodgett that they're sending a forensics specialist (Molly Runningwolf),

whose job it will be to help the sheriff make a strong forensic case for the state prosecutor.

12. Bentley is astonished to see Shakti. She does not tell him about her vision (he doesn't believe in visions), but says she came because he'd promised her he'd stay away from the elk-hunt protest and she wanted to remind him of his promise. She wants to know what happened. He tells her these rednecks have framed him, that this will be national news and it will be a terrible blow for the animal rights movement—which distresses him more than the murder charge. He says this is a dangerous place and he wants her to leave immediately; there's no telling what the local elk-killing, redneck jerks might do. Before the jailers take him away, he pleads with Shakti to go back to Berkeley and get help from friends in the animal rights movement. He needs money for a top legal team.

13. Shakti, trying to maintain her spiritual serenity, makes some phone calls to get some monetary help. She also calls her teacher and asks for prayers. He tells her that, despite her "monkey mind," she must be further along with her spiritual practice than either of them had suspected if she had a vision foretelling this. She wants to know if Bentley is going to be strapped to the death gurney for sure, and he says he doesn't know.

14. Shakti meets with Matt at a cafe and can't resist having some chocolate ice cream with marshmallow sauce. Her dealings with lawyers in the past (when she was tried and convicted for conspiracy) have predisposed her not to like lawyers. She's stunned by how much she's attracted to this lanky, polite, soft-spoken cowboy. She tells herself that she has no

room for a man in her life as a spiritual seeking Bhakta. Besides, she has to concentrate on helping her brother. She asks Matt if he believes Bentley is innocent and he says, as a defense lawyer, his job is to see to it that her brother gets the best defense he can give him and it doesn't matter if he's guilty or innocent—that is not his department. He points out that the case is very strong against Bentley and that his best hope of avoiding the death penalty is to accept a plea agreement. The state won't want all the national media coverage that a trial is sure to generate; the prosecutors don't like looking like a bunch of gun nuts.

Shakti loses her composure: Her brother is not going to plead to anything! He's innocent! She's instantly embarrassed: A Bhakta should never lose her temper. Matt points out that in Montana most people would hang a blood-sport protester for jay-walking; he's only trying to do what's best for his client. She says they should find out who really did it, and he says a PI costs $500 a day, and the state will give them authorization to spend state money only if it is to refute particular parts of the state's case, which will not be ready for four or five months. Could she afford to hire a PI privately? She says she and Bentley have no money, but she is trying to raise some. In the meantime, she will have to see what she can find out on her own. He scoffs at the very idea.

He asks her some technical forensic and legal questions she doesn't have the answers to, but she says with a wry smile she read a lot of Nancy Drew when she was eleven. Okay, Nancy Drew, where does she want to start? he asks. She asks him what he thinks. Always start with the scene of the crime, he says. That's what the Hardy Boys always did.

DISCUSSION

This ends Act I. Shakti, our hero/detective, has taken the case. It's important, when you get to this point, that you never go back, in the sense that the hero/detective should not pawn off this mission on someone else. This, in dramatic structure, is called a *plot point*. Once a plot point occurs, a story goes off in a new direction, or, as some creative writing teachers put it, a plot point puts the story on a "higher plateau." In this case, as of now, Shakti is going to act as our hero/detective and we're going to sympathize with her, empathize with her, and identify with her because of it.

You'll notice that, in my original plan, I was going to have Hegg shot with a gun that would later be found in the trunk of the car Bentley was driving. I decided, instead, to go with the head bashing and the broken neck. The lapel pin idea occurred to me later; it seemed like a good idea, so I put it in. When I actually draft this, I may take it out. Or I may take it out on rewrite. As I said, a stepsheet is flexible, a general plan for a direction of the story—it is not a straightjacket. It's okay to move things around, change circumstances, even give characters different motives and character traits—as long as you change their backgrounds and back stories to account for it.

Now, then, does Act I accomplish what it needs to accomplish? Does it get the reader involved in the story? I think it does. Are there strong story questions raised? Yes, there are. One is: Who killed Caleb Hegg? Another is: Will Bentley be proved innocent? Even before the murder, there are story questions raised by Shakti's visions. Readers will wonder if there's going to be a romance between Shakti and Matt, another strong story question.

There are conflicts: the interrogation of Bentley by the sheriff and the conflicts between Bentley and Shakti and between Shakti and Matt. There is suspense and menace: The town itself is menacing to outsiders, especially animal rights activists, and there's a murderer on the loose who may kill again. For the few pages we've gone into this story, there's a lot going down.

Act I, as stepped out in this stepsheet, would take up about 60 to 80 pages. I'd guess, of what might turn out to be a 300-page manuscript. So it would be about 20 percent of the story, give or take. Act I may be longer or shorter; there are no rules about how long it should be. It should be long enough to raise key story questions, create a mystery, and exploit the conflicts.

Let's move on, then, to the heart of a damn good mystery: the cat-and-mouse game that begins in Act II.

The Hero/Detective Gets to Work

PLOTTING ACT II

In Act II the hero/detective and the murderer begin the cat-and-mouse game Marie Rodell calls "the vicarious thrill of the manhunt."

Now, how's Shakti going to proceed with her investigation?

Hero/detectives follow one of two different detective styles when pursuing their quarry. One of these two methods is like *gathering* and the other is like *hunting*. When plotting, it's a good idea to keep these two methods in mind.

Some detectives work this way: They gather clues and interview witnesses in a willy-nilly fashion. The hero/detective will go to the scene of the crime, say, pick up this or that, then interview this witness, then that witness; later the hero/detective might do a little lab analysis, get the autopsy report, talk to some more witnesses, and so on. Only occasionally will the hero/detective give an indication of what the clues and witness statements mean. Then toward the end, usually either just before or during the obligatory scene (the point in the story where the hero/detective has figured out who the murderer is), the hero/detective will have a sit-down discussion, usually with his sidekick, and explain what all the clues and all the good information gathered from all this willy-nilly investigating has led the hero/detective to conclude. This is the hero/detective as gatherer. Hercule Poirot works this way. So does Sherlock Holmes at times.

When working as a gatherer, the hero/detective is like a sponge, soaking up information, taking it all in. The clues are collected more or less at random and then, from a huge mass of lies, deceits, real clues, observations, mistakes, and deceptions, the hero/detective will identify who the murderer is and why he or she committed the murder, giving us a reconstruction of the plot behind the plot.

In stories where the hero/detective acts principally as a gatherer, the story is like a game played between the reader and the hero/detective: Let's see who can figure out who done it from a huge amorphous pile of clues and witness statements, some of which are real clues, and the rest, red herrings. Red herrings are, of course, things that look like clues, but ain't.

The other method a hero/detective might follow is to act as a *hunter*. When working in this style, the hero/detective will latch onto a clue or a witness will give him something valuable, and this will send him to the next clue and the next witness and then onto the next and the next. The hero/detective as hunter is on a trail of clues, not just gathering them at random.

As an example, the hero/detective looks over the scene of the crime and finds that the dead man had an empty velvet ring box from a jewelry store on the table. He or she goes to the jeweler and discovers that, Yes, the dead man did buy a ring for a young lady with blond hair and a heart-shaped birthmark on her chin. The hero/detective goes to the dead man's favorite hangout and the bartender says, Yeah, he seen this doll with the heart-shaped birthmark—she plays in the symphony. When the hero/detective finally tracks her down, she says she was there that night, but they had a fight and she gave him back his ring and left. The ring is missing. Did she see anyone else? She says, No, but she did see a gray Mercedes parked in the alley and she says someone was getting out of it when she drove off.

Now the hunter hero/detective goes and looks for the gray Mercedes.

In most damn good mysteries, there are times when the hero/detective is acting as a gatherer, and there are times when the hero/detective is acting as a hunter. It is my view that the cat-and-mouse game between the hero/detective and the murderer is most compelling when the hero/detective is acting as a hunter.

Steve Brown, the author of a great resource for writers of detective fiction *The Complete Idiot's Guide to Private Investigating (2002)*, is a former FBI agent and has been a highly successful PI in Florida for twenty years or so. He told me once that most investigators actually work as hunters in real life; they follow a chain of clues just like fictional detectives.

Often on the TV show *Law and Order*, the detectives start out as gatherers and then become hunters when some of their leads look promising. This seems to me to be a good strategy for the fictional hero/detective as well. (Be warned, though, that *Law and Order* is as addicting as Swiss almond chocolate. If you are not already hooked, don't watch it.)

Anyway, the important thing is that when the hero/detective gets a hot lead, even when acting as a gatherer, the hot lead should be pursued. You should never leave your reader with the feeling that the hero/detective is ignoring some important line of inquiry. The reader will think your hero/detective is an idiot, and that's the last thing you want. Once your reader has judged your detective to be an idiot, the reader will toss your book out the window, even in a city with the harshest antilittering laws, and will forever after speak of your great deficiencies as a mystery writer to anyone who will listen.

Okay, then, our hero/detective is ready to get to work.

The secret of plotting this stuff is to just keep looking at each of your characters and keep asking, "If they're smart, what'll they do now?" This applies to the detective, the murderer, and all the other characters—the whole, scheming, devious bunch of them.

Stepsheet: Act II/*A Murder in Montana*

OFFSTAGE:

Okay, what's been happening? Lots of interesting stuff. Most everybody's been real busy.

- After murdering Hegg, Forest Volner is horrified to find out the next morning that there was an elk's head on the body when it was found. Somebody was there! Yikes—so he's now very worried.
- Meanwhile, his wife, Penny Sue, has been acting squirrelly because she knows he's guilty of murder, but she'd never, ever, tell anyone. What would happen to her daughters if she did? It's not just that they'd lose everything. How could they face life having a murderer for a father? Even though she's a pretty dim bulb, she also knows that if he suspects she knows, he would not hesitate to kill her, too. Everybody in town thinks he's a jolly old bear, but she's terrified of him.

- Sharon Sundance slipped her blackmail note under the door to Volner's office. She came in the back door of the Eagle and left the note without anyone seeing her. She's all excited, feeling as if she's won the lottery. In her whole, miserable life, this is the first time anything this good has ever happened to her. Volner has not found the note yet.
- Clyde Apple is still in the mountains looking for the gold mine, but he's getting mighty cold and having no luck at all.
- Sheriff Blodgett is very distressed to hear that the state is sending a forensic expert, Molly Runningwolf, to assist him in the investigation. Since the sheriff is corrupt, he doesn't like state police people snooping around in his jurisdiction. Volner convinces him to make sure they nail this blood-sport protester son-of-a-bitch good, so they put some of Hegg's blood on Bentley's clothes and shoes, then wash it off, but they know that Molly Runningwolf can still get the blood evidence using luminal and look like a hero. Then they put some California mud they scrape off Bentley's shoes in Hegg's truck. More forensic evidence.
- The deputies, elk hunters all, are harassing Bentley in his cell, goading him.
- Then there's poor Matt. He's strongly attracted to Shakti, but thinks it's not proper to feel that way toward a client's sister (and a religious person who is not interested in a romantic relationship). He's really in a pickle.
- And then there's poor Shakti, who finds herself worried down to the bone for her brother, yet keeps thinking about Matt.

THE READER SEES:
15. Shakti has never been a detective, so she figures she's going to try to get as much information as she can.

She sets off for the Eagle Tavern. Matt goes with her, telling her about the town. The townspeople they encounter already know who she is—word travels fast in a small town. They look upon her with suspicion. In the parking lot of the Eagle Tavern, Shakti and Matt see deputies sifting the snow for evidence and her brother's car being impounded. When Shakti tries to learn what the deputies have found, she's told to get lost. When she insists, the deputies escort her away from the scene. She's flunked her first test as hero/detective, but that's okay; in Act II, the hero/detective is still finding his or her way. Shakti heads for the door of the Eagle Tavern; Matt wants to go with her, but she says she thinks a lawyer might intimidate people. Okay, he says, he'll wait outside.

16. Inside the Eagle, Shakti takes out her pad and pen and starts haltingly to ask questions. Two local elk-hunting jerks heckle her. They grab her Divine Mother medal and toss it back and forth over her head to tease her. The bartender (who is not Volner) gets it back for her, but ushers her to the door, saying they don't allow sports in the barroom. Shakti is miffed.

17. Outside, Matt, trying to hide his I-told-you-so grin, says he's sorry for the rudeness of the town: They just don't like outsiders telling them what they can shoot and what they can't shoot. She tells him that he does not understand the power of love. She kneels in the snow and prays for a few minutes and then goes back inside.

18. Inside, Shakti tells the hecklers she forgives them for being cruel. She makes a speech appealing to their sense of justice and fair play, and wins over one of the hecklers. The second one makes a threat and leaves. The one she's won over tells her who was in the Eagle when her brother was there and what cars

were in the parking lot and gives her a timetable of events. He tells her it's the most he can remember, which isn't much, since he was nearly passed-out drunk. At this point, Matt comes in and is impressed that she's managed to get any information at all.

19. Outside, Shakti tells Matt she wants to see Volner, who, she's just found out, is the Eagle's owner, a member of the town council, the bartender on duty at the time of the murder, and a part-time sheriff. She asks Matt for directions to Volner's house and drives there in the van.

20. Along the way a kid throws an ice ball at the van and curses at her. She says a prayer for his soul.

21. We're with Bentley in jail. The guards harass him and there's some pushing and shoving. It gets rough: He tosses some of them around and gets the hell beat out of him.

22. At Forest Volner's house, Shakti meets Penny Sue Volner, who is the first person in town to show her real warmth and sympathy and to warn her that the men who hunt really and truly hate the animal rights people. Shakti sees Volner with his two lovely daughters, whom he obviously adores, but she senses some tension between him and his wife. Volner takes Shakti aside and tells her his wife is upset because of the murder—which is the first one in the county since the fifties—and the coming elk-hunting protests. Volner tells Shakti that he indeed saw the fight, and saw how angry her brother was, and when he ushered him outside, her brother said he'd better keep Hegg away from him, that he'd break his neck if he ever saw him again. The avuncular Volner, a seemingly nice guy who's taken a liking to Shakti, says he didn't put that in his witness report—he didn't want to jam the kid up. Just then there's a phone call: It's from Matt. They've just found some

new evidence and he wants to meet Shakti at the sheriff's office.

OFFSTAGE:

- Volner doesn't want Shakti poking around. He doesn't actually think she'll find out anything, but he's not going to take any chances on her getting lucky. After she leaves, he has a guy who does handyman work for him go to Reverend Diggs, a fire-and-brimstone Christian pastor, and tell him that Shakti was wearing a pagan symbol and proselytizing, for what he doesn't know. Satan worship, maybe. The reverend gets riled up.

THE READER SEES:

23. Shakti and Matt meet with Bentley and Sheriff Blodgett and a couple of his deputies. Bentley's face has been battered and he's boiling with anger. Matt threatens legal action for police brutality; the sheriff promises to see to it that Bentley and the guards both behave. Now for a dramatic moment: The police have found the murder weapon in Bentley's trunk—it's part of Bentley's camera tripod. The state is sending a forensic expert who will prove, no doubt, that it's the victim's blood on the thing. Bentley shrieks that the fix is in, that the frame-up is complete. Shakti calms him down; she wants to talk to him alone.

24. When she has Bentley alone, Shakti wants to know exactly what happened from the moment he came to town. Did he really say he would break Hegg's neck? When he left the bar and went into the hotel, did he see anybody? He wants to know why, and when she tells him she's going to try to find out who really murdered Hegg, the idea horrifies him. He insists that he does not want her involved because he thinks

the town is hostile and dangerous and he wants her out of there. He refuses to tell her anything.

25. Back with Sheriff Blodgett and Matt, Shakti says she wants to see Hegg's body, her brother's car, and Hegg's truck—and all the rest of the evidence they've gathered. The sheriff bends only when Matt dazzles him with legalese.

26. Matt and Shakti look over Bentley's car very carefully and find some scratches near the window. Shakti said she had a tow-truck driver open a car this way once, using a metal bar. A "slim jim," the sheriff says—only it won't work on this model of car, so she's out of luck.

27. Shakti looks at Hegg's camper. The dead bolt inside was not thrown. Could it be that it was broken open before the man got in it? The sheriff says she's clutching at straws. The camper is a pigsty: dirty dishes, dirty clothes, beer cans all over. What was taken, nobody knows. An old toolbox with a lock has been pried open; there's nothing inside. It's not all banged up or dirty and Shakti doesn't think it was used for tools. There's a map of the area with all kinds of Xs and Os all over it. On the floor, Shakti finds an eight-year-old envelope addressed to Hegg at a post office box in Indiana. No return address, but a North of Nowhere postmark.

28. Sheriff Blodgett shows Shakti and Matt Hegg's body. She prays for Hegg's soul. This is not her brother's doing, she tells Matt. He would not bash in a man's skull.

29. Molly Runningwolf from the Montana State Police forensic science team arrives (remember, she's a brilliant young Blackfoot woman, totally all business, with a Ph.D. in forensic pathology). Shakti hopes that she can win Molly over, but no dice. Molly says right off that the sister of the accused has no rights

when it comes to inspecting the evidence or the body. Molly Runningwolf tells the sheriff to tell Shakti nothing—all evidence and witness statements will be turned over to the defendant's counsel when the investigation is complete—and to escort Shakti from the building, which he does.

DISCUSSION

At this point, Shakti is acting as a gatherer. She has no solid leads. One of my preferred strategies when plotting is to get the murderer in close to the hero/detective, so that when he's unmasked, it will have greater impact. Volner, if he's smart, will be highly motivated to stick close to Shakti, to make sure she doesn't find out anything. I hope the reader will like him so that when he's unmasked as the murderer, the reader will have some positive feelings for him, which will add to the surprise and shock.

THE READER SEES:

30. Shakti goes to a phone and calls Bentley's editor and asks him to check around the town in Indiana the letter was addressed to and find out if anyone there knew Hegg. She wants to know what he was doing in North of Nowhere.

OFFSTAGE:

- Volner is really having a bad day. First, there was the elk's head that somebody who might have witnessed the murder put on Hegg's head. Now he's being blackmailed for $5,000, which he is certain is only for starters. How could someone have seen him—he was so careful! But no matter, he can't take the chance that this is a bluff. He figures he can put a small signal transmitter called a "tracking device" in with the payoff (the sheriff's department has one on hand from a

kit provided during an FBI training course) that will
lead him to the blackmailer. He plans to make this
person pay with a great deal of pain before dying.

- Sharon Sundance is hanging out at the Eagle, watching
  Volner sweat, and knows she's got her man hooked.
- Matt makes arrangements for his mother to look after
  his daughter so he can move into the hotel and protect Shakti. He gets an excited call from a friend that
  Reverend Diggs is on the way over to Shakti's hotel
  for a confrontation. He groans. Reverend Diggs is a
  royal pain.

THE READER SEES:

31. Shakti goes to her hotel. The desk clerk says some
    guy was calling for her—the editor. She calls him back
    and finds out that the return address on the envelope
    was for a post office box for a prison. So the letter was
    from someone in town to Caleb Hegg when he was in
    prison. She goes to her room to pray and chant her
    mantra and not think about chocolate ice cream.

32. Soon Shakti is called downstairs. Reverend Diggs
    and half a dozen men from his congregation are wait-
    ing for her there to tell her they don't like her spread-
    ing her heathen beliefs in their town. She calmly asks
    them if they believe God is love and eternal and that
    one should live a righteous life and so on, which they
    all agree to. She says she carries the medallion to
    remind her to pray; she kneels and says her favorite
    prayer, the Lord's Prayer. They're confused and don't
    know what to do; she doesn't seem like a devil wor-
    shipper. Some pray with her, others just go away.
    Matt breaks in to save her, which he sees is not nec-
    essary. She passes another test.

    Since she's made some friends, she asks them
    questions about Hegg. She discovers that he'd been
    in the area about four months. He'd go off into the

wilderness for days at a time and when he came back to town he'd be asking about a guy named "Swift" or "Swifty" who lived around there eight years ago and had a limp. No one knows such a person. Shakti finds out that Hegg spent some time with the town "party girl," Sharon Sundance, who Shakti knows was in the Eagle the night of the murder. Matt says he's moving into the hotel to keep an eye on Shakti and would she join him for dinner—ah, to discuss her brother's case. She says no.

33. Shakti goes to see Sharon Sundance, who is not exactly in mourning, but she seems to be sympathetic toward Shakti and is particularly interested to know if they've uncovered any other suspects besides her brother. Shakti says no. Sharon says she left the Eagle after the fight and didn't see anybody in the parking lot. Sharon says that Hegg was looking for Indian artifacts at a burial site out there in the mountains: artifacts—real totem poles—supposedly worth thousands that he was very excited about. The guy Swift supposedly knew where they were. (All to put Shakti off the scent, of course.)

34. When Shakti gets back to her van, she finds her windshield smashed. She's exasperated, but manages to pray for whoever did it. This shakes her up. She goes and gets some of her favorite comfort food: chocolate ice cream.

35. Shakti tracks down bar patron Billy "the Blob" Kruger, a tobacco-chewing, fat alcoholic with a bad back (who has been added to the cast of characters). He yells at her to get off his porch. Can't she see he's hurting? She shows him some yoga movements to help relieve the pain. In gratitude, he tells her that he saw Clyde Apple, the African American taxidermist, sneaking out during the fight. If anybody'd bash a head in, it would be him.

36. On the way to Clyde Apple's place, Shakti stops at a convenience store to get some cheap gas. There's a break in the snowstorm and she can see the magnificent peaks of the snow-covered mountains. She pauses for a moment to drink in the beauty God has made. Inside, the Indian woman clerk is cold to her and when Shakti asks if somehow she offended her, the woman says when the whites get stirred up against the animal protesters they vent some of their anger on the Indians—which to Shakti is an example of how bad karma spreads like dust in the wind. Shakti says she will work quickly to prove her brother's innocence. The Indian woman says that when the sheriff has decided you are guilty in this town, there will be no proving otherwise, as many of her people know. As Shakti goes out to her van, she sees a TV camera crew's truck arriving.

37. Shakti goes to Clyde Apple's place. There's no one around, which is strange. With the opening of hunting season on elk a few days away, she thinks he would be available for his business. A neighbor (reluctantly, of course) tells Shakti that he packed up his camping gear and left. Hard to believe he'd go camping in such bad weather. She asks if he had an interest in Indian artifacts, and the neighbor says no.

38. Shakti goes back to the Eagle Tavern in hopes of finding more people who were there the night of the murder. She finds Volner tending bar. She gets the address of one of the patrons, Red Steckles (the one who first insulted Bentley when he came into the Eagle) and asks Volner if he knows anybody named Swift. He says a long time ago—the guy only hung around a few weeks. She asks if Hegg ever talked about him or any Indian artifacts. He says, Yeah, he did ask about how much you could get for artifacts. Then he tells her, too bad, it's looking worse for her brother.

What does he mean? she says. About finding the blood on his clothes and shoes. She heads off to the sheriff's office.

OFFSTAGE:
- Volner is astounded that Shakti's found out as much as she has. He's hopeful that now that the evidence nails her brother she'll stop this investigating.

THE READER SEES:
39. Shakti arrives at the sheriff's office just as Matt is driving up—he's been summoned by Molly Runningwolf. In her portable lab, Molly Runningwolf shows Shakti, Matt, and Bentley one of Bentley's shoes and his blue University of California sweatshirt found in his hotel room. Both have blood on them—Hegg's blood with 98.6 percent certainty based on tissues typing matches—and she has sent samples for more in-depth DNA testing. They also found Bentley's keys using a metal detector in the middle of the street on a direct line between the parking lot and the side door of the hotel. Dirt on Bentley's shoes matches a speck of dirt found in the camper and she's certain laboratory analysis will prove it's the same dirt. This about wraps it up as far as she's concerned. Bentley has no explanation for how the blood got there, since Hegg was not cut in the fight. Word comes that the TV people have arrived for a press conference. Bentley has agreed to be interviewed. Matt groans. Shakti does too.

40. The TV interview. In front of the cameras, Molly Runningwolf and Sheriff Blodgett congratulate each other on a fine investigation; they have incontrovertible proof that they have the murderer in custody. Matt gives a brief statement that the defense has not had adequate time to go over the evidence, but that,

in the end, he is certain his client will be exonerated. Then Bentley, against his sister's and his lawyer's objections, makes a statement. He says that Hegg's death is trivial compared to the slaughter of the "innocent" animals that will be taking place in three days. This sounds like an admission of guilt; the TV people are ecstatic. Bentley, too, is a happy man; he has defended the elk. Shakti is miffed at her brother, who she can see is grandstanding, mugging for the cameras.

41. As Shakti leaves with Matt, Volner asks if Shakti will be vacating her room since her brother is soon going to be moved to the county seat. She says absolutely not: The real murderer is in this town and she intends to stay here and find him. He says her brother just more or less admitted it, and she says he was only joking.

OFFSTAGE:

• Volner is determined now to get rid of Shakti. He arranges to have a thug beat her up, to force her out of town. He hates to do it—he likes her—but he's got to get rid of her before she stumbles onto something.

THE READER SEES:

42. At a restaurant, Matt tells Shakti that he thinks she should leave; there's no point in her sticking around. He tries to convince her that maybe Bentley did do it. Molly would not try to frame him, and the best thing Shakti could do would be to raise some money for a high-priced defense team. No dice—she's staying. He says for her own safety he wishes she would go, but if she's staying, maybe they could have dinner sometime, get to know each other better. She tells him, please, she's a sort of like a nun; she doesn't date men, okay? Okay, he says, but if she's a nun, where's her habit? She's not a Catholic nun, she follows the

Eternal Religion; he would probably call it Hin-
duism. Has she taken a vow? he asks. Not exactly,
she says, but, well, relationships get in the way of her
spiritual progress so she has to avoid them. She
excuses herself. There's chocolate ice cream on the
menu and she's trying to avoid that, too.

43. Shakti goes to see Red Steckles. He gives her a hard
time, but she manages to break through and get some
info from him. He says he was provoked because her
brother came into the Eagle Tavern wearing an "Animals Are People Too" sweatshirt and the animal
rights lapel pin, which set him off.

44. Shakti returns to her hotel room to pray and meditate. When she gets into her room, a man wearing a
mask is waiting for her. He hits her several times and
twists her arm, but she does not cry out. Instead, she
says that he's creating a lot of bad karma for himself
and that she will pray that he will wake up to the
truth of his immortal soul so that he can escape the
karmic consequences of his bad acts. He hits her
harder. She cannot maintain her spiritual detachment; she begs him to stop hurting her. He hits and
kicks her, then runs away. She fights back tears and
cleans herself up. She's bruised and battered, but
nothing is broken.

45. The hotel clerk comes in and says they can't have
trouble here, she'll have to get a room someplace else.
He has no sympathy for an animal rights nut.

46. Outside the hotel, Shakti is putting her stuff into her
van. Down the street animal rights advocates are
massing and the elk hunters are shouting at them, all
to the TV people's delight. Sheriff Blodgett, his
deputies, reserve deputies, and deputies from surrounding towns are gathering as well. Matt arrives.
Shakti says it's amazing how bad karma can infect
everyone. He can tell Shakti is profoundly shaken.

The pain was greater than her spiritual power. She tells him about the great yogis who can stand on ice barefooted for four days in a blizzard. He holds her in an embrace; she doesn't resist.

47. Matt takes Shakti to his mother's place outside of town to treat her wounds and tempt her with Death by Chocolate ice cream, which she manages to refuse. Shakti meditates for a while and calms down. Matt's mother is a hardworking ranch woman, sharp and shrewd. She likes Shakti but is a little worried that her son is falling for this very strange woman with this strange religion who would never fit into his life. But she offers Shakti a place to stay. Matt's daughter comes home from school and she and Shakti hit it off. Shakti says she spent summers on a farm when she was a kid and she loved horses, too.

48. Sheriff Blodgett and Deputy Volner show up, vowing to find out who beat Shakti up, and pleading with her to leave town, but it's no use. On the way out, they tell her Bentley wants to see her.

49. In the jail visiting room, her brother hugs her. He heard about her beating and he feels responsible. He tells her to look into his eyes and says he's not lying: He killed Hegg. She's stunned. They fought, he says. Hegg made threats against the protesters, so in a fit of rage, Bentley went to Hegg's camper and smashed his head in. Now the only thing Shakti can do is to get Bentley money for an O.J.-style defense team.

50. As she leaves the jail, Volner profusely apologizes for the town, then offers to help her if she needs money. No, she says. Her brother would say anything to get her to leave, she tells him. She says it is not in her brother to kill anyone. She says she knows Hegg was looking for someone who had some Indian artifacts (this is her theory, which, of course, is wrong) and

that person perhaps had a strong motive to murder him and probably did.

OFFSTAGE

- Volner decides that as much as he doesn't like it, he's going to have to kill Shakti. Only he's got to make it look like an accident. He knows just the way. He has also borrowed $5,000 in cash from his partner, the madam at the whorehouse in Nowhere, to pay off the blackmailer.
- Meanwhile Sharon Sundance is getting ready to pick up her first installment on her relocation to a place where things are happening.

THE READER SEES:

51. Shakti gets back to Matt's mother's place and it's all over the news—her brother is saying that all animal murderers deserve to die. Matt is beside himself. Shakti says her brother has decided to throw himself to the lions.

52. During dinner, Matt reviews the evidence. They have nothing to show that anyone else might have done the murder and there's a ton of evidence that Bentley did—now isn't it wise to put their efforts into trying to save his life? He says she has to think with her head, not her heart. Shakti sees the logic in it. Feeling gloomy, she gives up resisting chocolate ice cream and has two bowls of it. Then she gets a phone call, a disguised voice. Hegg, the voice says, was looking for a guy named "Swifty," that would be Swifty Jackson who lives at an abandoned mine, the "Devil's Lady" at the end of Devil's Bend Road. She says thanks to the caller and gives a prayer of thanksgiving. There! At last a lead! She heads for her van.

53. Matt says he's going along, even though he thinks it's just some joker having fun. Shakti could get lost

and it's predicted to get below ten degrees in the mountains overnight. His mother makes them some hot chocolate; Matt takes some flashlights, warm coats, and his gun.

54. Along the way, Shakti tries to convince Matt that Bentley could not have done it. She tells him about Bentley as a child, what a loving and kind boy he was, blah, blah, blah, how committed he is to the cause of animal rights. She's down on herself because for a moment—even though he admitted it—she considered that he actually did it. No, it just isn't possible.

55. They find the mine—nobody around, but there are fresh tracks in the snow. The mine has been closed up for years. They find a heavy iron door open to a path that leads down into a cave and Matt explains that the cave used to be the vault where they kept the gold until it was shipped out. They hear a voice calling for help, faint and garbled, from inside the cave. Matt says to wait at the door, but of course Shakti follows him in. It's bitterly cold. Matt has a flashlight. They find they're in a small room; the door slams shut and they're locked in. They can see a vent in the roof where apparently the voice was coming from—suddenly, whoosh! Water comes splashing down all over them and they're soaked. They can't get out. They work on the huge steel door, but it's hopeless. Soon they're chattering with cold. Shakti meditates to calm herself. She says she's never tried it, but yogis who are far advanced can generate heat by meditation, enough to melt a block of ice thirty feet away. She tries to generate a little heat, but can't do it. They try again to get the door open, but no luck. They embrace for heat, but they're freezing, and it looks as though they might die. To get their minds off the cold, they talk. Matt tells Shakti more

about himself—how he loves horses and writes bad cowboy poetry, bad country and western songs, and how he's the best lawyer in western Montana. He used to be a deputy sheriff, but the sheriff is corrupt in a petty sort of way and Matt wouldn't go along with the payoffs, so they got him de-budgeted. And Shakti tells Matt about herself—that she was a spoiled rich kid, then a whacked-out antiglobalization protester, how she did dope, sold dope, got sent to prison on false testimony with hatred and murder in her heart, and then met a woman in prison who showed her the way to her spiritual awakening. Kathy Boxleiter became Shakti Boxleiter, a totally different person, except for her addiction to chocolate.

DISCUSSION

The scene above, in which the hero explains himself or herself, is common in drama. This is a very good way for readers to gain a deeper understanding of the hero and to establish greater intimacy with the hero they are already identifying with. This "hero-explains-self" scene is often presented too early in the story, even, at times, at the point of attack (the very beginning). This scene will play well here because the reader is in full sympathy with our hero/detective, empathizing with her, and identifying with her goals—both to save herself and Bentley, and to find the murderer.

This is the pivotal scene—the hero will have a death and rebirth that will change the hero in some significant way and the scene will have significant reverberations in the scenes that follow. In this case, the change will have to do with the romantic subplot and the development of the relationship between Shakti and Matt, as well as her renewed determination to prove her brother innocent.

THE READER SEES:

56. It gets colder, and Shakti and Matt are numb with cold. Death is approaching. He tells her he never wanted to love again, since he loved his first wife so much and she hurt him so badly, but here he is, like an idiot, falling for a nun. She tells Matt that she's sorry she got him into this and that she cares much more for him than she ever intended to, but it wouldn't have worked between them. She can't love a man; she's committed to her spiritual path. He's getting lethargic from the cold, turning blue. She tries rubbing him, slapping him, trying desperately to keep him awake. In desperation she again tries the heat meditation and goes into a sort of trance, deeper than ever before. While meditating, she has a vision of her brother wearing two sweatshirts.

Thus ends Act II.

How Our Hero/Detective Figures It All Out

Act III: The Thrill of the Chase

Remember: Act III is a continuation of the cat-and-mouse game with the murderer in Act II. The hero/detective, having experienced the pivotal scene and a death and rebirth, is now continuing the search for the murderer, pursuing justice more vigorously than in Act II.

So in Act III, the hero/detective has a change in psychology in some crucial way.

- Max, the PI (from Chapter 10), whose slovenliness and drunkenness led to a woman's death, is transformed by guilt in the pivotal scene into a reliable guy in Act III.
- Alice Cicero, the cynical stand-up comedian, finds a kind of peace after her rebirth in the pivotal scene.

- Simon Craft, the detective who plants evidence to
  stop a serial killer of little girls, was a too-sensitive
  cop bordering on a breakdown; now in Act III, after
  the pivotal scene, he's a cold and ruthless vigilante.

Besides the change in psychology, in Act III the menace
increases, the conflicts get stronger, and the pace quickens.
As the hero/detective closes in, the murderer gets frantic.

When she wakes up in that cave, Shakti will be reborn and
we'll be in Act III. She'll be a new person in that she'll realize that the attraction she felt for Matt is really love, and she
must fight against those feelings. Also, she realizes that the
two-sweatshirt vision she had means something.

In Act III, now, for Shakti there will be more of a sense of
urgency and mounting tension as we drive toward the climax
of the story. The reader has seen, at the end of Act II, that the
hero's life is in imminent danger. The murderer may strike
again at any time. Let's see how Shakti finally figures out
that the murderer is Forest Volner.

Stepsheet: Act III/*A Murder in Montana*

THE READER SEES:

57. Shakti comes out of her meditation. It's morning.
    Matt is up and about. He says he's never seen any-
    thing like it: She radiated so much heat it dried their
    clothes. In fact, the room got too warm. It was a mir-
    acle! He has just a T-shirt on, and she sees he has the
    scar from a bullet wound on his arm. He explains
    that he was in a shoot-out once and was trained to
    turn sideways if there was no cover, and that's how he
    got shot in the arm. He thanks her for saving his life.
    She realizes that some time ago she had progressed
    spiritually to the point that she no longer feared

death, but now she's regressed; she fears death because she's become attached to Matt. A bad thing for a Bhakta. She knows she must not touch him ever again, or even look at him unless she has to.

She tells him about the strange dream she had— her brother wearing two sweatshirts.

Then it hits her. The sweatshirt with the blood on it was not the sweatshirt with the "Animals Are People Too" slogan on it. This proves he was framed! Besides, why would the murderer go to all this trouble to kill them if Bentley were guilty?

He says she's got a point.

She must see Molly Runningwolf immediately! But they're locked in. He says his mother will discover he's missing and she knows where they went, so all they have to do is wait. Shakti does not want to wait, now that she has proof of her brother's innocence. There's a small opening near the hinge and she says if he were to fire his gun, he might blow the hinge off. He says the ricochet could kill them. She says the hinge looks rusty—they have to take the chance. She suggests they pray. They do. Then he fires the gun at the hinge. He gets winged with the ricochet, but they manage to get the door open wide enough for Shakti to squeeze her arm through and pull the bolt. They're free!

58. Shakti and Matt go to see Molly Runningwolf at the sheriff's office and they pick up Red Steckles on the way. Molly is packing up to leave town—her work is done. She reviews the incontrovertible, forensic, physical evidence against Bentley once again in her cold, scientific way. Then Shakti tells Red to tell Molly why he started heckling Bentley at the Eagle, and he says because Bentley was wearing the animal rights sweatshirt. Molly Runningwolf says, So what? That's what he told the police. But the sweatshirt in

the evidence locker is Bentley's UC Berkeley sweat-shirt, Shakti says—that's the one that has the blood on it! Molly shrugs. She says they found the "Animals Are People Too" sweatshirt behind the coke machine at the motel where her brother must have stashed it. Blood must have gotten on the University of California sweatshirt by touching the other one. Shakti says her brother isn't so stupid as to try to hide evidence behind a coke machine. Besides, somebody tried to kill them at the mine, which proves there's a murderer out there covering his tracks! Molly Runningwolf is not convinced.

59. Matt wants the sheriff's department to look into who tried to kill them at the mine—obviously the killer is trying to stop Shakti from discovering his identity. Sheriff Blodgett tells them they were trespassing and that the big door might have closed by accident, but if they'll fill out a complaint, he'll send a man out there—if he can find one who's not busy with the protester stuff.

60. Shakti and Matt visit Bentley in his cell. He has more bruises from brawling—this time with a prisoner. Shakti scolds Bentley for lying to her last time. He's got to tell her what he saw and did that night when he got to town—did he see anyone around outside? Any other cars? How could someone have gotten his keys? Who could have put his sweatshirt behind the coke machine? No dice. He won't cooperate with her. She tells him it was a vision that brought her here; he scoffs. He begs her to leave town; he's ten times more worried about her than he is about himself. He pleads with her tearfully—he couldn't stand it if the murderer tried again and succeeded. He's worried to death. No, she will not desert him.

61. Shakti and Matt (who now believes that Bentley is innocent because the murderer tried to kill them)

canvass the town, trying to find out if anyone knows the man called Swift. No one knows him, but they do find out that Hegg was spending a lot of time near the Valley of the Moon bird sanctuary where he had some kind of run-in with Clyde Apple. Shakti knows that Clyde Apple was in the bar the night Hegg was killed and that he left for the wilderness shortly thereafter.

62. Shakti and Matt go to Clyde Apple's place. He's not there. They break in. They discover that Clyde has a stash of nuggets and receipts for what he paid for them, mostly from Forest Volner because he has a bar (and, it's rumored, part ownership of a whorehouse in Nowhere). Sometimes customers pay in nuggets. They pan for gold in mountain streams supposedly, only these nuggets were taken from a vein or a pocket of gold. Shakti and Matt discover some of the letters from Sam Hegg to Caleb Hegg when Caleb Hegg was in prison. These must have been taken off Hegg's body after he was killed, Matt thinks. Or he broke into the truck and got them, Shakti says. She knows from her timetable that Clyde left during the fight her brother had with Hegg—he could have sat out in the parking lot and lay in wait. Clyde returns and opens fire on them. Shakti and Matt run for it. They're not recognized.

63. Shakti and Matt go to his place (not his mother's). Matt can't tell Sheriff Blodgett about the letters they saw; he'd be disbarred for breaking and entering. But, clearly, the letters indicate that this man Swifty might have killed Hegg's brother and Hegg was looking for him, and certainly that would be a motive for murder. Could Swifty be Clyde Apple? Matt says no one in town likes Clyde Apple much; he's the best at his craft, but has no friends except a lonely widow. Shakti is shaken—not by her brush

with death, but by how much she worried about Matt when the shots were fired. They comfort each other, then—ah—they make love. The next morning, Shakti is upset with herself for being weak and not sticking to her spiritual path—even worse, she knows for sure she's in love with Matt. That will ruin her meditation—she won't be able to banish him from her thoughts—and it will make further spiritual progress almost impossible. She's in total, existential despair and wishes she had some chocolate cherry ice cream with whipped cream.

64. Later that morning Shakti goes right back to Clyde Apple's place and apologizes for breaking in. She says she knows he took stuff from Hegg's camper, including some letters she'd like to see. She says she also knows he didn't kill Hegg, he's not the kind of man who could lay in wait for a man and bash in his head. And she knows he just wanted the letters to help him find the gold mine. He agrees to show her the letters. The letters talk about the former football player "Swifty," the man Hegg's brother doesn't trust. Shakti wonders if Hegg ever talked about him to Sharon, who she now knows made up the stuff about the artifacts business.

OFFSTAGE:

- Meanwhile, Volner leaves the $5,000 in blackmail money in a sack with a tracking device in it that he got from the sheriff's office, then follows Sharon to her home.
- Sharon gets home and dumps the money out of the bag, giddy with delight. But then she sees the tiny tracking device taped to the bottom. She guesses what it is and throws it out the back door. She grabs her luggage and heads for the door, but too late. Volner comes in. He forces Sharon to show him a letter she wrote to

incriminate him if something happened to her. He has her write another letter naming Clyde Apple and then kills her with a scalpel that taxidermists use and breaks the blade off to leave as evidence. He tears the place apart looking for the tracking device, but can't find it. He thinks she may have thrown it into the snow. It's no longer activated. He goes out into the snow to look for it. When he hears Shakti drive up, he runs.

THE READER SEES:

65. Shakti arrives at Sharon's place hoping that she's still awake. The lights are on, but no one answers the door. Shakti goes in and finds Sharon dead, her throat cut. The place has been torn apart and the back door is open and there are tracks in the snow going back and forth. There's a bloody, curved scalpel on the floor with the blade broken off. Shakti calls the sheriff.

66. Sheriff Blodgett and his people come, including Molly Runningwolf who has not yet left town. Molly Runningwolf says the scalpel is a taxidermist's scalpel. A search reveals that under one of the kitchen drawers there's a letter handwritten by Sharon naming Clyde Apple as Hegg's killer. Shakti's brother is off the hook! Only thing is, Shakti knows that Clyde Apple couldn't have killed Hegg and Sharon.

67. Over Shakti and Molly Runningwolf's pleas for caution, Sheriff Blodgett and his deputies, including Forest Volner, raid Clyde Apple's place and have a shoot-out. Clyde Apple is killed in a hail of bullets. Putting together afterwards what happened is difficult. It seems somebody—Clyde? A deputy? The sheriff?—started shooting and Clyde ended up dead.

68. Looking over Clyde's place, Shakti notices that he was very meticulous and that all the different sizes of

scalpels are in their sheaths, and none of them are missing. Where did the one that killed Sharon come from? And a man as meticulous as Clyde Apple sure was sloppy to leave a scalpel behind at a murder scene. She tells her suspicions to no one.

69. Bentley is set free. Now he thanks his sister profusely. He starts setting up to shoot pictures of the protest that's getting under way. Ooooo, he says, the fireworks are going to be fantastic! So it looks like our damn good mystery is over. The only thing left to settle, it seems, is what Shakti is going to do about Matt.

70. Shakti says good-bye to Bentley, Matt's mother and daughter, Molly Runningwolf, and even Forest Volner, thanking him for his kindness.

71. Shakti says good-bye to Matt. He says he wants to come to Berkeley and learn some of this meditation stuff. Tearfully, she says no, she can't ever see him again. She gets into the van, drives down the street, and turns around and comes back to Matt. He's ecstatic, thinking she's going to stay, and he starts gushing about how she'll love living in Montana, blah, blah. But instead she tells him she doesn't quite believe that Clyde Apple killed Hegg. She wants to go back to Sharon's place—the murderer was looking for something in the snow and she has to know what it was. He tells her she can't mean it—there's a handwritten letter naming Clyde Apple, there's a taxidermist's scalpel for a murder weapon! He fired on the deputies! Matt's glad Shakti's come back, but the case is over. She can't let it go, she says. There's a murderer still on the loose.

72. At Sharon's place, to Matt's astonishment, Shakti goes out into the snow in her bare feet so she can search by touch and finds a tiny tracking device. When she finds it, Matt explains what it is. Shakti

finds the bag the payoff money was in (she can smell the money that was in it) and finds the taped place on the bottom where the tracking device fits. She realizes this was a blackmail payoff.

73. At the Sheriff's Office, they look at the supplies and discover a tracking device is missing. Okay, somebody forgot to sign one out; no big deal. Shakti talks to Sheriff Blodgett—she wants to know how the blood evidence got on Bentley's clothes and dirt from Bentley's shoes got in Hegg's camper. He says it must have been a mix-up; there's no way to explain it. She backs him into a corner and he says nobody walks for murder in his town—he'll do what he has to do, and he's not saying any more. She doesn't believe the sheriff killed Hegg: Volner had confirmed Sharon's lie about Hegg looking for Indian artifacts.

74. Shakti and Matt go to Bentley and Shakti gets Bentley to tell her what he didn't tell her before—that there was a late-model SUV parked across the street from the Eagle when he went to the hotel, but he couldn't tell if there was anyone in it. Matt knows only two people in town with newer SUVs. One is owned by a widow woman who lives on the edge of town, a woman Clyde Apple worked for, and, some say, was having a love affair with. The other SUV belongs to Forest Volner, but his pickup truck was out back that night, so why would he have two vehicles there?

75. Shakti and Matt check with the widow, who says the night of the murder her SUV was in a shop over in Kallispell and she has a receipt to prove it. Shakti tells Matt that Volner told her that Hegg was looking for Indian artifacts. This was a lie and he knew it. Matt and Shakti talk it over. Volner could have gotten this device. Volner could have started the shoot-out and killed Clyde Apple. But the note Sharon wrote nam-

ing Clyde Apple? Volner could have tortured her into signing it. Matt thinks this is too far-fetched. Volner is old friend of his, one of the best, most generous men in the county—a pillar of the community.

76. Shakti and Matt go to see Penny Sue Volner, who is shaken by the visit but says her SUV was in her garage. Then, on the wall, Shakti sees that family photos are missing; Mrs. Volner says her husband took them down. Shakti wants to see them and Mrs. Volner shows them to her. One, a photo of a football team signed by most of the players, has a caption that says "Good luck, Swifty, finding that pot of gold." So her husband was the man Caleb Hegg was looking for, the man who worked the mine with his brother, Sam—the man who may have killed him. Mrs. Volner breaks down in sobs and shows Shakti the bloody shoe she saved from the ashes.

This, then, is the obligatory scene, the end of Act III. The hero/detective has unmasked the murderer.

All About Bringing Off a
Gripping Climax
and
Other Good Stuff

THE CLIMAX

And now for the gripping climax.

Pulling off a gripping climax is important if you're going to satisfy your reader, and every damn good mystery leaves the reader very well satisfied.

We are past the obligatory scene now, as we begin Act IV. Being unmasked, the murderer must now, in Act IV, be brought to justice in the showdown scene between the hero/detective and the murderer. This is the climax of our damn good mystery. Then comes the resolution—the consequences of the capture of the murderer, which makes up Act V.

In *How to Write a Damn Good Novel*, I wrote about creating an effective, dramatic climax of a dramatic novel. The principles of creating an effective climax certainly apply to a damn good mystery as well. I wrote "a dramatic novel, no matter how elaborate, how well told, how intriguing, is nothing without a good climax-resolution."

As in any damn good novel, you will want your premise proved. In a mystery, that premise is *Reason triumphs over evil*. But it should not just be proved; it should be proved in a surprising way.

John Lutz, in *Writing Mysteries*, says that when you "read the last paragraph or sentence of a successful mystery story you think, 'This is how everything *had* to turn out.' The ending does more than simply surprise you. It seems not only possible but plausible. That's because the writer knew from the beginning where the story was going." When my readers find out that Forest Volner is the murderer, I think they will have just that reaction.

Okay, then, here are the important things to consider including in your climactic sequence, starting with the surprise:

Surprise about the identity of the murderer. One thing we want for sure is a surprise when the murderer is uncovered. Among the characters in the novel is an innocent-seeming person who is in fact despicably evil, a murderer. One of the qualities we created in the murderer was the desire to hide his or her evil nature. Volner is certainly such a character: He's hiding his evil nature behind a friendly, helpful demeanor. It seems to me it's always best if the murderer turns out to be someone the reader knows pretty well and even better if the reader likes the character. When drafting the scenes, I'll try to make Volner likable.

Other surprises. Remember what Elizabeth George said about delivering what your reader does not expect? Let's say your reader expects your hero to make a commitment to his or her lover, and doesn't. The reader expected Clyde Apple to be the murderer, and we even had a pseudoclimax in which he was killed. Then, *surprise!* We've got the wrong guy.

Intense menace. At the climax, the murderer is in a trap. He or she has already murdered and has been conniving to cover it up, and now, as the hero/detective is about to snap the cage door shut, the murderer is going to become a very dangerous beast indeed.

Intense conflict. We've had slowly rising action all along, but now, at the climax, the conflicts are explosive. This is where the finger of guilt is going to be pointed at the murderer; this is where desperation on the part of the murderer is going to be greatest. These conflicts, as well as the menace, should be exploited to the fullest.

Seeing justice done. At the climax, the reader gets to see justice done, as already discussed. One of Marie Rodell's four reasons that readers read mysteries.

Reason does it. It is logic—deduction, brain power, the little gray cells—that does the murderer in. Not luck or chance, or somebody other than the hero/detective figuring it out.

Action. There should be significant actions (finding clues, a chase, fisticuffs, shooting, that kind of thing) at the climax.

However, there are exceptions. In certain kinds of mysteries, like tea cozies, there might be just dialogue. Some actions are nonviolent. An example of a nonviolent action: The hero puts the hat on the murderer and it's a perfect fit.

THINGS TO AVOID: TABOOS OF THE MYSTERY WRITING GAME

Prolixity. Long explanations as to motive, means, and opportunity of the murderer by the hero/detective are out. Of course, there will be some of that, but it's best if it comes through the conflict of accusation and defense—which is dramatic conflict. Warren D. Estleman, in *Writing the Private Eye Novel: A Handbook by the Private Eye Writers of America* (1997), puts it this way:

> *While the reader will, for the sake of a good story and challenging mystery, accept the fact that your detective behaves in a fashion more worthy of St. George than the workaday professional investigator of the real world, he will question why that same St. George is allowed to hold forth at jaw-breaking length on timetables, motives, and minute clues without someone interrupting him.*

By acting like St. George, I guess he means things like the hero's propensity for risking his life for others, as St. George and other self-sacrificing mythic heroes are wont to do. You should nix prolixity on the part of the murderer, too. If there are some important things to be cleared up after the murderer is caught, such as the motivation for the murder, okay. Your murderer might mention how fear drove them to it, say, or obsessive love, but don't let them prattle on, whining about how they had to do it.

Corkscrewing. Don't overdo the twists and turns at the end. Having a few surprises is a good thing; too many is a bad thing. It's like Goldilocks's porridge; it needs to be "just right." Now, then, how many surprises are too few? How many are too many? Two or three big ones and a couple of little ones might be okay, but when you have too many, it starts to become comic.

Maximum capacity lapses. The enjoyment of reading the cat-and-mouse game of the trackdown comes from both the hero/detective and the evil one/murderer being clever and resourceful and never operating at less than their maximum capacity. In other words, the reader never says, "Gee, that's a stupid thing to do." There's always a temptation for mystery writers to have the murderer slip up somehow and get caught as a result. Of course, if the crime were perfect, the murderer wouldn't be caught, so in some sense there always is a slipup. But the reader should not sense that the author has deliberately contrived it. The reader should always think that the murderer is clever and resourceful and always working at top form, and that the murderer is caught because the hero/detective was even more clever and resourceful.

Self-destructing murderers. Sometimes in bad mysteries the murderer—overcome by conscience, say, at seeing the wrong person being carted off to prison for a crime the murderer committed—will break down and confess all. Please, no pangs of conscience—it ruins the mystery. What pleasure can there be in seeing a *repentant* murderer getting his or her just deserts? The hero/detective must compel the murderer into a confession if the murderer is to confess and only if the case is so strong that keeping quiet wouldn't matter.

A Special Note About Fortune, Good and Bad

As a rule, good fortune is on the side of the murderer, until the obligatory scene when the murderer is no longer wearing a mask.

Let's say that before the obligatory scene the hero/detective is following the murderer, but loses him or her in a snowstorm. The snowstorm is a lucky thing for the murderer. That would be okay: Lucky happenings are obstacles for the hero/detective.

But after the obligatory scene, when we move into Act IV, we are in different territory. The reader is impatient with luck going against the hero/detective, who has, after all, solved the murder (but has not as yet captured the murderer). The reader senses that the showdown is coming, and further complications with luck on the side of the murderer feel anticlimactic (even though the climax has not happened yet). Therefore, after the obligatory scene and moving into Act IV, if there's a snowstorm, it will not help the murderer escape. In Act I, II, or III, if the murderer races for the train to escape and if it pulls out just as he jumps aboard, that's fine. But after the obligatory scene, it pulls away leaving him desperate to find another route of escape from his pursuers.

Types of Climactic Sequences

The dependable standard. In the standard mystery climactic sequence, the hero/detective is usually acting as a hunter following chains of clues from one suspect to the other until the obligatory scene at the end of Act III, where he or she gets the clue that leads to the (surprise!) murderer. Then in Act IV the murderer is tracked down and there's a showdown scene and the murderer is turned over to the law for punishment or will be punished in some other way. In Act V we see what happens to the hero/detective and to the other important characters in the aftermath of all that's taken place.

The dependable standard, legal variation. In the legal variation, the lawyer hero/detective has gathered a lot of clues—acting usually more like a gatherer than a hunter—and when he or she gets the murderer on the stand, hammers away at the murderer until the truth comes out. Often in the legal variation the obligatory scene is not shown to the reader, so that in the showdown scene the reader might not know if the witness being hammered is the murderer or not, even though the hero/detective does.

The gathering of suspects. This is the Hercule Poirot–type ending. Often when the hero/detective is in the gatherer mode rather than in the hunter mode for the whole of the story, the climax comes with a gathering of the suspects. The hero/detective dazzles us with his brilliance by interpreting the clues he's gathered—all of which the reader has seen if the author has been playing fair—and exposes the murderer, telling not only how the murderer did it, but why, and how he or she tried to cover it up. This type of climactic scene is little used now; it's considered old-fashioned.

The trap. In this type of climactic sequence, the hero/detective knows who did it in the obligatory scene, but there's no proof and the murderer may not be brought to justice. So a trap is laid. Some bait is put out and the murderer goes for it, thus fingering himself or herself as the guilty one. The trap must be clever; otherwise, the clever and resourceful murderer would not be at maximum capacity to fall into it. On TV's *Murder She Wrote*, Jessica Fletcher uses a trap quite often. If you use this device, try to make your trap more clever than Jessica's, where frequently the murderer is an idiot to take the bait.

The thriller ending. This type of climactic sequence can be very exciting. As the hero/detective is closing in on the murderer, the murderer freaks out and does something desperate, such as take a hostage or threaten to blow up a bunch of innocent people, that kind of thing. My advice is not to overdo it. A thriller ending is usually okay—it's great to have an exciting action-packed ending (as long as you're not writing a tea cozy)—but be careful that your carefully constructed damn good mystery does not become too much of a thriller, or you might lose your audience. A too-thrilling climax would be one that involved, say, an atom bomb blowing up Paris.

The pseudoclimax. This is my personal favorite; in fact you already saw it in *A Murder in Montana*. In this type of climactic sequence, the cops or the hero/detective finger the wrong guy. If it's done well, the reader will believe that the murderer has been caught. Ah, but no! The hero/detective says something doesn't quite fit—we had it figured wrong. This sequence may include a pseudo-obligatory scene where the hero/detective goes "ah-ha!" but has made a mistake, so it's not the real obligatory scene.

15

Gotcha! Putting the Murderer in the Bag

Stepsheet: Act IV and Act V/
A Murder in Montana

ACT IV: TELLS HOW THE HERO/DETECTIVE TRAPS THE MURDERER

Since I elected to plot *A Murder in Montana* using the pseudoclimax option, I will have to be careful when I write the pseudoclimax and the pseudoresolution that follows (where Shakti says her premature good-byes) not to let the reader slip into too much of a comfort zone, feeling that the story is over. I'll have to show right away that Shakti is upset with Clyde Apple's death and that, despite the convincing evidence—such as Sharon's note naming Clyde Apple as the murderer—Shakti thinks there's something amiss.

Okay, now that we've had the real obligatory scene at the

end of Act III, we can plot the real Act IV of *A Murder in Montana*.

THE READER SEES:

77. Shakti goes to the Eagle with Matt and a sobbing Penny Sue Volner. She leaves them in the car while she goes in and asks to speak to Molly Runningwolf and Sheriff Blodgett, privately. They go outside and Shakti tells them they should put Deputy Volner under arrest and handcuff him—Volner killed Hegg and Sharon Sundance and she can prove it with Mrs. Volner's help. Blodgett and Molly Runningwolf are both skeptical. After all, Forest Volner is a sworn deputy sheriff and a nice guy, a pillar of the community and all that blah, blah, blah. "But, okay, bring in Mrs. Volner," Sheriff Blodgett says, "Let's hear what she has to say."

78. The sheriff goes back in and relieves Volner of his service revolver—he's not a total fool. Volner wants to know what's going on. The sheriff tells him he's just heard some crazy story and he wants to sort it out; he doesn't want Molly Runningwolf getting her tail all twisted up. The last thing he needs is to be second-guessed by the state big shots. Volner also gives the sheriff a gun he keeps behind the bar. "See, Sheriff, just to let you know I'm not guilty of nothing and so I don't need no gun." He offers his hands for cuffing, but the Sheriff tells him to forget it— after all, there's half a dozen peace officers in the barroom.

79. Shakti, Matt, and Mrs. Volner come in. Shakti says she wants to compliment Forest Volner on his cleverness, and tells him that he was the guy, the former football player called "Swifty," referred to in Sam Hegg's letters. He must have killed Sam Hegg and been taking gold out of Sam's stash for years and selling it to gold hounds like Clyde Apple on the sly.

That's how he ended up owning half the town and the best whorehouse in western Montana.

Volner's wife keeps sobbing.

Volner defends himself by saying he's worked hard for what he's got, and he never murdered anybody. He insists it was Clyde Apple who killed Hegg and Sharon.

Shakti produces the tracking device she found in the snow. And the money bag that must have held a payoff for blackmail.

Volner says the Sheriff's Department has very sloppy security; anybody could have gotten one of those things. It might have been dropped in Sharon's backyard anytime.

Shakti shows the picture of the boys on the football team with the caption calling him "Swifty." "He took it off the wall—he didn't have the heart to destroy this wonderful picture of his glory days," she says.

Volner gulps.

Shakti says he had the keys to Bentley's room and asks the sheriff if he could have gotten keys to the evidence locker so he could put blood on Bentley's clothes.

The sheriff says he might have gotten some fool to help him (meaning himself, of course).

Then there are the scraps of clothing his wife saved from the ashes of the potbellied stove that Shakti now produces. Volner has no explanation for this.

Volner has yet another gun, which he now pulls out. He makes them all drop their gunbelts. Everyone but Matt. He tells Matt to keep his hands way up in the air—everyone knows Matt is the fastest gun in Montana.

Volner says he did it and would have gotten away with it were it not for his stupid wife and Bentley's crazy sister.

Shakti notices that the sun is reflecting off her Divine Mother medallion. She maneuvers to blind Volner with the reflection, but it doesn't work. Shakti can see that Matt is getting ready to draw, and if he does, he will no doubt be shot. Volner tells Shakti to stop trying to blind him or he'll shoot. He's leaving, he says. He's got a plane fueled and ready to go, and he's going to take Shakti with him as a hostage. Now Shakti is certain Matt will try to shoot him—he's not going to let Volner take her away to certain death. Now quickly:

Matt draws on Volner.

Volner fires at Matt, but Shakti has leapt in front of him, turning sideways to take the bullet in the arm—as Matt told her police are trained to do.

Matt fires twice; Volner goes down.

Shakti is bleeding from the arm, but she goes to Volner.

As Volner dies, Shakti counsels him on what he will find after death and tells him he can work off the bad karma he has made for himself in this life and he shouldn't give up hope. The hell that he will find himself in is of his own making, but he will get another chance. Shakti says he was a loving father in his heart, not a killer. He says to give him his gun; he'll show her how wrong she is. He curses his wife for turning on him, and dies.

DISCUSSION

Okay, the murderer is brought to justice. This is the end of Act IV. What follows is the resolution, in Act V.

A *Murder in Montana* Stepsheet Continues

ACT V: TELLS HOW THE EVENTS OF THE STORY IMPACT THE MAJOR CHARACTERS

80. Matt says if Shakti doesn't love him, why did she take a bullet for him? "Love, it's my spiritual ruin!" she cries, falling into his arms. "So why am I so happy?" she asks.

    Mrs. Volner, meanwhile, kicks her dead husband. The sheriff turns in his badge.

    Molly Runningwolf apologizes to Shakti. As the volunteer fireman medics are taking Shakti away, her brother, Bentley, comes in and tells her he warned her something like this would happen.

81. Some months later. We're at the new Western Montana Meditation Retreat, and Mrs. Shakti Dillon is conducting a class in front of a garden now in full bloom. Her best student is Matt's mother, but Reverend Diggs and Lyle Blodgett, the former sheriff, are doing well, too. Matt, however, seems to have trouble concentrating on anything but Shakti.

    Oh, yes, she still craves chocolate ice cream once in a while but, for some strange reason, she no longer feels guilty when she gives in to temptation.

The End of *A Murder in Montana*

DISCUSSION

Okay, we now have a "tentative" stepsheet. Tentative, because when the story is drafted the stepsheet will change as new elements are added and some elements are dropped, and the plot may even take other twists and turns. But the plot feels to me like a good one, one I have confidence in, at least enough confidence to let it guide me through the first draft.

We'll be writing our damn good mystery using damn good prose, which comes next.

16

Writing Damn Good Prose

ELEMENTS OF DAMN GOOD PROSE

A damn good mystery is first a damn good story. Up until now in this book we've been going through the steps for making a damn good mystery, story-wise. Now, creating a damn good story is one thing; writing it with damn good prose is another.

When editors or agents first gaze upon your work, the quality of the prose better impress, if not dazzle, them. A damn good mystery is not just a damn good story, it's damn well written, too. Most editors and agents will not read much beyond a page or two if they're not gripped by the story elements, but they won't read more than a sentence or two of poorly written prose.

Let's take a look at the elements of good prose; it's really not that difficult.

- *Good prose is clear.* Often a lack of clarity comes from carelessness.

At the mall, Fred met Bob. He had just robbed the bank.

Which one is it who just robbed the bank? Fred or Bob? Some square-headed grammarian may know a rule that applies here, but most readers don't.

Many clarity problems occur because the reader does not know where the camera is. Is a scene being described through the eyes of a character, or through the eyes of the narrator?

The dazzling sunset lay under the dark clouds to the west. A soft wind blew. The fog would be rolling in. A shadow crossed the wall. The captain got out of his chair.

Are we inside? Outside? Are we supposed to be taking in the scene from the captain's viewpoint? It would all be clear if it had started, *The captain looked out the window from his bedroom and saw . . .*

Have the people who read your drafts tell you whenever they're confused. Good prose is first of all clear prose. One trick is to read your narrative aloud. If you stumble over a sentence, it's often because the sentence is not clear. If you read your work into a tape recorder and play it back, you can often find your own clarity problems.

- *Good prose is efficient.* This means that there are no extra words. This does not mean that the descriptions are not adequate, but that there are no repetitions (except the occasional repetition deliberately used for emphasis) and there are no meaningless extra words or phrases. Here's one common fault: A scene is flowing along nicely and it's perfectly clear from the dialogue and action what is happening, yet the narrator will also tell the reader what is happening, as if the reader were too stupid to figure it out.

"Gee, I never held a gun before," she said, the Colt .44 shaking in her hand, beads of sweat forming on her forehead. She was frightened.

Obviously, the "shaking hands" and "beads of sweat" indicate fear, so the sentence *"She was frightened,"* is unnecessary. Whenever you write a sentence that you suspect is not needed, it probably isn't, and the prose will be improved if it is cut. Oftentimes, there are literally hundreds of words or phrases that can be cut, such as the words *times, literally,* and *whatsoever* in this sentence, making the prose more efficient, faster-paced, and more elegant, with no loss of meaning whatsoever.

- *Good prose uses sensuous detail.* These are details that appeal to the five physical senses—sight, sound, hearing, taste, and touch—and the "sixth" sense, the psychic sense. Much bad prose appeals only to the sense of sight:

He walked into the room. There was a desk under the window and a bed along the wall with a picture of George Washington hanging over it.

This scene would be so much better, would be more real, if it appealed to more of the senses:

He walked into the musty room. An old, metal desk stood forlornly under the window, the wind whistling through the crack in the glass. He touched the surface of the desk, wiping a swath of soft grime from the hard surface. A picture of George Washington hung on the

> *wall at an odd angle, making old George look some-*
> *what odd, intoxicated perhaps.*

- *Good prose makes good use of metaphor.* A metaphor
  is simply a comparison of one thing to another. When
  as or *like* is used, it is a special kind of metaphor called
  a *simile.* Often writers have trouble with metaphors
  because they don't ask themselves this very important
  question: Is it true? Is the comparison I am making a
  true comparison? They'll use a metaphor that might
  sound good at first but, upon reflection, the comparison is not valid.

Unless you're using exaggeration for comic effect, you
wouldn't want to write: *The gun in his coat made him list to
one side, as if he were carrying a piano in his pocket.* A
piano? Really? Is this metaphor apt? I've seen metaphors
like, *He was poor as a Mexican.* Well, yes, some Mexicans are
poor, but there are millions of middle-class Mexicans, too,
and thousands of rich ones. You are trying to make the
reader see and feel the scene; a bad metaphor can jerk the
reader right out of a scene.

Avoid using too many metaphors. Your prose will begin
to turn "purple," a serious fault.

You will have to rely on your readers to tell you when
you're overdoing it, the way a cook needs tasters to tell him
if he has too much salt in the soup. A little metaphor goes a
long way, and a few good ones, say one or two per page, are
fine—twenty or thirty, probably too many. If you *suspect*
you've got too many, I can guarantee that you do.

Often, with metaphor, the central comparison might
work well, but there may be other connotations that you
don't want. *Her eyes were as soft and brown as hemp.*
Hemp, of course, is rope made from the marijuana stalk, so
if she smokes dope, it might be a good metaphor, but otherwise not.

Fr. Tom, the most gentle and loving of the monks, was short, round, and had the face of a cherub works. But *Fr. Tom, the most gentle and loving of the monks, was short, and round as a thousand-pound bomb* does not. Sure, a thousand-pound bomb is round, but you don't want Fr. Tom to be thought of as lethal or explosive.

Clichés are overused metaphors: *soft as a baby's bottom, dry as dust, dumb as a post.*

In genre mysteries, clichés are not a serious fault, especially if they are not overdone. Editors and readers of genre fiction don't seem to mind them. In mainstream mysteries, they should be avoided except in dialogue that characterizes a character.

Clichés in literary fiction of all kinds produce nausea in the literary reader, and on rare occasions have been known to cause hives, shingles, or worse. One reader in Berkeley, California, with a highly elevated literary sensibility choked on a gob of brie cheese and died on the spot when she came across the cliché *sour as a pickle* while reading a nonlinear, post-Christian, existential novel titled *Let's Dance on Freddy's Grave.* Or so some writer of popular fiction claimed.

Anyway, if you want to be literary, avoid clichés like the plague.

• *Good prose uses active verbs.* This means fewer "to be" verbs. If you were to write *he was on the couch* (*was* is a form of *to be*), it would not be as effective as if you wrote *he perched on the couch* or *he slumped on the couch.* Active verbs provoke images in the reader's mind, and that's a good thing if you're trying to create a fictive dream. Using active verbs makes the prose more vigorous. *To be* verbs tend to flatten the prose.

• *Good prose uses the active voice.* Passive voice is less vigorous than active voice. Passive voice makes the actor the object of the action—*The ball was hit by John*—rather than the subject of the action, as in active voice—*John hit the ball.*

- *Good prose is emotional.* In the "sensuous detail" example above, there was no emotion.

Putting emotion in a scene is simply a matter of having the character react emotionally to what he or she encounters in the scene:

> *He walked into the musty room, feeling a sense of dread. An old metal desk stood forlornly under the window, the wind whistling through the crack in the glass. So this is where she lived, he thought grimly. Lived and died. He touched the surface of the desk, wiping a swath of soft grime from the hard surface. A picture of George Washington hung on the wall at an odd angle, making old George look somewhat odd, intoxicated perhaps. The painting made him feel sad for old George and for her . . . and for himself.*

- *Good prose uses telling details.* This is true in any damn good fiction, but it is especially true in mystery writing. A "telling" detail is simply a detail that tells us something about a character or a place, as opposed to a "generic" detail that tells us nothing. *It was a sunshiny day* is a generic detail. *The Arizona sun pressed down on them like a hot iron on an anvil,* is a telling detail (even though it's a bit of a cliché).

  Generic description does help the reader dream the fictive dream, but it does not bring the character to life as a particular, unique person. To make characters come alive on the page as unique people, you need details that not only describe, but characterize:

> *Bledsoe was a tall dude, decked out in buckskin, a tall Stetson cocked on his head to one side as though he had not a care in the world. He had narrow eyes and scars on his face, the kind you get from other people's knuckles.*

- Obviously, this description characterizes him. He's cocky and tough. Sometimes such details can really put a stamp on the character that is unforgettable. Think of the clacking steel balls that Captain Queeg rolls around in his hand in *The Caine Mutiny* (1951), or the godfather in Mario Puzo's *The Godfather* (1969) saying, "Make him an offer he can't refuse."

  The details of a character's abode, place of business, campsite, car, or any possession can help to characterize him or her. They say that if you look into the trunk of a car that a person's owned for more than two years, you can learn all there is to know about him or her.

  In the trunk of Bennie Knockworst's '65 Chevy Super Sport: a flat spare tire, no jack, beer cans, a bowling ball, dog hairs, a dozen old copies of Playboy *magazine, two cans of no-name brand motor oil, a half-smoked joint of marijuana in a tobacco tin, a broken fishing pole, an empty box that once contained an auto generator, a rusty pair of pliers . . .*

- What would the reader conclude from this description? Right. Bennie is a redneck, lowlife slob.

  In the trunk of Bonnie Beneveau's 1998 VW Golf: a spare tire, a jack, a wilted radish that rolled into the spare tire well out of sight, two safety flares, tire chains wrapped in plastic with instructions (both never used), a small 12-volt vacuum cleaner, a half-full bottle of Windex, *a roll of paper towels . . .*

- Right. The reader concludes that Bonnie is neat, clean, and doesn't do much besides work, go grocery shopping, and go home.

  Telling details, then, are very important in making the reader understand the characters and the scene.

How to Check Your Prose

Okay, here's a way to check to see how good your prose is. Select a book written by an author you consider a good stylist. Pick a few pages at random. Go through the pages and draw a circle around every "to be" verb and a square around every "active" verb. Now do the same thing with your prose. Chances are, the author you have selected will have far fewer "to be" verbs per thousand words than you, and far more "active" verbs.

Now mark all the sensuous details in both.

Now mark all the emotions conveyed in both.

Now check the metaphors in both.

Now check the telling details in both.

Do this with several good prose writers. You will now know exactly what your prose lacks.

Choosing Your Viewpoint and Voice

When you draft your novel, you will write it in a certain tone, with a certain voice, from a certain viewpoint. You will make your choice depending on the story you wish to tell.

Say you want to tell a "tough-guy" detective story. You might use a first-person narrator like this:

> Johnny D. and me were pals in Q back when that fruitcake Carter was in the White House, when for ten, maybe fifteen large you could get a pickup truck full of weed and wholesale it to surfers for fifty, spend the winter in Hawaii, and do the same trick next year. He was a big man, forty or so, as easy to like as a Texas whore. He always wore faded bib overalls, and he had a black beard that smelled of axle grease and breath that smelled of cheap hooch. A couple of freaked-out Cubans with pump shotguns, their eyes rollin' like windows in a nickel slot machine, took us down the second

year, so we was broke. The last I seen of our weed it was heading south on Hacienda Boulevard in Compton going about sixty in a thirty-five zone. So I talked Johnny D. into us takin' down this DuperSuper Pharmacy in Vegas where they take in two milski cash in a weekend and don't get to the bank until Monday. This, Johnny D. said, was opportunity knockin' loud.

Him going for my scheme wasn't what got him popped. That was another matter that happened after we took down DuperSuper for a dribble—like ten large was all—and we hooked up with Buddy Westin of Philadelphia, PA, the city of brotherly love. That's where things went bad. Buddy had this other idea. That we should kidnap this British kid, the Queen's son, who was coming to New York to help save the friggin' whales or some damn thing. . . .

Okay, but for another story you might choose quite another first-person narrator using another style altogether. Here's an example:

Now that I'm retired from my bookkeeper career at Mimi's Confections, I have little else to do but take care of my tabby cat, Marjory, and sit in my parlor watching my neighbor, Mr. Haskins, getting ready to murder his wife.

Now I know what you're thinking—that I'm a little daft, haven't got both oars in the water. I'm almost eighty years old—that's if you leave off about four years, which I usually do. The four years I lived in Milwaukee with my second husband, Charles, who I'd rather forget. And so you think I don't know what I'm talking about: Mr. Haskins is not, in your opinion, going to murder his wife. You think I have an overactive imagination or Alzheimer's, don't you?

That's what the policeman thought, I'm sure. Lieu-

tenant Henley. A stupid man, if you ask me. As stupid
as my third husband, Albert, who was too dumb to tie
his shoes. Lieutenant Henley sat at his desk and listened
to me, arms folded, with that supercilious, sanctimo-
nious smile like he was talking to the village idiot. He
said they went and talked to Mr. Haskins and he had a
good explanation for everything I offered as proof.

Like why he bought a big, shiny table saw when he
never does any repairs or remodeling.

He was planning on learning, the dumb lieutenant
answered. Like sure, a man in his late forties, he just
decides to become a do-it-yourselfer, just like that. So I
asked what he was planning to do with the fifty-pound
bag of lye . . .

As an author of damn good mysteries, you should be able
to create endless narrators, each with a distinctive voice.
This is true with third-person narrators as well, of course.
You might want to write one mystery in a hard, lean and
clean, Dragnet-type style, like this:

Bledsoe and his new partner, Marian Pink, arrived
just after the coroner's black hearse had loaded the
body. Bledsoe was big and beefy, all hard muscle. He
wore a herringbone tweed sports jacket, tight at the
shoulders, black permanent-press pants, and no tie.

Marian Pink was not Bledsoe's type. She was a tall
number with straight, black hair and no makeup,
wearing a beige business suit that made her look like
an executive on the way up. She didn't know beans
about football and refused to listen to anything about it
from him.

They got out of the squad car and into a cold, mist-
ing rain and fog blowing in from the Pacific. Marian
Pink shivered and folded her arms across her chest.

"Look," he said to her. "Your job is to do what I tell you and don't talk."

"Anything you say, mein Führer."

He didn't smile at her joke. She did.

"What's in the package?" Bledsoe said to the coroner.

The coroner was fat, old Doc Thompson, a sharp-eyed buzzard. Doc Thompson lit a Marlboro, cupping his hand in the wind. "Twenty-something female, been marinating a week." He unzipped the body bag.

Bledsoe stepped aside to give Marian Pink a look at the bloated white corpse that smelled like rotten fish and ammonia. The coroner and Bledsoe figured she'd puke.

She held back the flap of the body bag and looked at the corpse. "She took a bullet in the forehead," Marian Pink said. "Got her dead center. Must have been a magnum or maybe a high-powered rifle, blew away the back of her head. What do you bet a fish got the left eye?"

She stepped back to give Bledsoe a look.

"You missed the ligature marks on the wrist and the little tattoo on her thigh. Might have been a rose."

"I didn't miss them. I left them so you could find them and look good."

He shot a glance at her. In the dim light he thought he caught her smiling. She wasn't afraid of him: that was good.

Old Doc Thompson nudged him with an elbow. "I think you got a keeper," he said with a chuckle.

Another time you might want a slower, more dense, detailed style, for, say, a mainstream mystery:

Lt. Ellen Parr saw the flashing red lights illuminating the fog as she made the last turn and parked next to the coroner's black hearse. All they'd told her on the phone when they'd tracked her down at Bennie's Lounge was that a fisherman had snagged a floater. Another one. Number 4. It would be a young woman again, she thought—again there would be no clothing, no identification, and no apparent motive. It would turn out she'd be a college student or a beautician or a fast-food worker. Some clean kid, sweet as a chocolate bar. A good kid, the parents would say; the friends would say so, too. She might have played the piccolo in the high school band, something innocent like that.

It was going to be a repeat showing of the same film—of that she was certain. And she'd be having more haunted dreams.

She turned off the engine. The coroner's assistants, with the help of a couple of eager young sheriff's deputies, were loading the body onto a gurney. God, was she ever that young? Did she know then that she'd ever be this old? Feel this old? Christ, 42, and she felt 82. She took a silver flask out of her glove box and took a few swallows of vodka. People couldn't smell it on your breath, supposedly. She could smell it on her captain's breath, but what the hell. It might as well be gin. She liked gin. She liked bourbon, scotch, brandy. Damn, she had a wide range of tastes, developing more all the time. She took a couple more swallows and got out of the car.

Ellen was almost 6 feet, a thin, dishwater blonde with a square face and deep-set, dark eyes that, rumor had it, could see through walls. She still wore her wedding ring, a narrow, gold band, even though the husband was long gone. He didn't say good-bye when he left. She gave him eleven years and four months and he didn't even give her a damn good-bye.

The mist felt good on her face. She liked the fog and the sound of the waves. She could hear them now far below the cliff. That would be Johnson Beach. That's

*where they found Number 2 and Number 3. Janice
Beecher Rice and Penny Ann Armstrong. Janice was a
cheerleader; Penny had a dog named Scooter.*

*She pulled up the hood of her slicker as she threaded
her way through the soft mud. There was old Doc
Thompson, looking as if the weight of the universe
were on his shoulders.*

"Is this number three?" he asked.

"Four," she said.

*"Oh, yeah, four. You want to have a look? She's
been in the water more than a week."*

"That's what they pay me for."

*They walked over to the gurney and unzipped the
bag. The same old ammonia–rotten fish smell. The
body was bloated and partially blackened. She turned
the head so she could look at the forehead. Same as the
others, a .357 mag dead center. Her hair was dark and
curly, reminding Ellen of her niece back east. Going to
Bryn Mawr, smart as a whip. Too smart to ever be a
damn homicide cop.*

Anyway, you get the idea. Work on your voices.

THE SECRET METHOD OF MASTERING THE ART OF WRITING DAMN GOOD PROSE

There's an old method of teaching the writing of good prose
that works wonders and it will help you find a distinctive
voice. Doing the following exercise a half-hour to an hour a
day has made some of the worst prose-writing students in
my classes into some of the best prose-writing students in a
few months—or less. Often the improvement is very rapid
and the degree of improvement is astonishing.

Here is what you do: Every day when you sit down to
work, you take a good prose writer's work and you copy it.
That's right, you type it out, word for word. Do two or three

pages: You will not only get a feeling for how good stylists use words, you will feel the timing and the rhythm of their prose and the snap, crackle, pop of their dialogue.

Next, write a page or so in imitation of what you've just typed. That's right. If, say, you've just typed an outdoor scene with a lot of action, you write an outdoor scene with a lot of action, trying your best to write it in the style of the piece of writing you've just copied.

After a while you will find that you can imitate this style at will; now try another author and another, until you can imitate various styles and voices any time you like. You will then discover, wow, you have the ability to change your style and tone and voice effortlessly. And soon you will find your own, distinctive voice.

A Sample Imitation

A while back I was studying Hemingway's prose for a novel I was writing, *The Hemingway Man.* I love Hemingway. As a man, he was a drunken, loudmouth bore and a bully, but he was a fabulous prose stylist. I offer the following as an example of writing imitation; can you tell which of the two examples is the real Hemingway and which is my imitation Hemingway?

1. We stayed that afternoon in a village in the pine-forested foothills and sat on the verandah of the inn in the late afternoon drinking a strong, sweet sangria and talked politics with the old innkeeper, who was a royalist and a Catholic. Cantrell was in one of his dark moods, and he kept saying that the Pope in Rome was a *Fascisti*, which only made the old innkeeper chortle at what he took to be an absurd joke, and he poured us more wine and we sat there until it was quite dark.

2. Back in Paris in the heat of August when the city was deserted, Anna and I began to quarrel and it was

worse in the evening and the lovemaking was bad. We fought about small things, the housecleaning and the buying of the day's bread and cheese, and more important things, too, about our future and the baby, and should I go to Istanbul and Switzerland. We fought about these things because the real thing was not even whispered. The real thing hung in the air above us like a cloud of doom, silent and foreboding. Then one morning I went out to the post office on the *rue de Rivoli* looking for the check from Mr. Foster in New York which as it turned out had not come. I returned to our rooms to find that Anna had gone and taken her clothes, her books, and the painting of the canals we'd bought in Amsterdam that winter, and she left a note hastily scribbled on a piece of brown butcher paper that I could not bring myself to read until later when I was quite drunk.

By doing these exercises, you'll soon discover that your own, individual, distinctive styles will emerge, styles suited to your personality and to the particular story you are writing, styles unlike any of the styles you've been imitating. Your friends and fellow writers who read your drafts will begin to tell you what a fine writer you are.

Tell them it's a natural talent you were born with; let them think you're a genius.

The Fine Art of Writing the Mystery Scene

CREATING THE FICTIVE DREAM

It is the job of every writer of dramatic fiction to create the fictive dream and to keep the reader dreaming it. In *How to Write a Damn Good Novel II: Advanced Techniques*, I suggested five ways to strengthen the fictive dream: by raising story questions and creating sympathy, empathy, identification, and exploiting inner conflict. In writing our damn good mystery, we'll need to keep these techniques in mind. So I offer this brief review:

Story Questions
Story questions *make the reader curious*, thereby engaging the reader's mind. Story questions are cast in declarative sentences, such as:

> *As Fred went to bed just after nine, he heard a squeak in the attic.*

Obviously there's a question in the reader's mind: What made the squeak? Here's another example:

> *Alice loaded the .45, put it in her purse, and, just before she went out, reread the letter from Andrew.*

The reader, of course, wonders who Alice intends to use the gun on. Okay, just one more:

> *He was sure the red Porsche had been following him since Phoenix.*

The reader wonders, Who could it be? And why are they following him?

Sympathy

We will *get the reader to sympathize* by making the reader feel sorry for some character. This will connect the reader's emotions to the story. Sympathy is perhaps the easiest emotion to arouse in a reader. Here's an example:

> *Fred arrived at work at ten after ten, having had a flat tire, two speeding tickets, an overheated engine, and possibly a cracked block. But ten minutes late was ten minutes late, the boss said, and fired him.*

If the reader does not feel sorry for Fred, the reader is made of stone. Example #2:

> *The doctor came into the waiting room and walked over to Fred and Alice, who looked at him and knew by the expression on his face that he hadn't saved their son.*

Again, the reader will feel sympathy.

Empathy

We will *get the reader to empathize* by making the reader feel emotions that the characters feel:

> *Alice saw something on the floor and at first she thought it was a rolled-up rug. Then the smell of gunpowder and the coppery smell of blood hit her—Oh, God no, she thought, her heart beating fast, and then she turned the corner and saw a pool of blood on the floor as large as a tabletop. Henry's body lay in the blood, strangely bent, and where Henry's head should have been was a mass of pulpy, raw meat and bone.*

Made me feel nauseated to write it. I hope you, dear reader, felt the same reading it.

Identification

We will *get the reader to identify* with the characters by giving the characters goals that the reader wants to see accomplished.

> *Alice left the police station burning with rage. Okay, they didn't have any evidence, they hadn't turned up a suspect or a significant clue, but somebody, by God, pulled both triggers of that shotgun and blew Henry's head off, and she, by God, was going to find out who.*

Inner conflict

We will *exploit inner conflicts* (a character being torn by conflicting desires). This will bring the reader into the story so completely that the fictive dream will overwhelm the real world and the reader will be transported into the story world and will not easily be able to escape.

> *Alice couldn't believe it: So it was Malcolm who had stolen the letter; it was Malcolm who ran to the house and got the shotgun; it had to be Malcolm who put the gun to Henry's head—but how could it be? Malcolm was the sweetest man in the world, a true man of God who loved Henry, who had fed him and cared for him through his long illness. . . . No, no, anyone but sweet Malcolm. But then she looked at the stamp in her hand, the stamp that she'd found in his writing desk— Henry's stamp. It was true: Malcolm was a vile murderer. It had to have been Malcolm. He had the key to the gun locker and was the only one who . . .*

Don't get stressed out—most of these things writers do by instinct; in fact, in most how-to-write-a-mystery books they are not even mentioned. But it's helpful to think of these things both before you draft a scene and before you rewrite; they are powerful tools to help you bring the fictive dream to life.

DRAFTING A DAMN GOOD SCENE

Much of the enjoyment in reading a damn good mystery comes from being absorbed in the fictive dream created by a well-written scene. Here's what you need to keep in mind when you write a scene for a damn good mystery—or any other damn good novel:

Before you sit down to write the scene, you should prepare by asking yourself what the characters *want* in the scene. What characters want is part of their agenda. You should know precisely what the character's *agenda* is. For instance, the hero/detective's agenda is to catch the murderer. But in a particular scene, the character's objective is, say, to find out what another character saw at the murder scene. It is the other character's objective, say, to deny having seen anything, to make it look as though he's not involved.

When the various characters in the scene are trying to achieve their objectives and the others won't bend, dramatic conflict is created. This is the "insistence vs. resistance" I discussed at length in *How to Write a Damn Good Novel* that is at the heart of all dramatic writing; it is to a scene what air is to a soccer ball.

One of the most common failings of first-time mystery writers is that their scenes are slow to develop. There's a long, dreary lead-up into the scene with the arrival of the detective, introductions, chitchat—all before we get to the conflict. This is called the "warm plunge," named after the practice of swimmers who wade in slowly, first getting their toes wet, then their feet . . . The preferred way in the modern mystery is the "cold plunge," jumping right into the part of a scene where the questions and conflicts are starting to heat up. Most damn good scenes will begin with a cold plunge, but every damn good mystery can have some slowly developing warm plunge scenes as long as there are adequate story questions, inner conflicts, and foreshadowing of conflicts.

The characters need to experience dramatic growth in any dramatic scene. That is, they should change emotionally, rather than keeping the same emotional tenor. If they don't change, the scene will be static and dull.

The conflicts will rise to a climax in the scene. That is, the characters will be pushing to achieve their objectives and will either succeed in obtaining them or will withdraw from the conflict. That moment is the climax. The climax of the scene is a reversal of sorts; the characters quit trying to attain their objective. A cop, say, has been smacking around a suspect who, at the climax of the scene, gives up his mother as the murderer. At this point the cop may give up his objective because he's accomplished his previous one.

Following the scene climax, there will be falling conflict: This is the resolution. Often, the hero/detective has broken down the resistance of another character—a witness or a suspect—as in the last example of the creep who fingers his mother. So in the resolution of the scene, the hero/detective, at last, gets some information. Some of it may be bogus, of course.

We need to be on the lookout for what we might use as clues in these scenes. Some clues will pop out at you; others sort of dawn on you as you write. Sometimes they may not be noticed by either the hero/detective or the reader at the time, but may be considered on reflection. A clue may be one of the details, or something someone says or does. Clues are important—it's best to jot them down when they strike you. They are malicious little devils that can hide on you. You better look out for red herrings, too: They are false clues, which are just as important as real clues. Often in a damn good mystery the hero/detective is following a trail of red herrings. In *A Murder in Montana*, Shakti is looking for a man named "Swift" who doesn't exist, and Indian artifacts that don't exist. It can be just as gripping following red herrings as following real clues. And often it's a nice surprise in the end when it turns out that the only thing to come out of it is that wrong suspects are scratched off the list.

There is other information about the crime or suspects that should be coming out. Often the hero/detective is gathering a lot of information other than clues or red herrings, such as the background of the characters, the relationships between the characters, and so on. The reader and the hero/detective are constantly sifting through this mounting pile of information for clues.

DAMN GOOD ENDLINES

The last line of a scene or a section, the *endline*, is extremely important. A good endline will form a bridge to the next scene by creating a story question that will make the reader curious and want to read on.

First, let's see an example of a scene with a poor endline:

> *Bledsoe sat in his car and thought things over for a while. He just didn't have a single damn clue as to who shot Mrs. Applegate. He went through his notes twice, didn't get any new ideas, so he decided to go home and go to bed.*

Notice how the last line, ending with "so he decided to go home and go to bed" just goes flat. There's no story question being raised that would make the reader curious to read on. Let's see if we can give the same material a better endline.

> *Bledsoe sat in his car and thought things over for a while. He just didn't have a single damn clue as to who shot Mrs. Applegate. He went through his notes twice, didn't get any new ideas, so he decided to go home and go to bed.*
>
> *In the morning he'd have to start on the witnesses once again. This time, he'd take Teddy Roosevelt's advice and he'd carry a big stick.*

Okay, now there's a story question. He's going to get rough, but it's really not a strong story question. Let's try again:

> *Bledsoe sat in his car and thought things over for a while. He just didn't have a single damn clue as to who shot Mrs. Applegate. He went through his notes twice, didn't get any new ideas. He ran through his list of*

suspects. They were all lying, but he was certain Miles Morgan was telling the biggest lie—he had seen somebody leave the house by the back door right after the murder. Either that, or he was the one leaving.

Maybe if old Miles were looking down a gun barrel, he'd be a bit more truthful. Gun barrels have that effect on some people. Bledsoe knew he was risking his PI ticket, but what the hell, he was desperate. He got out and opened his trunk and rummaged through the accumulated junk. That old gun with the broken firing pin had to be there someplace.

Okay, better? The story question (what will happen when he uses the gun) is stronger and there's a nice bridge to the next scene. The other end of the bridge might then begin:

Miles Morgan looked funny, clownishly funny, Bledsoe thought, with a .38 stubby stuck in his nose.

PUNCHY ENDLINES

Sometimes a good endline will not raise a story question that forms a bridge to the next scene. Instead, it simply ends with a strong dramatic statement, such as:

Bledsoe sat in his car and thought things over for a while. He just didn't have a single damn clue as to who shot Mrs. Applegate. He went through his notes twice, didn't get any new ideas, so he fished out a bottle of bourbon from under his seat, took the top off, and proceeded to get quite drunk.

Okay, it's not all that great, but it's better than going home and going to bed.

A scene might end with a line of dialogue. Here's an example (Bledsoe's a cop this time):

"Okay, Mrs. Timmor," Bledsoe continued, "you claim you weren't anywhere near the Barkely place when old Joe got his brains beat out. Where were you exactly?"

"I was seeing a gentleman friend," she said through pursed lips.

"And just who might this gentlemen friend be?"

"I never kiss and tell, Lieutenant."

Bledsoe said, "This time you either make an exception or I'm taking you in on suspicion of murder."

"I'll get my coat."

Bledsoe sighed. He knew he didn't have anything on the old dame. He held up his hands in mock surrender.

"Look, Mrs. Timmor," he said, "let me be frank, I don't think you did this, but my boss insists that I check out everyone's alibi, I'd really appreciate it if you'd cooperate."

She sighed and fanned herself with her fan. Then she sat down at her vanity and ran a brush through her hair.

"I'm sorry, sir, but as I said, the identity of the person whom I was with is my secret."

"Okay, play it the hard way."

"I'm not going anywhere."

"Good afternoon, then," he said.

This is a fairly weak endline. Not terrible—most editors would let it pass—but it's far from damn good. You'll notice in this scene there is a very nice dramatic line before the end of the scene: "I'll get my coat." It's nice because he threatened her and she didn't back down, and it's a nice indirect line. A direct line such as "All right, take me in" would have been dramatic, but the indirect line is better and would make a damn good endline.

But wait, you say, how can that be the endline when he doesn't take her in? Easy, you simply end the scene with:

> "*Okay, Mrs. Timmor,*" Bledsoe continued, "*you claim you weren't anywhere near the Barkely place when old Joe got his brains beat out. Where were you exactly?*"
>
> "*I was seeing a gentleman friend,*" she said through pursed lips.
>
> "*And just who might this gentlemen friend be?*"
>
> "*I never kiss and tell, Lieutenant.*"
>
> Bledsoe said, "*This time you either make an exception or I'm taking you in on suspicion of murder.*"
>
> "*I'll get my coat.*"

Okay, so we have the good endline. Now we'll simply start the next scene with:

> As he drove down Mrs. Timmor's long drive, Bledsoe thought, he should have taken the old dame in; it would serve her right for calling his bluff. But he knew she didn't do it: She was a coldhearted bitch, but she'd never bludgeon a man. Too messy. If she was going to kill somebody, it would be with a neat poison, administered in a nice cup of English tea served with crumb cake on the veranda.

SCENE WRITING MADE SIMPLE

Of course, you cannot keep every possible element of a scene in mind as you write. You should draft your scene and then read it over, reflect back, see what it may lack. See that it has rising tension and snappy dialogue and a great endline.

In practice, when you start to draft a scene, think of the characters' agendas and objectives and put the characters in conflict, then let the characters have a go at it. You know from the stepsheet what is supposed to happen. Put the characters in conflict, dream the fictive dream, and let the characters write the scene for you.

Let's take a look at a scene from our damn good mystery under construction, *A Murder in Montana*. Okay, Shakti has been to the Eagle and has found out a little about what happened the night of the murder. One thing she found out is that a guy named Red Steckles was there, one of the men who was heckling her brother and goading him about being an animal rights activist. Let's say he lives in a mobile home at the edge of town. It's mid-afternoon. Shakti drives up in her van and goes up to the door:

Shakti rang the bell and heard the chimes inside. The door opened and a man about her height stood before her, a beer in his hand.

"Yo?" he said, looking her over.

"Are you Red Steckles?"

"Yes."

"I'm Shakti Boxleiter."

He sneered. Word must have gotten around, she thought. The whole town probably knew who she was and what she was doing.

"You mind if I ask you a few questions?" she asked.

"No, I've got nothing to hide. C'mon in."

"You were at the Eagle the night of the murder."

"That's right."

"I understand you gave my brother a hard time."

"He had it coming."

"Did you see the fight with Hegg?"

"Yeah."

"Did you see my brother leave?"

"Yeah."

"Did you see him outside?"

"No. I left a couple of minutes after. There wasn't nobody in the parking lot."

"Were you driving?"

"Yes. My old Jeep, right there. I got in it and drove away."

"Did you see Mr. Hegg leave?'

"No."

"Do you know anyone else who might have had a reason to kill Mr. Hegg?"

"He was always fighting with Sharon Sundance, but I never thought they'd kill each other. He had a temper, Hegg did."

"Well, thank you, Mr. Steckles."

I know, I know, it's so bad it makes you want to puke. This is a scene that my writing coach, Lester Gorn, would say is all "backing and forthing." Shakti asks the questions, Red answers, blah, blah blah, back and forth. No rising conflict. I've read hundreds of student mysteries that read like this, and I've seen many published books loaded with long, boring stretches of backing and forthing.

Besides conflict, the scene lacks details, and nothing is accomplished, really, except the pile of information Shakti was collecting got a little higher.

Let's think about Red for a moment.

What's his agenda? In the draft I just showed you, he has no agenda, and so he's not presenting Shakti with any obstacles. Hence, no conflict. So, very boring.

When you're writing a story and you get to a step and it involves a minor character you have not done a full biography of, you will need to take a few moments to think about the character—who he or she is, what he or she wants, what his or her agenda might be in life, and his or her objective in the scene.

Okay, who is Red Steckles?

Let's say he works occasionally in a transmission shop and on the side is an apprentice alcoholic. He's thirty-four, divorced with a retarded kid, and very close to his arthritic mother. Red has a passion for killing animals in and out of season. He's mean, hates animal rights activists to the bone, and, when he's not hunting or working, is usually down at the Eagle drinking beer and lamenting his sad life with the other losers who hang out there, or at home watching violent films and drinking beer. He has a girlfriend ten years older than he is, but he only sees her on Saturday nights because she lives twelve miles away.

So what's his agenda? He wants to see Bentley go to the death house for killing Hegg, even if he didn't do it. He cares nothing about Hegg, he never did like the creep, but he hates animal rights protesters. So he is about to shower his hate and venom for the animal rights movement on Shakti, whom he sees as one of them. His objective in the scene? He wants to convince Shakti that her brother did murder Hegg. Anything he can do to bury Bentley deeper, he's glad to do it. Right now, though, his biggest problem in life is that he's broke.

Okay, the scene I'm about to show is a "warm plunge" scene (one that starts with a warm-up), which is okay if there's inner conflict and foreshadowing of conflict. Here's Shakti and Red Steckles, version #2:

> *Shakti parked her van off the road in a parking place marked for visitors of the trailer park with a crude, hand-painted sign. She got out of the car; the frigid, gusting wind swirled snow around her* [a generic detail, but still building the reality of the scene]. *Red Steckles's old mobile home was on a small hump of ground and had a faded plywood patch on the side where one of the windows had been broken long ago* [a telling detail—he's a lazy slob]. *The awning was propped up with a couple of two-by-fours* [more telling detail—the place is a dump]. *Old, rusted, bedsprings stood by the door, and a dented old Jeep with its canvas door in tatters sat in the driveway* [building more reality with more telling details].
>
> *Shakti made her way through a drifting snow bank, the soft powder trickling down her boots. Part of her*

mindfulness, she thought. Focus on the sensation, be in the moment [telling details that characterize her].

She felt a knot in her stomach. Fear. Fear that this man might do what? Hit her? [emotion, raising story questions, and hopefully creating empathy]. *She should not be thinking such thoughts* [inner conflict]. *She'd asked Forest Volner about him and he'd said that in the afternoon, before Red Steckles got really drunk, he was never a problem* [raising the story question, Will he be a problem now?].

Shakti took a few deep breaths. Fear was a bad sign that she was not achieving the detachment she thought she had been achieving back in Berkeley, which at the moment felt like a thousand thousand light years away [more inner conflict].

She knocked on the door and heard movement inside. A TV was turned off. The door opened.

A man stood before her in an old flannel bathrobe open in the front. Underneath he wore jogging pants, worn at the knees, and a faded Dallas Cowboys T-shirt. His face was narrow and gaunt, with a scraggly, gray-streaked beard and dark-reddish hair, almost to his shoulders. He looked to Shakti like an inmate of a gulag in a Russian novel [she pities him]. *He sneered. His teeth were yellow and crooked* [a glimpse of his character].

"The fucking animal-loving fuck's sister, right? Heard you were goin' around making a nuisance of yourself." [shows his view of the animal rights people]

"Are you Mr. Steckles?"

"Yeah, so what?"

"My name is Shakti Boxleiter," she said. *"I'd like to ask you a few questions."* [her objective]

"I ain't answering no questions, bitch." [resistance—conflict]

He started to close the door. "Have I been rude to you, sir?" she said. [she's still pressing her objective]

"I got nothin' to say but 'fuck you.'"

"Sir, I believe my brother is innocent of the ridiculous charges against him. As any loving sister would, I'm trying to do what I can to aid in his defense. I know that you do not approve of his activities in support of the rights of animals, but, nevertheless, he is entitled as an American to advocate any position he likes, is he not? It's called free speech—you do believe in free speech, don't you?"

He nodded vaguely. [she's touched a button; this is emotional "growth"]

"Please, I won't take but a moment of your time."

She tried to move past him to go inside, but he blocked the way.

"There ain't nothing I got to say to help you, Zakti, Bopti, Shitski—whatever your name is. Your animal-fucking-loving brother killed Hegg. Nothin' I can do about it."

"Did you see him do it?"

He grinned, taking a swig of beer. "Yeah, I seen him do it. I was an eye-fucking-witness." [This of course is a lie.]

She felt a jolt. This just wasn't possible.

He chuckled. "Yeah, I was in the Eagle, see, when your dipshit bro came in. The fuck's parka's open and he's wearing this stupid fuckin' sweatshirt says "Animals Are People Too." You fucking believe it? I had to say somethin'—try to straighten him out."

"You saw the fight with Hegg?"

"Yeah. Your brother was lucky Hegg was half-gassed or Hegg would have torn his arms off. And then I seen your brother leave. A few minutes later, Forest, the guy who owns the joint, says he's closing up."

"What time was that?"

"One forty-five, a few minutes early. I down the rest of my brewski and haul out. Out back I get in my

old Jeep, but I got trouble crankin' her over. Other guys and that half-breed girl Sharon Sunfuck, they come out, they drive off. I seen Hegg come out, your brother was hiding behind a car, jumps out and whacks him. I seen Hegg go down." [devastating, but of course it's all a lie]

"Then what?"

"I seen him put this hood or something on him— that elk's head thing—and run off. Yeah, I seen it all. He done it."

Shakti stared at him. He was grinning, gulping down some more beer.

"Maybe we can talk about how much it's gonna cost you to keep my mouth shut," *he said.* [now we get to the point]

"Where did he get the elk head?"

"I don't know. He had it with him. Yeah, that's right."

"Why have you not told the sheriff this?"

"I was waiting to see if there wasn't a few bucks in it for me, somehow. You want me to swear on the Bible?"

"No, I want you to come with me now. We'll go to the sheriff. I want you to tell him what you saw." [she's calling his bluff]

"Why would you want me to do that?"

"It's the truth, isn't it?"

"Of course it's the truth."

"Good, then let's go to the sheriff and tell him. Let's call him, have him come over here. An eyewitness— I'm sure he'd want to hear what you have to say. But don't slip up! That woman, Molly Runningwolf, she's very good at catching liars and prosecuting them for perjury."

He gulped some air.

Shakti stepped inside, feeling the warmth coming

from an old wood stove. The place smelled of beer and wood smoke and old sneakers. There was litter every-where, and an old green couch had the stuffing coming out of it. The TV was large and new, and one wall was covered with photographs, mostly of Red and an older woman, looking gnarled and bent over. His mother, she guessed.

"Now," Shakti said, "do you want to tell me what you really saw?" [this is the climax of the scene—he reverses himself and tells her what he knows]

He drained his beer and tossed the can into a bin near the stove.

"All I seen was some old codger come out, drive off. Then Sharon Sundance came out and got into her car."

"You didn't see her leave?"

"Nope. I thought she was waiting on Hegg. I got my old Jeep cranked up and I came on home. That's it, that's all I seen." [we're now in the resolution of the scene]

Shakti walked over to the wall of photos and looked at the woman standing beside Red. In her eyes, Shakti could see a strong woman, a loving woman. "Your mother?"

"Yeah."

"I'll bet she tells you you have unrealized potential." He chortled. "Yeah, she does say stuff like that."

Shakti started to leave. She opened the door and turned to him. "She's right, you know? You could be a good man, a very good man."

"She says that, too." He said this with a shy grin. [more emotional "growth"]

"I believe her, Mr. Steckles."

He looked a little confused for a moment, then smiled and nodded. "Watch your step, the stairs can be icy," he said. "You go see Sharon Sundance. She might'a seen something."

> *"I intend to do just that, Mr. Steckles,"* she said, *making her way down the steps.* [the bridge to the next scene]

DISCUSSION

I noted some of the character growth in the scene, the change in Red Steckles. There is a small change in Shakti, too. In the beginning she's frightened and by the end she's made a friend. Being in conflict with Shakti has caused Red to change and become less hostile, more human. In all good, dramatic fiction, the drama causes characters to change and develop, to experience different emotions, to shift their moods. When we read good fiction, we are witnessing the vast and wondrous river of life, and the river of life is ever-changing.

It's no wonder writers love writing so much. We get to live so many lives, feel so many emotions, dream so many dreams.

DRAMATIC NARRATIVE AND HALF-SCENES

This narrative might come right after the above scene:

> *But already she was thinking, that blow to the head with Bentley's tripod. Sharon Sundance could have done it! It wouldn't take a lot of strength. And Hegg knew her, he might have turned his back on her without giving it a thought. Hadn't they been arguing about something earlier in the tavern? Yes, Shakti thought, Sharon Sundance just might be a murderer.*

This sort of thing is sometimes called the *sequel* to the scene. It's how the character is reacting to the conflicts. Sequels are a kind of dramatic narrative and are very useful for keeping the reader involved by rehashing clues and witness statements, giving us a review of what's going on.

Dramatic narrative is also used when creating the fictive dream that shows the reader what a character does over a period of time. Dramatic narrative is *not* a summary of events. Summary has no place in a damn good mystery. A summary would read like this:

> *Shakti spent the afternoon knocking on doors all up and down Main Street, asking everyone she met if they knew a man named* Swift. *No one admitted that they did. By evening, she was tired, and went back to her hotel and prayed and meditated till past nine, then went to bed.*

Dramatic narrative needs to have all the fictive values that a scene has—sensuous detail, other details, emotion, conflict, character growth, everything. The only difference is, in a scene the events are happening more or less in real time. If the actions of the scene were happening in front of us, it would take about the same length of time to read the scene as to watch it happen.

In dramatic narrative, the events and conflicts being shown take place in a longer span of time than it takes to read them. It reads like this:

> *Shakti began canvassing the town, desperate to find this "Swifty" person. About noon, just as there was a break in the snowstorm, the sun burst through the clouds, making North of Nowhere sparkle under a heavy blanket of snow. Shakti worked her way north, stopping first at the hardware store and asking the moon-faced clerk, who shook his head blankly, and an old ranchhand with a corncob pipe, who said he never did hear of the man, and a man with dark features wearing a hunting jacket, who told her to leave town. She covered the west side of Main and started back, her feet frozen in her unlined boots. More clouds were*

moving into the valley in the afternoon—dark clouds,
meaning there'd be more snow by morning.

No one admitted to knowing any Swifty. Four peo-
ple told Shakti to leave town: half a dozen refused to
speak to her. On a side street, a kid in a red jacket
threw a snowball at her from just outside a house with
a large, wraparound porch, the kid's father standing
next to him. Shakti smiled and waved at him, but
inside she felt angry, not at the boy, but at ignorance
and what it could do to people.

The difference of course, is that summary does not suggest the fictive details that evoke the fictive dream in the
reader, but dramatic narrative does.

A half-scene is simply the insertion of a piece of a scene
into the middle of a dramatic narrative.

Shakti turned the corner and called at the first three
houses—no one would answer the door. Then at the
fourth house, a young man answered, a thick book in
his hand. [so far dramatic narrative, but we now go
into a scene] *He was short and fair and blinked at her*
through thick glasses.

"Yes?" he said.

"I'm looking for a man named Swifty. He used to
live in this town."

"You must be the sister of that man who killed
Mr. Hegg."

"I'm the sister of the man accused, who is innocent."

The young man laughed, and shut the door in her
face.

As she went down the stairs, she could hear him
inside, still laughing. [end of half-scene, back to dramatic narrative] *She finished the block and then stopped*
at a rundown cafe for a salad and some tea and endured
the nasal country and western songs pouring too loudly

from the jukebox while a couple of cowboys looked her over and chuckled to themselves. [back to a half-scene]
  "Glad I amuse you," she said.
  They looked away.
  Twenty-five minutes later she was back going from door to door. [return to dramatic narrative]

Before drafting any of your damn good mystery, it will be necessary for you to choose a voice and a viewpoint. Which will you choose? Read on.

All About Viewpoints and Voices
or
Who's Telling This Damn Story Anyway— Me or Him? Him or Me?

DECISIONS, DECISIONS, DECISIONS

The voice and viewpoint you choose are important decisions and the time to make them is before you start making your stepsheet. You'll need to know because the voice and viewpoint will determine which scenes you show the reader and which scenes you keep offstage—the ones the reader does not see.

I'll give the advantages and disadvantages of the various possibilities that are commonly used.

Let's start with your first decision, which is whether this story should be told in "first person" or "third person."

FIRST-PERSON NARRATION

A "first-person" narrator is a character in the story who has, supposedly, witnessed the events and is recounting them from his or her point of view.

The advantage of the first-person narrative is that the narrative voice can be strong, colloquial, and colorful. There's a long tradition of tough-guy fiction written in a first-person narrative voice.

> *The young woman at the spotlessly white, enameled desk looked up at me. She had a round face, looked sort of Slavic and unpleasant. A tattoo on her hand, a small red and blue heart with a black arrow through it.*
>
> *"You must be Frey, the PI—hey, that kind of rhymes," she said to me.*
>
> *"Buzz Mr. Penol, tell I'm here, would you please?"*
>
> *She buzzed. He didn't answer. She flicked her fingernail; it was long and blood-red to match her lipstick.*
>
> *"You'll never find her, you know," tugging on her large, round, gold earrings, playful now.*
>
> *"I'll never find who?"*
>
> *"Whom," she corrected. "You'll never find Mr. Penol's dog."*
>
> *"That's why I'm here—a dog?"*
>
> *"Yes it is." Now she smiled. Sunny and sardonic.*
>
> *I smiled back, my best crooked, cocky, PI smile. "I'm good at finding dogs. They like me."*
>
> *"I like you, too," she said.*
>
> *She buzzed again and handed me a slip of paper. "In case you get lonely so far from home. That's my name there, Jolene Quickly."*
>
> *A man's voice barked from an unseen speaker: "Send the dick in."*
>
> *"Showtime," said I.*

DISCUSSION

In this example, the hero/detective is the narrator of his own story.

The narrator does not necessarily have to be the hero/detective. The narrator might be, say, the hero/detective's sidekick, such as Dr. Watson in the Sherlock Holmes stories.

In the story under construction here, *A Murder in Montana*, we choose a sidekick. He could be the hero's lover, Marshal Dillon, who is not the hero's sidekick at the start of the story, but who might become the hero's sidekick as the story progresses.

Suppose you're in a bookstore browsing around and you come across *A Murder in Montana* by James N. Frey. Ah, you think, I've heard of him, a damn good writer. You open it to Chapter 1 and you read:

CHAPTER ONE

My name is Marshal Dillon, attorney at law.

I know, it's funny, the name. My parents loved Gunsmoke *and our family name was Dillon and so I got to be called "Marshal" Dillon—that's what the birth certificate reads. You can look it up yourself in the county courthouse in Kallispell, Montana.*

Most people call me "Matt." I thought of changing my name legally to something other than Marshal, but an old Indian told me once that was bad luck: The Great Spirit knows me by the name I was born with and might not recognize me with any other name. Maybe the real reason I keep it is because people don't forget it.

Now I live near a dusty, ramshackle, rundown little town called North of Nowhere on Highway 12 that I happen to love.

I was hired by the state to represent this weird elk-hunt protester who everybody knows is guilty as O.J. His name is—get this—Bentley Boxleiter, and he has a sister, Shakti. No kidding, Shakti.

Talk about names. Shakti. I thought it sounded like something you might order in a Japanese restaurant. I didn't know what to expect. All I knew about her was she taught yoga classes in Berkeley and was really into some weird religion.

I guess for me the story really began when I met the bus she was on from Salt Lake on that snowy day two days before the opening of elk season, which in these parts has all the excitement of the World Series. The first thing I noticed about her was she was a little on the thin side and she had big, brown eyes that seemed to take everything in. . . .

Okay, you can see the merit of a first-person narrator: The language can be nice and colorful. The drawback is, it's difficult to show the reader scenes in which the first-person narrator is not present. It can be done, but the narrator has to do a little fancy footwork so as not to wake the reader up out of the fictive dream.

Since the story is being told after the events occurred, the scenes the narrator didn't personally witness can be told. Here's how:

I went over to the jail with Shakti that first day and we talked to her brother. Sitting in the visitors room in his orange jail jumpsuit, nervous as a day-old colt, he told us how he had come to town the previous Saturday. It had been snowing, he said, and the defroster was fogging up the window, so he had poor visibility. Also, he was tired, his eyelids drooping; he'd come all the way from Boise that day.

Trying to park, he'd bumped into an old pickup.

Around here, nobody'd give a damn, but he was edgy, being an animal rights activist in a town where about the only rights an animal has is to breed and to be used for target practice in season.

Anyway, he looked at the damage. It wasn't that bad, so he figured to give a guy a few bucks and that would be that.

He went into the Eagle Tavern to find the owner of the old pickup, who turned out to be Caleb Hegg, a mean drunk. Somebody knew Bentley from the year before and started ragging on him, saying he liked to have sex with animals. Caleb shoved Bentley, and Bentley had to throw a judo hold on him and Caleb passed out, but came to instantly. Everyone in that bar went dead silent.

Bentley then went and checked into the flea-bag, mildewed, old log house motel on the creek run by that retired circus clown, Moses Montgomery. Moses, he told us, was busy juggling some coke bottles when he first came in and Bentley asked for a room and was given one in one of the cabins along the road. He said he was tired from his trip and so he took a steaming shower, put on some fresh pajamas and went to bed. . . .

I know I changed the story a bit, that's the way it goes when a story is being developed—things keep changing.

The fictional values of the story can come through this way, but you end up with a lot of "he later said" or "he must have" and that kind of thing, in order to maintain the flow of the narrative without the reader saying, Whoa, how could he know that? This is especially true when the narrator is relating a blow-by-blow account of an action he or she did not see. It is difficult, but a skilled writer can do it.

One way to surmount this problem is to have the first-person narrator be the hero and to try to create the fictive dream only in scenes the hero participates in. In *A Murder in Montana*, Shakti might narrate her own story like this:

CHAPTER ONE

Ms. Chan, the receptionist at the meditation center where I work, interrupted my yoga class for senior citizens one morning and said I had an important phone call. This interruption was a violation of our usual practice, and by Ms. Chan's demeanor I could see she was distressed. My class of six oldsters and I were practicing the eel posture, an easy one for beginners.

"What is it, Ms. Chan?" I asked.

"Your brother is on the phone—he says he's in trouble."

"Did he say what kind of trouble?" To my class, I added. "He has poor night vision and is always bumping into things, but he's a good person who has dedicated his life to art and animal rights."

"Perhaps you ought to speak to him," Ms. Chan said. She obviously did not want to reveal the nature of my brother's problem in front of my class. I told my class to do some stretching and I would return in a moment.

I followed Ms. Chan into the lobby and picked up the phone.

"What is it, Bentley?" I said. "Please be brief. I'm in the middle of a class."

"I'm sorry, Shakti, but you see, I'm in a real pickle this time."

I could hear the fear in his voice.

"I've been arrested, Sis . . . They think I killed a guy."

I felt the room close in on me.

There is an obvious advantage to this. Remember, as Marie Rodell said, one of the primary reasons for a reader to read a mystery is to identify with the hero, and a first-person account in the voice of the hero is a powerful way to get the reader to identify.

Also, it gives the reader the same clues the hero/detective gets. The reader sees and hears only what the hero sees and hears, so what could be more fair? The reader then gets an up-close-and-personal look at the cat-and-mouse game: We are with the hero at all times and can appreciate the hero's cleverness and resourcefulness.

But most damn good mysteries today are written in the third person.

THIRD-PERSON NARRATION

When using a third-person narrator, the author, in effect, creates a sort of nameless character as the narrator of the story. As the author, of course, you are this narrator, but when you write as a fictional narrator you use different diction than you normally use in your everyday life.

> *Through the dusty windshield of his car, Chief of Police Georgios Skouri watched the office buildings and hotels of downtown Athens collapse in a slow dance of disintegration, one after the other like rows of giant pins in some cosmic bowling alley.*

This is from Sidney Sheldon's *The Other Side of Midnight* (1973). Now I ask you, do you know anyone who talks like this? No chance. This is written in fiction writer's diction, which is as far from normal speech as Florida is from Iceland. You use fiction writer's diction when you narrate a story in third person. When you use it, you pretend to be a sort of disinterested witness to the events. You do not say things like:

> *Fred got up that morning and the dumb bastard went to work with a gun. He was never all that bright.*

This is the narrator giving an opinion. This is a no-no, except in comedy.

In a serious damn good mystery, your narrator is a neutral third party just giving us the facts in an unbiased way. The narrator, the character created to tell the story, has no attitude whatsoever. Just a sexy voice that uses fictive diction well. There are, of course, shadings that do reveal the character of this narrator, which I discussed at length in *How to Write a Damn Good Novel II: Advanced Techniques*. But it's best if you keep the narrator's opinion out of it.

"CLOSE" THIRD PERSON

There are two modes of third person: one is "close" and the other is "distant." Some books are written in close third person, some in distant, some in a combination of both. The difference between close and distant has to do with the way in which the thoughts of the characters are revealed.

In close third person, the narrator quotes the thoughts of the character like this:

> *Freddy walked in the door of the convenience store and spotted Julie behind the counter. Golly, he thought, that's one mighty fine-lookin' gal.*

Some authors use italics for quoted thoughts, others use quotation marks, but more commonly the thoughts are in plain text as in the example above. The convention of using italics or quotation marks has gone out of fashion.

The reader can tell by the diction that this is a direct quote of his thoughts; we really don't need either quotation marks or italics. A neutral narrator would not use an expression like "mighty fine-lookin' gal."

When writing in close third person, using this narrator character to do the storytelling, you are constantly slipping into character viewpoint from the narrator's viewpoint and back again. Like this:

> *Freddy stood for a moment gawking at Julie and didn't see the man coming in, didn't see him pull the gun, but he heard the shot and felt the slug hit him in the back* [from narrator's point of view] *and as he lost consciousness he could see Julie at the cash register* [switch now to the character's point of view] *and he thought, Golly, that's one mighty fine-lookin' gal.*

"DISTANT" THIRD PERSON

In "distant" third person, the narrator describes but does not quote the thoughts of the characters.

> *Freddy walked in the door of the 7-Eleven and spotted Julie behind the counter and thought she was an extremely attractive young woman.*

When writing in distant third person, your narrator supposedly knows what all the characters are thinking and is giving you a sort of report. In actual practice, the narrator is switching from one viewpoint to another all the time.

> *Freddy drove up to the convenience store just as it opened* [narrator's point of view]. *He got out of the car and didn't see the man in the van parked across the street* [describing what is in his mind; this is distant third]. *He went inside and spotted the good-looking young woman—the long blond braids, the bright blue eyes—behind the counter. She glanced his way. Wow, he thought, wow, wow, wow,* [close third]. *He decided on the spot that he was not going to stick the place up on her shift* [distant third].

Switching Viewpoints from Character to Character

There are creative writing workshop leaders and teachers who preach that it's an ironclad rule that you must stick to one viewpoint per scene and that the only time you should change viewpoint is when you change scenes. What they mean, of course, is that it's permitted to switch between the narrator's viewpoint and a character's viewpoint in the scene, but not to switch from one character's viewpoint to another. This rule is complete nonsense. You may follow that rule if you wish; in fact, for many writers it's a valuable rule to follow. You'll be much less likely to violate the principle of clarity if you stick to one character's viewpoint in a scene, but if you do it deftly, it's perfectly okay to switch viewpoints between characters in the same scene.

That is, it's okay once you set your contract with the reader. If, from the start of your mystery, say, you show the reader that sometimes you'll stay in the same viewpoint in a scene and sometimes you won't, there will be no problem. At the start of a story, you make a contract that establishes the pattern you're going to use and, once established, it's best not to break it. All you have to do is show the switching of viewpoint in the same scene from character to character early on and you can keep right on doing it.

Here's an example:

> *Freddy was waiting for Jean-Ann for almost an hour and was getting agitated, pacing back and forth with his hands in his pockets* [from the narrator's point of view]. *Jeez, women. Always friggin' late* [now we're in Freddy's point of view; the change in diction indicates it] *but what'ya gonna do—can't live with 'em, can't live without them, he mused* [attributives like "he mused" put us clearly in his viewpoint]. *Then he spot-*

ted her coming down the stairs, holding her skirt from blowing in the breeze, Marilyn Monroe–style.

She paused to stare at him; she was thinking to herself that she didn't really know what she saw in Freddy: He was a shrimp, not too bright, and always broke [distant third from her point of view]. But he did take her to Harry's, and there were always interesting men to talk to at Harry's, and one of these nights she was going to go home with one of them.

"Hi, Freddy!" she called.

"Hi, ho, love!" He ran to her and threw his arms around her. She felt great in his arms, soft, warm, cuddly [from his point of view]. Freddy was a man who loved all soft, warm, cuddly things [narrator's point of view].

THE USUAL VOICES AND VIEWPOINTS

Today almost all mysteries—genre, mainstream, and literary—are written either in first person, using the hero/detective or the hero/detective's sidekick as narrator, or in what is called a "third-person limited omniscient narrator."

This narrator knows everything that is going on in the course of the story and selects a few (usually no more than about five) characters to be "viewpoint characters." A viewpoint character is one whose thoughts are either quoted (in close third-person viewpoint) or described (in distant third-person viewpoint).

Sometimes a third-person limited omniscient narrator will slip into the viewpoint of a character who is not one of the chosen viewpoint characters, but a minor character. It might be, say, the character who finds the body, or even the victim.

Okay, let's say you start your novel like this:

Cluny Boyce loved three things: his Big Bertha golf driver, his old Algonquin deerskin slippers, and a cat *named Sugarpops. On the evening of October 16, 1999, Sugarpops went out the cat door for her nightly pee at seven-fifteen and never came back. Cluny noticed about eight-thirty—right in the middle of* Law and Order, *the only thing on earth he was ever addicted to—that she was not in his lap where she usually sat, so he went out into the backyard to see what the hell had happened to her. There was no way that old fluffball could get over the fence, he thought—that's why he was worried. She might have had a heart attack.*

He turned on the backyard light and there she was, right in the middle of the junk-and-debris-filled backyard, lying near a pile of old tires and a rusted swing. He rushed over there, but when he got to her he could see that her head was split clean open and she was cold dead.

He froze. He'd seen it in 'Nam. A bullet in the head, dead center, could split open a skull like that.

A wave of fear washed over him. He looked back toward the stairs, back into the house: it was forty, maybe fifty feet. And here he was in the open, standing in the light like a big ole target.

That's when he heard a sound he had not heard since 'Nam. The receiver on an automatic weapon being pulled back.

He screamed, ducked, and ran for the back door as fast as his sixty-seven-year-old legs could carry him.

And he almost made it.

Okay, this is a minor character and we never get into his viewpoint again. But you have established in the contract you're making with the reader that you will be using more than just one viewpoint.

THE RARE EXCEPTIONS

You might, for some stories, elect to write your damn good mystery using various first-person narrators. The first section is named, say, "Freddy"; the second section, "Linda"; and so on, with each section written from the point of view of a different narrator. You gain a little freshness, but you sacrifice the reader's involvement somewhat. When you switch from one narrator to the other, you take the reader out of the fictive dream.

You might use present tense with a first-person narrator. It's difficult to sustain it, and very tricky to write it. Scott Turow used it in *Presumed Innocent* and did a nice job. It gives your work a sort of literary gloss and critics like that. The reader, though, often finds it tedious. I tried it once or twice. My readers didn't like it, so I switched back to third person. Here's how it goes:

> *I get up in the morning the day I'm gonna do the convenience store job and already my stomach's jumping. I sit at the table in that stuffy old kitchen while Ma makes Aunt Jemima pancakes and sausages and I clean my gun again for the nineteenth time.*

Supposedly, present tense gives the prose an immediacy that past tense lacks. For many readers, though, it's like music played off-key.

Another viewpoint used sometimes is "objective viewpoint." In objective viewpoint, the narrator shows the actions but does not know what is going on in the characters' heads.

> *Freddy sat in his car outside Moon's Magic convenience store and rubbed the barrel of his gun. He opened the cylinder and inserted six bullets, one at a time. He wiped the gun with a rag and put the rag under the seat. He inspected his hand to see, perhaps, if*

it was trembling. Then he put the gun in his belt, mum-
bled "Showtime" to himself, and got out of the car.

Because the narrator does not know what the character is thinking, readers can only discover the nuances of a character's inner life through the narrative. Objective viewpoint, if done well, has a strong sense of reality. If it is not done well, the reader becomes confused, because the motives for the characters' actions may not be clear.

Okay, once you have made the decision as to voice and viewpoint and have your stepsheet, you're ready to start drafting, which is discussed in the very next chapter.

Drafting, Rewriting, and Polishing Your Damn Good Mystery

CREATING IN THE FAST LANE

I met a well-known mystery writer who has published over fifty novels in the past twenty-five years or so. She told me her secret of speed writing after about four margaritas at a party one rainy night at the Squaw Valley Writers' Conference. She made me swear one of those wonderful Sicilian oaths to never quote her, so I can't tell you who she is, the awards she's won, or the model of Mercedes she drove. I'll call her Alice Flint. Okay, I'm going to give you her secret, but don't tell anyone where you heard it or the penalty for violating my oath may be invoked and I'll have hair growing out of my eyelids.

Alice Flint told me she'd read Lajos Egri's book, *The Art of Dramatic Writing*, when she first got into the writing racket, and she created her characters with their physiology, sociology, psychology, and ruling passion in mind.

And she knew who the murderer was whenever she plotted a mystery, and why the murderer committed the murder. She said she thought of a mystery as a trail of clues leading to different suspects, one of whom turned out to be the murderer, so she created maybe three other characters who had motive, means, and opportunity. I told her we were right in synch.

Then, Alice said with a sly wink, she'd work out the scenario for the whole story in a shorthand fashion: She called it her plot outline. Okay! I said, right on! I told her I call it a stepsheet—more or less the same thing.

Now here, she said, was her secret. Her first draft was just a quickie knockoff, written at a hundred miles an hour, pedal to the metal. She'd write some of the important dialogue, then summarize the actions. This way she could do her first draft in, say, ten days.

I gasped. Ten *days*. I wrote a first draft of a 70,000-word novel once in six weeks and thought I was Superman. A first draft in ten days—it sounded impossible.

"Fast," she said, "is not only fun, it energizes me, like a tall margarita with lots of salt."

Later she showed me an example of a draft of a novel. It's not the one I'm going to show you, but it was similar. I've changed the name of her detective to "Sam Bass." The part that's in ALL CAPS is meant to be descriptive summary of what she intends to write.

A Speed Sample

SAM ARRIVES AT DANIELLE'S PLACE, SNEAKS AROUND, THEN USES HIS LOCK-PICKING KIT TO BREAK IN. HE'S SEARCH-ING FOR THE DIARY WHEN DANIELLE COMES IN WEARING A SLINKY NIGHT-

GOWN, BUT HOLDING A GUN. SHE CLICKS
ON THE LIGHT.

"*Well, well,*" *she said.* "*Look what I caught, a large-
mouth bass.*"

"*Hi, Danielle, I was looking for my wallet, I must
have left it here earlier. I didn't want to disturb you.*"

"*I guess what you really want is Lionel's diary.*"

He nodded. "*Guilty as charged.*"

"*You know, I could shoot you right now, put a
weapon in your hand—a knife out of the kitchen
maybe—and no one would question it.*"

"*You do have the diary, don't you?*"

She laughed, tossing her head back. "*Bravado in the
face of certain death.*"

"*No bravado needed. I know for a fact you
wouldn't shoot me.*"

"*Oh, why not?*"

"*You go for guys like me—sensitive, yet virile.*"

"*You sound like an after-shave commercial.*"

HE EDGES SOMEWHAT CLOSER.

"*Tell you what, Sam, maybe we could make a trade.
You give me something. I give you something.*"

"*What would that be?*"

"*The ring?*"

"*What ring?*"

"*I know you have it.*

SHE TELLS HIM HOW SHE KNOWS HE'S
GOT IT; YET TO BE WORKED OUT.

"*Say I did have it, or could get it—would you give
me the diary for it?*"

"*No, but I will let you keep your most prized posses-
sions.*"

*She points the gun at his groin. He looks at her and
smiles.* "*How well you understand me.*"

"Can I have it?"
"You've made an offer I can't refuse."

HE TOSSES IT AT HER, SHE LUNGES FOR IT, HE LUNGES FOR HER GUN, THEY WRES-TLE, HE KISSES HER AND SHE SEEMS TO LIKE IT, HE RELAXES, AND THE GUN GOES OFF.

Sam stepped back. He looked down at his shirt. It had a black hole in it and a ring of blood around it. He felt a searing pain in his belly. She was gawking at him, then she looked at the gun in her hand, a wisp of smoke coming from the barrel.
"How could you do it?" he said. "I love you."
She dropped the gun. "Oh, Sam. My God, what have I done?"

SHE DOES SOMETHING TO INDICATE SHE LOVES HIM TOO, THEN HE PASSES OUT.

DISCUSSION

Okay, you get the idea. Some of my students have tried this technique and found it useful. They simply look at the stepsheet and start pounding on the keys. Since a lot of the first few drafts is usually thrown out, there's not a lot of time wasted writing descriptions that end up in the garbage.

THE PROFESSIONAL MYSTERY WRITER AT WORK

A published friend of mine was recently invited to be on a panel at a writers conference. One of the other writers on the panel was a famous mainstream-mystery writer who was getting $600,000 advances and hit the *New York Times* best-seller list every time out. My friend, who gets $30,000 advances, was in awe. They hit it off and went to lunch, and soon the conversation drifted onto the subject of rewriting.

My friend is always struggling through what she thinks are endless rewrites, sometimes four or five complete drafts with major plot revisions. The famous writer said he was impressed. He often has to go through fifteen or twenty, and then he goes through what he calls a polish, trying to punch up the prose, find better lines of dialogue, and so on, thirty or forty more times.

My friend just about fell off her chair. She had always thought of this guy as a major talent, and somebody so talented, why . . . it ought to be easy. His writing was so smooth, his stories so seamless . . .

You, too, can have that smooth, polished feel to your work. Keep rewriting and polishing. You rewrite until it's right. If it comes out right on the second draft, or the tenth draft, fine. But if it still is not right, then rewrite some more. Being willing to go back again and again and rework your material is the hallmark of a professional mystery writer.

BEING SELF-CRITICAL

Rewriting is first a matter of knowing that something is not working as well as it could. Not that it's bad; it's just that it could be better—maybe.

Learning to evaluate your own work takes a while. In this book I've given you the elements of a good story, a good scene, and good prose. All you need to do is be objective about your work and ask yourself the right questions. Do I have enough conflict? Good details? Emotion? Are the characters well motivated? Is the dialogue fresh?

You need to be both critical of yourself and ruthless with your cuts and trims.

THE PROCESS OF REWRITING

In *How to Write a Damn Good Novel*, I demonstrated how to turn a rough draft into a working draft, and a working draft into a better draft. I've had countless letters about that section from new writers, so I'll do it again here to demonstrate the process with what is a typical mystery scene: The hero/detective interviews a witness.

I'll do a warm plunge scene, starting with the arrival of the detective.

Draft #1

The neighborhood was that tree-lined, faded-elegance kind of place. I parked in front of 212, a huge, white structure with pillars in front and hedges on both sides of the walk trimmed as square as a set of dice. I went up the walk and rang the doorbell, and a pretty, young, Asian maid answered. I gave her my card.

"Mr. Frey?"

"That's what it says."

"Whom do you wish to see?"

"Mrs. Starford."

"Could you wait a moment?"

She showed me into a foyer about the size of a movie theater lobby. I could see into the living room: pretty nice, like the showroom of a furniture store.

Mrs. Starford appeared. A tall number, in her fifties, not bad looking.

"How may I help you, ah, Mr. Frey?"

"I was told by a pet shop that you've been looking for a rare Siberian sheepdog.

"That's right. I have."

"I was also told that you used to own such a dog and it recently died."

"Yes, that's true."

"And that you offered a thousand dollars, somebody could get you one."

"Right again."

"My client is missing such a dog."

"Oh, my. And?"

"I was wondering if the guy who snatched it, a guy with an old green station wagon, might have offered you one for sale."

"No, he hasn't. I would not buy a dog from anyone other than a legitimate breeder. Is that all Mr. Frey?"

"Yeah. I guess so."

The maid showed me out. I stood on the front porch for a moment and thought I heard the yap of a dog. In fact, I was certain of it.

Maybe I'd have to come again when the lights were out, take a look around. Yeah, now that was a plan.

DISCUSSION

Like all first drafts, there are things about this that I like, and things I think might be improved.

First of all, it seems slow starting to me. Next, there is not enough detail. The character of Mrs. Starford is completely stereotypical, same with the maid. The first-person narrator is colorful, but there could be even more color. The dialogue lacks freshness, which is one of the reasons Mrs. Starford is a stereotype. Look at her lines: They are all just the standard, predictible blah, blah, blah. There are no clues but the yapping of the dog. Mrs. Starford's home is not well described; her character is not coming through.

The dialogue is, of course, all backing and forthing, and way too direct and not too colorful. Good dialogue is

often "indirect," because people tend to say things in an
oblique way.

Okay, let's try a rewrite:

Draft #2

*Twenty minutes on the freeway and I was in the
foyer of the grand old Starford place. The Filipino
maid, a sweet little motherly type, the kind that makes
you feel welcome with a look that said she wasn't in
tune with the richies she works for, had let me in. Mrs.
Starford appeared a moment later, a tall number, had to
be in her fifties, liposuctioned and facelifted, a face and
body as perfect as a Barbie doll's. She was wearing a
business suit and an expression that was all business to
go with it.*

"How may I help you, ah, Mr. Frey?"

*"I was told by a pet shop owner, Mr. Morris Chin,
that you were in looking for a Siberian sheepdog."*

*"Is Frey your real name? Is that German or En-
glish?" She had my card in her hand; she kept looking
at it.*

*I could see behind her a living room about half the
size of a ballpark, full of Chinese furniture and ornaments, the kind of place you'd be afraid to put your
feet up.*

*I said, "I was also told that you used to own such a
dog and it . . . departed."*

*"How is this any of your business, if you don't
mind my asking?"*

*"You offered a thousand dollars if somebody could
get you one."*

*"I've raised my offer to two thousand." She smiled
the superior smile of the super-rich, who wipe their
asses with thousand-dollar bills.*

"My client is missing such a dog. Her name is Lolita."

"Do I look like a dog thief to you, Mr. Frey?"

"I was thinking a guy with an old green station wagon might have offered you one for sale."

She blinked at that. I could see she was surprised I knew about the guy with the old station wagon.

"I would not buy a dog from anyone other than a legitimate breeder," she said firmly. "Is that all, Mr. Frey?" A brittleness crept into her voice. Lying makes the female voice brittle, I've noticed. The male voice drops an octave.

"Only that maybe we could make a deal, if you had bought Lolita. I don't have to report back." I was trying to make her cop to it. I wasn't really going to sell out a client.

"Good day, Mr. Frey, please do not bother me again with this nonsense."

The maid showed me out. She gave me a knowing smile as I went out the door. I stood on the front porch for a moment and thought I heard the yap of a dog. In fact, I was certain of it.

I took a quick look to see if the place was wired for a burglar alarm. It wasn't, far as I could see. Now wasn't that like an invitation?

DISCUSSION

This is an improvement, I think. The dialogue is snappier, more metaphorical. The place is better described, but Mrs. Starford is still a cliché and doesn't have adequate growth. In fact, there's not enough emotion and the details still do not bring her to life. Okay, let's try again.

Draft #3

Twenty minutes on the freeway brought me to Hillsborough, the richest county in California, as rich, they say, as France. Here I was knocking on the door of the grand old Starford place. It looked like the size and style of the White House. The Filipino maid, a sweet little motherly type, the kind that makes you feel welcome with a look that said she wasn't in tune with the richies she works for, let me in. She took my card, the real one that says I'm a PI, and Mrs. Starford appeared a moment later—a tall number, had to be in her fifties, liposuctioned and facelifted, a face and body as perfect as a Barbie doll's. She was wearing a business suit and an expression that was all business to go with it.

"You may have fifteen seconds of my time, Mr. Frey."

"I was told by a pet shop owner, Mr. Morris Chin, that you were in looking for a Siberian sheepdog."

"Is Frey your real name?" She had my card in her hand; she kept looking at it.

I could see behind her a living room about half the size of a ballpark, full of Chinese furniture and ornaments, the kind of place you'd be afraid to put your feet up. On the wall was a Russian flag, the imperial flag of Mother Russia. Maybe she thought of herself as a czarina.

I said, "I was also told that you used to own such a dog and it . . . departed."

"It died, Mr. Frey. It did not depart. How is this any of your business?"

"You offered a thousand dollars if somebody could get you one."

"I've raised my offer to two thousand." She grinned

the superior grin of the super-rich, who wipe their asses with thousand-dollar bills.

"My client is missing such a dog. Her name is Lolita."

"Do I look like a dog thief to you, Mr. Frey?"

"I was thinking a guy with an old green station wagon might have offered you one for sale."

She stiffened at that. I could see she was surprised I knew about the guy with the old station wagon.

"I would not buy a dog from anyone other than a legitimate breeder," she said. "Is that all, Mr. Frey?" A brittleness crept into her voice. Lying makes the female voice brittle, I've noticed. The male voice drops an octave.

"Only that maybe we could make a deal, if you had bought Lolita. I don't have to report back." I wasn't sure if I was trying to make her cop to it or if I was trying to gather up some of her ass wipes.

"Good day, Mr. Frey, please do not bother me again with this nonsense."

"You want to keep the dog, you'd better deal with me."

"My gardener has a fourth-degree black belt in tae kwon do, Mr. Frey. Should I have him break some of your bones as a gesture of my sincerity?"

"I'm a fifth-degree black belt," I said.

She scoffed and turned her back on me.

The maid showed me out. She gave me a knowing smile as I went out the door. I stood on the front porch for a moment and thought I heard the yap of a dog. In fact, I was certain of it.

I took a quick look to see if the place was wired for a burglar alarm. It wasn't, far as I could see. Now wasn't that like an invitation?

DISCUSSION

It's getting there. I'm going to try to increase the conflicts and smooth it out, maybe find some telling details.

Draft #4

Twenty minutes on a freeway filled with lunatics pushing ninety, bumper to bumper, brought me to Hillsborough, the richest county in California. As rich, they say, as the whole country of France. The neighborhood I drove to, Gregson Manor, was tree-lined, quiet, elegant, nestled into the foothills, snug and comfy. The Starford place turned out to be a huge, white-and-brick colossus with pillars in front and hedges on both sides of the walk trimmed as square as a set of dice. I got out of my car and scraped some dried mustard off my tie and went up the front walk. The air was perfumed by a multicolored flowerbed that ran along the base of the hedge. Here I was, little ole private eye me, knocking on the door of the grand old Starford place.

The Filipino maid, a sweet little number, the kind that makes you feel welcome with a look that says she's regular folk, let me in. She took my card, the real one that says I'm a P.I., asked me to please wait, then she floated down a hallway.

I looked down into the sunken living room; it was about half the size of a Cadillac dealer's showroom, full of Chinese furniture and ornaments, the kind of place you'd be afraid to put your feet up. On the wall was a Russian Flag, the imperial flag of Mother Russia. Maybe Mrs. Starford thought of herself as a czarina.

Mrs. Starford swept in from another room, a tall number, had to be in her fifties. Liposuctioned and facelifted, she had a face and body as perfect as a Barbie doll's, hair as yellow as crime-scene tape. She had on a business suit and wore an expression as dour as a funeral director's.

"You may have fifteen seconds of my time, Mr. Frey."

"I was told by a pet-shop owner, Mr. Morris Chin, that you were in looking for a Siberian sheepdog."

"Is Frey your real name?" She had my card in her hand; she kept looking at it, puckering, as if it gave her a bad taste in her mouth.

I said: "I was also told that you used to own such a dog and it . . . departed."

"It died, Mr. Frey, it did not 'depart.' Your fifteen seconds are up."

"Isn't it true you've been shopping for another Siberian sheepdog?"

"How is this any of your business?" She dropped my card on a table, crumpled. They cost me $12 a box, people should have more respect.

"You offered a thousand dollars if somebody could get you one, I believe," I said.

"I've raised my offer to two thousand." She grinned the superior grin of the super-rich, who wipe their noses with thousand-dollar bills. I noticed her skin was stretched too tightly over her cheekbones, the plastic surgeon skimped on the plastic, maybe.

"My client is missing such a dog," I said. "Her name is Lolita."

"Do I look like a dog thief to you, Mr. Frey?"

"I was thinking a guy with an old green station wagon might have offered you one for sale."

Her eyes went wide at that. She was surprised I knew about the guy with the old green station wagon.

"I would not buy a dog from anyone other than a legitimate breeder," she said. A certain brittleness had *crept into her voice. Lying makes the female voice brittle.*

"Is that all, Mr. Frey?" She gestured toward the door. The maid was standing by to open it for me.

"Look, lady, I thought maybe we could make a deal, if you had bought Lolita . . ."

She blinked at me.

"What I mean is, I don't have to report back that you have the dog, exactly." I said this with a friendly tone. At the moment I wasn't sure if I was trying to make her cop to it or if I was trying to gather up some of her nose wipes. I mean, I'd bet Lolita would love it here, they'd probably feed her nothing but salmon loaf and liver pâté.

She rapped her fist on the table like a night court judge rapping a gavel. "Good day, Mr. Frey, please do not bother me again with this nonsense."

"You want to keep the dog, you'd better deal with me, get what I'm saying?"

"I told you to leave." She pointed at the door, the czarina laying down the law.

"Mrs. Starford, I'm sorry if I said anything to upset you, I do want you to have the dog. But if I look the other way, I'm going to be out some scratch, that's all. Mr. Chin offered me a bonus, see, if I found the little darling."

I made no move toward the door, I was holding my ground.

Now, suddenly, she broke out in a derisive little laugh, through tight lips. "I don't deal with rodents," she said.

I gave her hard look, not too hard, but one hard enough for her to know I was going to make trouble if she didn't open her wallet and let a few little green birds take flight.

"My gardener has a fourth-degree black belt in tae

kwon do, Mr. Frey," she said. "Should I have him break some of your bones to impress upon you that I am not to be trifled with?"

"I'm a fifth-degree black belt," I said.

She scoffed, and turned her back on me, marching off like the conductor of a marching band to the crash of cymbals. That's when I saw the gardener standing by in the doorway, a rather large fellow, blond, muscled, grinning like a fourth-degree black belt dying to kick some ass.

I waved to him, a chipper little wave of pure bravado. I walked slowly toward the door, just to show I wasn't intimidated, even though my heart was beating about 1,268 beats a minute. The maid showed me out. She gave me a knowing smile as I went out the door. She smelled as good as fresh apple cake. Standing on the front steps for a moment, I thought I heard the muffled yap of a dog, an unhappy dog. Yap, yap, yap.

I'd bet my last roll of dimes that it was Lolita mooning for her master.

I had taken a quick inventory on the way out to see if the place was wired for a burglar alarm. No control panel inside the door. No wires. No motion detectors. I looked at the outside. Nothing showing here. Now wasn't that like an invitation?

DISCUSSION

You get the idea. Writing is rewriting. You go through your drafts, thanks to the miracle of modern computer technology, and you make changes. You keep rewriting. Polishing is a matter of making small refinements. Keep asking yourself, Is there is a better way to say what I'm saying? A snappier line of dialogue, better metaphors, better description? If it takes a writer making millions with years of experience ten, twenty, thirty passes—hey—maybe that's why he's making the millions.

Once you write it, you'll have to sell it. That is part of the business of writing. That, my friend, is the main subject of the last chapter, which comes next.

20

The Killer Attitude

or

Getting an Agent, Dealing with Editors, Promotion, Book Signings, and Living the Writer's Life

Writers are always coming up to me at writers' conferences and telling me how much they got out of *How to Write a Damn Good Novel*, how they massively underline every wise word, how they reread it all the time—but very few people have thanked me for the "Seven Deadly Mistakes" I laid down in *How to Write a Damn Good Novel II: Advanced Techniques.* Now that I think about it, I guess the advice I gave was pretty hard to swallow. I was calling on people to take the leap of faith, baby, and just do it. And people find such leaps very scary. It helps if—in the words of Zorba the Greek who is telling the boss to take such a leap— you have a little *madness.*

I don't intend to rehash the sermon I gave on how important we are in people's lives and how we have a duty to give our customers, our readers, our best work. But I do want to say something about being a mystery writer.

Every writer, when learning the craft, goes to workshops or classes on craft and sooner or later gets hooked up with someone who knows the craft and hopefully can teach it. Every writer, when learning the craft, reads a lot of books on craft and tries to follow the rules—and finds it's rather like trying to learn to juggle fourteen balls at once and the best you can do at first is keep one of them in the air. That's right, learning the craft is a bitch. Reading books on craft and listening to teachers talk about craft is like reading about the Tour de France and hearing people tell how they won it, then trying to ride a bicycle. You can study technique till you're blue in the face, but the only way to really learn it is to do it.

I've never had much luck learning a foreign language. I hear that learning one goes something like this: You memorize, memorize, memorize, then you keep trying, keep trying, keep trying, but even after years and years you still can't carry on a conversation beyond "Which way to the bathroom, por favor?"

But folks who have learned a language tell me it's an extremely odd thing: You keep slugging away at it, looking at your flash cards, trying to talk to speakers, and then—whammo—one day you can speak it! You're prattling along like a native. The day before you couldn't, but now, bang! One day you can't, then the next day, and forever after, you're bilingual!

With writing, I've noticed, people learn in stages. They have several bang! moments.

Gradually, as you've learned your craft, you've been noticing the flaws in books you've read and movies you've seen—you've even been driving your civilian, nonwriter friends nuts with your observations—but now, now all of a sudden you can create a story at will, from beginning to end. Of course it will have to be rewritten and the kinks worked out, but you know you've crossed a threshold and, from now on, you might not be writing all masterpieces, but at least they will be dramatic stories. Hopefully, damn good dramatic stories.

If you write imitations and work on your style, if you practice making stepsheets, you can cut down your time in the apprentice barrel. Then you rewrite and polish and one day the miracle happens. You have a manuscript ready for submission.

You know it's done when on a rewrite you discover you're putting it back the way it was three drafts ago. You'll also know it's done when your readers start talking about the fancy restaurants you're going to take them to when you publish.

Then, gads, you will have to get an agent.

The Killer Attitude and How to Get One

In my career as a writing teacher, I've seen many fledgling authors get to the point where they need an agent and I've thought to myself, Wow, this writer really has a shot at it. They've written a damn good novel and it ought to be published. It ought to make a lot of money. It ought to end up on the *New York Times* best-seller list.

But often, none of these things happen. And it's not that I'm a bad judge of fiction. The reason the book didn't make it is that the author, who got pretty good at the writing part, forgot that after you've created a damn good mystery, you have to sell it like any other product.

You might be astonished to hear this, but *most* writers who finish a damn good mystery send out a few queries to agents and, when their work is turned down, put the manuscript in a drawer and never look at it again. I have seen this happen *hundreds* of times. A talented writer has a damn good story written with damn good prose, but after one or two rejections, there it goes into the damn drawer.

Makes me crazy.

If you want to make it in the mystery game, you must think like a professional mystery writer. And not just any old run-of-the-mill mystery writer—you need to think like a professional mystery writer with a *killer* attitude.

Having a killer attitude means you will constantly be improving your craft. The truly wonderful thing about being a writer is that you can master the craft—but you can never master it completely. There are always new tricks of the trade to be learned, new approaches, new techniques. After more than twenty-five years of attending workshops and leading workshops, I still have lots left to learn. And I still have barriers within myself that must be knocked down.

I regularly read books and magazine articles both on craft and on promotion. Sometimes I go to a lecture and am bored out of my mind for 99 percent of it because it's about things I know down to the marrow of my bones, but then, suddenly, wham! The speaker says something and a whole new way of looking at things or doing things opens up.

Having a killer attitude means you will constantly be producing new work. Of the seven deadly mistakes I wrote about in *How to Write a Damn Good Novel II: Advanced Techniques*, that of not producing new work is the most deadly. It seems so obvious to state, but hey, if you don't write it, you absolutely ain't never gonna sell it. Most of the successful mystery writers I know set production goals every day. So many words. Say, 1,200. That's five or six pages of rough draft *per day.* After ruthlessly cutting and rewriting, that might come out to say, three net pages per day. Such a schedule will yield two to three finished books a year.

Here are some helpful tips:

Have a special place where you write, make sure it's quiet, and make sure you won't be interrupted. When you are in your place, you are on the moon and can't be contacted. That's it. Unless the building is on fire, you don't want to be disturbed for any reason by anyone. You may have to have this place away from your home.

Try to write at the same time every day. Play the same music, have the same lighting. Make sure that your computer and your keyboard are set up so that you're comfortable. The space does not have to be large, but it has to be quiet. If you can't find a quiet place, get a stereo and put on earphones.

You will have to make it clear to everyone that mystery writing is not a hobby, and not just a profession—it's your life. They wouldn't go into an operating room and interrupt a surgeon, would they? Just because your operating room is in your home does not mean that you allow interruptions when you're working. If you can't stand up to the people you live with and enforce the no-disturbance rule, then move out. At least get a writing place elsewhere, even if you have to buy an RV. I use my boat as my writing area. When I travel, I have an old camper van with a writing desk in it.

Having a killer attitude means you will be represented by as good a literary agent as you can get. There is no question I'm asked more often than this one: How do I get a good agent?

And my answer is: Write a damn good mystery!

That's right, you must first have a product to market before you can find someone to market it.

Okay, once you have finished your damn good mystery—and I mean *completely* finished—it is time to switch gears from creative genius to marketing maniac.

If you don't have a damn good agent and you have a

damn good mystery to sell, then you will need to get real busy finding one.

If you don't have an agent, or you have not been around the book business and don't really understand the process, it can seem like a daunting task. And if you're in workshops and attending creative writing classes, you've heard from other writers all their tales of woe. They'll tell you they had a bad agent, they had a crooked agent, they had a lazy agent—they'll tell you all kinds of stories. After all, they are storytellers; a lot of the stuff they tell you is bull.

Agents are not mysterious, ethereal creatures with magic powers. They are people who are in a sales profession. They sell books the way real estate people sell houses—on commission. They will take on a "project" (what agents call books) if they believe they can sell it and the commission will be large enough to compensate them for their time and trouble more than some other project they could be giving their time to.

That's it in a nutshell. They are in it for the money.

Of course they like books, but the main thing with them is the money. Hell, we all got to make a living.

To get an agent, learn to think like an agent.

Okay, an agent has to sell books to publishers to make a living. Most agents would prefer to sell fiction than nonfiction because fiction is fun, but nonfiction is easier to sell.

Your job is to convince an agent that if she takes on your book, she will make more money than she will from the other books she's being offered, including nonfiction works. You have to convince the agent that you're talented and skilled and work hard and you're going to give her lots of books in the future and she is going to make lots and lots of money on commissions from selling your work, and will be proud to represent you because you're a quality author who writes damn good mysteries.

SEDUCING AN AGENT

In general, agents have three ways of getting new clients.

1. Their current clients, or someone else they know and whose judgment they trust, will recommend a writer.
2. They go to writers' conferences and workshops and meet with writers face-to-face.
3. They receive a query in the mail, it intrigues them, they ask to see the manuscript, they read the manuscript and say to themselves, Wow! Here's a damn good mystery written by a damn good writer who's going to produce lots more damn good mysteries.

The first way—getting someone to recommend you—is difficult if you don't know any writers. If you do, don't be timid. Ask them if they like their agent. If they do, ask them if they would recommend you to the agent.

I often hear, "Gee, Jim, I'd be too embarrassed . . ."

This is not reflective of the killer attitude it takes to make it in this business. I'd say if you're too embarrassed to ask a small favor of someone you know, then get into some other line of work. Writers with a killer attitude would ask anyone who will listen, whether they know them or not.

The second option is to go to writers' conferences and workshops. Your local library can give you lists of them. *Writer's Digest* has a list every year. Go to the ones that advertise that they will have agents there. Do your homework, find out the agents who specialize in the kind of book you write, take a look at the list of authors they represent, familiarize yourself with those authors' work.

Then when you meet the agent you can say, "I understand you represent Alice Cornbread. She's one of my favorite authors. I love her blah, blah . . ."

The best way to present your work is to compare yourself to well-known, moneymaking authors.

You might say to an agent, "I'm glad to meet you. I understand that you represent Alice Cornbread. She has some of the cleverest plots. . . . I've tried to work out my plots as diligently and cleverly as she does, and my readers think I've done it. But my style is not like Alice's. People tell me it's more like Sue Muckton's, whose latest title, I'm sure you know, has been number one on the *New York Times* best-seller list for fifty-seven weeks . . ."

I've had new writers say to me, "What? Me, compare myself with Alice Cornbread and Sue Muckton? I'd be too embarrassed." They'd better get into some other business.

You are an artist, a craftsperson, and a tradesperson. You are in the business of selling books and you're looking for a partner to believe in you. If you do not believe in yourself enough to toot your own horn a bit, then you are not going to get anyone else to toot it for you, that's for sure. When enthusiasm gets attached to a project, it spreads from the agent to the editor to the publicity department. That enthusiasm must start with you.

If you approach an agent with this attitude, "Gee, well, I don't know if my book's any good. My mother read it, and she said it was sort of good. . . ." you are doomed, my friend. You have just cursed your own book.

I have had students with very little talent and a shaky command of craft, but they were great at pushing themselves, and believe me, they pushed themselves a long way. A long, long way.

BE READY TO PITCH YOUR PROJECT

At a writers' conference, people will ask, What is your book about? You will need to have a little capsule summary that will give the essence of the book and its commercial appeal. As an example, I might say,

> *My book,* A Murder in Montana, *is the first of a series about a young, deeply spiritual, woman meditation instructor in the San Francisco Bay Area, Shakti Boxleiter. Her brother, Bentley, an animal rights protester in elk-hunting country in Montana, is accused of bashing in the head of an elk hunter. Shakti goes to this small town, North of Nowhere, where the murderer and the elk hunters and the corrupt sheriff have fabricated a powerful case against Bentley. Determined to clear her brother, despite the insults and abuse she takes—they beat her up and later try to kill her— Shakti manages to nail the real killer. Complications include her falling in love with her brother's lawyer, Matt, which present problems not only for her detective work, but also for her spiritual quest.*

You'll notice that I said "first of a series." An agent wants to sell lots of books, so "series" is a word with mystical powers when it comes to an agent.

THE QUERY

The third common way of finding an agent is to write a query letter. Here's what I tell my students; it has proven to be a successful way to find an agent.

You send a one-page query letter; a three-to-five-page, single-spaced (double spaced between paragraphs) synopsis; and ten to fifteen pages, the beginning of the novel. You also enclose a business-sized, stamped envelope addressed to you and you mark on the synopsis and the sample pages "disposable copy."

You will want to tell the agent in the body of the letter:

- that you have a mystery, the first in a series
- that you want this agent to represent you
- what makes you qualified to write it

- something about its commercial value
- why the agent should take you on

Okay, say I was a first-time author and I'd written *A Murder in Montana.* Here's my letter:

Dear Ms. Smyth:

I've just completed a mystery, A Murder in Montana. *My amateur sleuth, Shakti Boxleiter, is a bit different: she's a loving, kind, gentle, sweet yoga instructor trying to make good spiritual progress; she has a well-focused mind just right for detective work. Her brother, an animal rights protester, is accused of murdering an elk hunter in the corrupt, redneck town of North of Nowhere, Montana, and even he says he's guilty. But he's not, and Shakti sets out to prove it, despite the people who might kill her to stop her.*

I understand you represent Malcolm Nurdly, whom I greatly admire. His Death Tango *is one of the most gripping, well-written novels I've read in years. I hope you will take a look at* A Murder in Montana: *I think you'll like it. Maybe I'm not as great a writer as Malcolm Nurdly, but I am very good for a first-time novelist, as you can see by the sample pages and short synopsis I've enclosed. I've been working with Sara Cunningham at the Chicago Creative Writing Institute for six years and every summer for the last five years I've attended the West Valley Writers Workshop with John Knox.*

Right now, animal rights is a hot issue constantly in the news and I feel that, fictionally, I have some interesting things to say on both sides of the issue. When I was a child I went hunting with my dad every fall and know that the wild animal herds must be controlled to prevent disease and starvation. Later, I was involved with a campus protest against using animals in experi-

ments because I feel very strongly that animals should not be tortured to create better eye shadow.

I'm already working on the next installment. In this one, Shakti's neighbor's head is chopped off and dumped in her fish tank and the police are determined to pin the crime on Shakti's friend, Peter, who's severely learning disabled and doesn't understand the trouble he's in.

Hope to hear from you soon.

Yours,

WORKING WITH AN EDITOR/DOING PUBLICITY

Writers are like the soldiers in war—interested in capturing or holding a few feet of ground, staying alive. Editors are the generals back at headquarters; they're thinking strategically.

As a soldier, you want the general to send you more guns, more ammo, more blankets, more tanks, more artillery, but the general has lots of areas to think about, not just your area. He can give you some stuff, but he can't give you everything.

So which writer gets more of the stuff—a bitchy, complaining, whining writer, or a friendly, cooperative, helpful writer?

Right. The bitchy, complaining, whining writer.

Just kidding.

The way to deal with the business of book publishing is to first do what the editor asks. Help them to help you. They'll want you to fill out a long form that will tell them what angle they might take in promoting your book. Give it some thought; do a thorough job filling it out. If they want you to go to a mall in your area and sit all day at a desk and sign a few books, do it. If they want you to contact your local newspaper and try to get an interview, do it.

And do some stuff on your own. Try to get jacket-copy

blurbs from well-known writers. Write to book reviewers at the big papers, and try to get them to review your book.

You and your editor are partners. Since the editor has bought your book, the publishing house owns the rights to it; you are therefore the junior partner, so don't make an ass out of yourself by being too demanding. Remember, the editor wants to sell your book just as much as you do.

Occasionally trouble develops between a writer and an editor over the rewrite that the editor requests. Most of the time, editors do make the book better with their editoral comments. But they sometimes want the writer to make changes the writer opposes. Say with this book, if my editor were to ask me to make it more academic, to cut the humor, to bend a knee to the gods of grammar, to change the breezy style, etc., what would I do?

I'd probably agree to tone it down a bit, but I feel that the tone is right, that my style for this book is easy to read, and that to make it more formal and academic would be intimidating to beginning writers. So I'd fight on those issues.

On other things, I might not fight. The editor might say to trim this or that, and even if I thought it would be better not to, I would make the trims in the spirit of cooperation. My experience has been that most of the time what the editors want is good for the book, even if my first reaction is that it isn't. After I make the change I often realize that, indeed, it is an improvement.

Most editors are quite flexible about their demands. They understand that writers have egos as fragile as snowflakes. They want to get along with you as much as you want to get along with them. Give them a break.

A Last Word

In the section on weird traits for the hero, I didn't tell you the weird way Louie Krep, the grizzled, old detective, became a butterfly collector. I never did work that out; my only excuse is that I'm as lazy as a throw rug.

Also, in the section on writing in various styles, I didn't say which of the two samples Hemingway wrote. You're probably dying to know, but I'm not telling. It's best, I think, if some things remain a mystery.

James N. Frey
Web site: www.jamesnfrey.com
E-mail: jnfrey@yahoo.com

Bibliography

Black, Cara. *Murder in the Marais*. New York: Soho Press, 1999.

——. *Murder in Belleville*. New York: Soho Press, 2000.

——. *Murder in the Sentier*. New York: Soho Press, 2002.

——. *Murder in the Bastille*. New York: Soho Press, 2003.

Brown, Steve. *The Complete Idiot's Guide to Private Investigating*. Indianapolis: Alpha Books, 2002.

Cain, James N. *The Postman Always Rings Twice*. New York: Alfred Knopf, 1934.

Campbell, Joseph. *Hero with a Thousand Faces*. Princeton, N.J.: Princeton University Press, 1948.

Carr, John C. *The Craft of Crime: Conversations with Crime Writers*. Boston: Houghton Mifflin, Inc., 1983.

Chandler, Raymond. *Farewell, My Lovely.* New York: Alfred Knopf, 1940.

Christie, Agatha. *Curtain.* New York: Dodd, Mead, & Co., 1975.

Cornwell, Patricia. *Cause of Death.* New York: Berkley Publishing Group, 1997.

Cuthbert, Margaret. *The Silent Cradle.* New York: Pocket Books, 1998.

Egri, Lajos. *The Art of Dramatic Writing.* New York: Simon & Schuster, 1946.

Frey, James N. *How to Write a Damn Good Novel.* New York: St. Martin's Press, 1987.

———. *Came a Dead Cat.* New York: St. Martin's Press, 1991.

———. *How to Write a Damn Good Novel II: Advanced Techniques for Dramatic Stoytelling.* New York: St. Martin's Press, 1994.

———. *The Key: A Fiction Writer's Guide to Writing Damn Good Fiction Using the Power of Myth.* New York: St. Martin's Press, 2000.

Freytag, Gustav. *Technique of the Drama.* Chicago: Scott, Foresman and Company, 1894.

Grafton, Sue, ed. *Writing Mysteries: A Handbook by the Mystery Writers of America.* Cincinnati: Writer's Digest Books, 1992.

Hammett, Dashiell. *The Maltese Falcon.* New York: Pan Books, 1930.

Haney, Lauren (Betty Winkleman). *The Right Hand of Amon.* New York: Avon Books, 1997.

———. *A Face Turned Backward.* New York: Avon Books, 1999.

———. *A Vile Justice.* New York: Avon Books, 1999.

———. *A Curse of Silence.* New York: Avon Books, 2000.

Kirst, Hans Hellmut. *Night of the Generals.* New York: Pantheon Books, 1963.

Michaels, Grant (Michael Mesrobian). *A Body to Dye For.* New York: St. Martin's Press, 1990.

———. *Love You to Death.* New York: St. Martin's Press, 1992.

———. *Dead on Your Feet.* New York: St. Martin's Press, 1994.

———. *Mask for a Diva.* New York: St. Martin's Press, 1996.

———. *Time to Check Out.* New York: St. Martin's Press, 1997.

———. *Dead as a Doornail.* New York: St. Martin's Press, 1998.

Norville, Barbara. *Writing the Modern Mystery.* Cincinnati, Ohio: Writer's Digest Books, 1986.

Puzo, Mario. *The Godfather.* New York: G. P. Putnam's Sons, 1969.

Raglan, Lord (FitzRoy Richard Somerset, Baron), *The Hero: A Study in Tradition, Myth, and Drama.* New York: Vintage Books, 1956.

Randisi, Robert J., editor. *Writing the Private Eye Novel: a Handbook by the Private Eye Writers of America.* Cincinnati: Writer's Digest Books, 1997.

Rodell, Marie. *Mystery Fiction: Theory and Technique.* New York: Duell, Sloan and Pearce, 1943.

Sanders, Lawrence. *The First Deadly Sin.* New York: The Putnam Publishing Group, 1973.

Sheldon, Sidney. *The Other Side of Midnight.* New York: William Morrow & Co., 1973.

Tapply, William G. *The Elements of Mystery Fiction: Writing a Modern Whodunit.* Boston: The Writer, Inc., 1995.

Turow, Scott. *Presumed Innocent.* New York: Farrar Straus & Giroux, 1987.

Vogler, Christopher. *The Writer's Journey: Mythic Structures for Storytellers and Screenwriters.* Studio City, Calif.: Michael Wiese Productions, 1992.

Wouk, Herman. *The Caine Mutiny.* New York: Doubleday and Company, 1951.